BOOK of REMEDIES

A Comprehensive Collection

Saurabh Avasthi

Meenakshi Awasthi

NOTION PRESS
INDIA | USA

Disclaimer

This book is intended to provide information about astrological remedies derived from various sources, including ancient texts, practices and modern interpretations. The content is for educational and informational purposes only and should not be considered a substitute for professional advice in medical, legal, financial, or psychological matters.

The remedies presented in this book are not suggested by the author but are a collection from various sources. The author does not claim any credit for the original work or the authorship of the remedies listed. There may be errors in the mantras, misprints, or inaccuracies in the information provided.

While every effort has been made to ensure the accuracy and authenticity of the remedies mentioned, the author does not claim guaranteed results or outcomes. Individual experiences may vary and the effectiveness of remedies may depend on multiple factors, including personal beliefs, circumstances and adherence to instructions.

Readers are encouraged to consult qualified professionals, such as medical practitioners, certified astrologers, or counselors, before implementing any remedy, especially if it may impact health, well-being, or personal decisions.

The author and publisher disclaim all liability for any direct, indirect, incidental, or consequential harm or damage resulting from the use or misuse of the information provided in this book. Readers are solely responsible for their decisions and actions.

By reading and using this book, you acknowledge and accept this disclaimer.

Saurabh Avasthi
Meenakshi Awasthi

Book Title:

BOOK of REMEDIES - A Comprehensive Collection

Genre: Self Help for Success
Edition: 1.0, January 2025

Language: English
Country of Origin: India
Author: Saurabh Avasthi

Other Books by Author (Saurabh Avasthi):

BHRIGU NANDI NADI: Astrology Simplified, 2024

COMPATIBILITY IS A MYTH, 2024

VEDIC NUMEROLOGY || ANK JYOTISH || The Proven
Methodology to Accurate Prediction, 2023
THE ART AND SCIENCE OF SIGNATURE ANALYSIS: A
Step-by-Step Guide to Deciphering Nature, Behavior,
Personality and Intent, 2023

PSYCHOLOGY OF DOODLES & SCRIBBLES: Visual
Expression of the Unconscious, 2023

ENCYCLOPEDIA OF GRAPHOLOGY: A Master Practitioner's
Guide - Volume I: Gestalt Method – Holistic Approach to
Handwriting Analysis, 2023

ENCYCLOPEDIA OF GRAPHOLOGY: A Master Practitioner's
Guide - Volume II: Trait Method – Feature Analysis Approach
to Handwriting Analysis (Letters A to Z, Numerals), 2023

BASICS OF GRAPHOLOGY, 2023

BESPOKE SALES PITCH: Date of Birth = Buying Behaviour =
Sales Pitch, 2019

DEDICATED TO

**To our dearest parents,
I. C. Awasthi and Kiran Awasthi**

ACKNOWLEDGEMENTS

I would like to express my sincere gratitude to all the authors and scholars whose works have inspired "BOOK of REMEDIES - The Comprehensive Collection." This book is a compilation of remedies from various texts in the fields of astrology, Vedic sciences and holistic healing and it would not exist without the invaluable contributions of these original authors. Their dedication to exploring and documenting the rich traditions of remedies has been instrumental in shaping this collection.

I also want to acknowledge the wisdom and insights shared by practitioners and experts in astrology and holistic healing. Your knowledge has greatly enhanced my understanding and appreciation of the subject.

Finally, I want to clarify that this book is a collection of remedies derived from existing literature and I do not claim any original authorship or credit for the content included herein.

I hope this compilation serves as a valuable resource for readers seeking to explore the fascinating world of remedies for self-discovery, healing and personal growth.

Thank you for being a part of this endeavor.

Saurabh Avasthi
Meenakshi Awasthi

INDEX

It is not the Remedy that Works

It is your Faith in the Remedy that Works

It is not the God that Works

It is your Faith in the God that Works

The Inspiration

All the remedies in this book are sourced from the following resources.

1. Brihat Parashara Hora Shastra | Maharishi Parashara / Translator/Editor: R. Santhanam
2. Lal Kitab | Pandit Roop Chand Joshi
3. Bhrigu Samhita | Sage Bhrigu
4. Vedic Remedies in Astrology | Sanjay Rath | Publisher: Sagar Publications
5. Astrology and Health | R. S. Agarwal | Publisher: Pustak Mahal
6. Secrets of Gems and Astrology | Prem Kumar Sharma | Publisher: Hind Pocket Books
7. Practical Lal Kitab Remedies | U.C. Mahajan | Publisher: Pustak Mahal
8. Mantras for Success and Prosperity | Swami Satyananda Saraswati | Publisher: Yoga Publications Trust
9. Astrological Remedial Measures | K.N. Rao | Publisher: Vani Publications
10. Vastu Shastra: Science of Architecture | B.V. Raman
11. Healing Spells and Mantras | V.P. Goel | Publisher: Sagar Publications
12. Aura and Energy Healing | Barbara Brennan | Publisher: Bantam Books
13. Tantra: The Path of Ecstasy | Georg Feuerstein | Publisher: Shambhala Publications
14. Gemstones and Their Healing Powers | Harish Johari | Publisher: Inner Traditions
15. Pitra Dosh: Symptoms and Remedies | Pawan Sinha
16. Vastu Tips for Wealth and Happiness | N. H. Sahasrabudhe | Publisher: Pustak Mahal
17. Herbs and Ayurveda | Vasant Lad | Publisher: Lotus Press
18. Mantra Pushpam: A Vedic Hymn Collection | Publisher: Chinmaya Mission
19. Astrology for Beginners | William W. Hewitt | Publisher: Llewellyn Publications
20. Modern Astrology and Remedies | Dr. Deepak Singhal
21. Yoga and Meditation for Health and Prosperity | Swami Sivananda | Publisher: Divine Life Society

22. 9 Planets and Their Remedies | S.P. Bhardwaj
23. The Secrets of Astrology | Dr. L.R. Chawdhri | Publisher: Sagar Publications
24. Gem Therapy in Vedic Astrology | Neeraj Lalwani | Publisher: Sagar Publications
25. The Complete Book of Chakra Healing | Cyndi Dale | Publisher: Llewellyn Publications
26. Vedic Mantras and Hymns | Swami Sivananda | Publisher: Divine Life Society
27. Tantra for the Modern World | Osho | Publisher: St. Martin's Press
28. Jyotish Ratnakar | Devkinandan Shastri
29. Astrological Remedial Gems and Their Powers | S.K. Kapoor
30. Vastu: Astrology and Architecture | Michael Borden | Publisher: Mandala Publishing
31. The Ayurvedic Cookbook | Amadea Morningstar & Urmila Desai | Publisher: Lotus Press
32. Charak Samhita | Acharya Charaka
33. Planetary Influences on Human Life | K.N. Rao | Publisher: Vani Publications
34. Healing Powers of Herbs and Spices | Bharat Aggarwal | Publisher: Sterling
35. Simple Remedies from the Lal Kitab | U.C. Mahajan | Publisher: Pustak Mahal
36. Mantras for Healing and Success | Eknath Easwaran | Publisher: Nilgiri Press
37. Vedic Rituals and Remedies | Swami Satyaprakash Saraswati
38. Remedies for Planetary Doshas | Komilla Sutton | Publisher: Wessex Astrologer Ltd
39. Practical Astrology | Dr. B.V. Raman | Publisher: UBS Publishers
40. Astrological Predictive Gems | Shalini Aggarwal | Publisher: Sagar Publications
41. The Tantric Path to Higher Consciousness | Goswami Kriyananda | Publisher: Kriya Press
42. Sacred Rituals and Practices of India | Pandit Rajmani Tigunait | Publisher: Himalayan Institute Press
43. The Light of the Vedas | A.C. Bhaktivedanta Swami Prabhupada | Publisher: Bhaktivedanta Book Trust
44. Astrology for Health and Longevity | Dr. Robert Svoboda | Publisher: Lotus Press

Why Remedies?

Correct Imbalances and Negative Influences: Remedies help fix problems or negative influences in life. They act as corrective tools to reduce the harmful effects of challenging situations.

Promote Positive Change: Remedies are not only for solving problems but also for improving various aspects of life, such as wealth, health, success and relationships. They help enhance our overall quality of life and guide us towards better circumstances.

Empowerment and Control: Remedies give us a sense of control over our lives. By performing specific actions, mantras, or rituals, we feel empowered and involved in shaping our future, rather than just waiting for things to happen. This belief in our ability to influence outcomes is comforting and motivating.

Holistic Approach to Life: Remedies cover many areas, from planetary influences to home arrangements (like Vastu), showing that all aspects of life are interconnected. They help align different parts of our lives, creating harmony and balance. This holistic approach focuses on overall wellbeing, not just fixing individual problems.

Understanding Remedies: How They Work

It's important to note that these explanations are rooted in cultural and spiritual beliefs.

1. Spiritual and astrological alignment:

Many remedies involve mantras, prayers and rituals directed at specific deities or astrological forces. The belief is that these practices help align the individual with positive spiritual energies, potentially counteracting negative influences. For example, the book mentions mantras for various gods and planets, suggesting that invoking these entities can bring about favorable changes in one's life.

2. Energy manipulation:

Concepts like auras and the use of gemstones imply a belief in subtle energies that can be influenced. Remedies often involve wearing specific gems, using certain colors, or performing rituals that are thought to adjust these energies. The underlying idea is that by manipulating these unseen forces, one can create more favorable life conditions.

3. Symbolic actions and psychological impact:

Many remedies involve symbolic actions or the use of specific objects. For instance, the book mentions using peacock feathers or performing certain rituals on specific days. These actions, while not having a direct physical effect, may work by influencing the practitioner's mindset and expectations. This psychological shift could lead to changes in behavior and perception, potentially resulting in real-life improvements.

4. Balancing elemental and planetary influences:

Astrological remedies often focus on balancing the influences of various planets or elements. This is based on the belief that planetary bodies and natural elements have tangible effects on human life. By performing specific actions or using particular substances associated with these planet entities, individuals hope to optimize their influence.

5. Creating positive vibrations:

The repetition of mantras and the performance of rituals are believed to create positive vibrations or energy fields. This concept suggests that by consistently engaging in these practices, one can gradually transform their immediate environment and circumstances.

6. Karmic adjustment:

Some remedies, particularly those related to concepts like Pitra Dosh (ancestral debt), are believed to work by addressing karmic imbalances. The idea is that certain life challenges are the result of past actions (in this life or previous ones) and remedies can help resolve or mitigate these karmic debts.

7. Holistic harmonization:

Practices like Vastu work on the principle that the arrangement of one's living space can impact life events. Remedies in this context are thought to create harmony between the individual and their environment, leading to overall life improvements.

8. Placebo effect and self-fulfilling prophecy:

While not explicitly stated in traditional explanations, the belief in these remedies can create a powerful placebo effect. When people believe strongly in the efficacy of a remedy, they may experience real benefits, partly due to their positive expectations and partly due to subtle changes in their behavior and decision-making.

Remedies: Planets and Bodily Connection

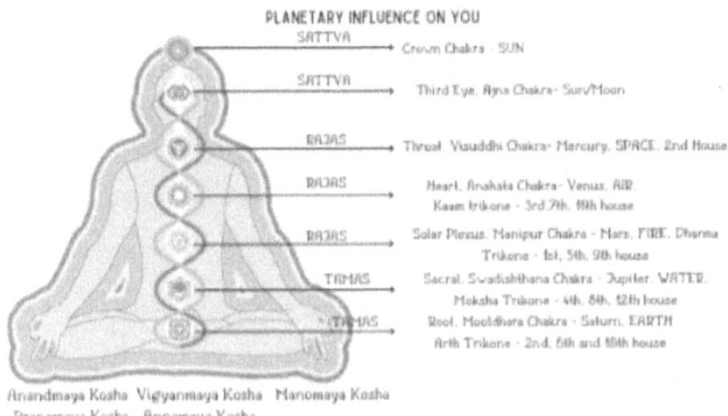

Chakra	Ruling Planet	Houses	Element & signs	Guna	Kosha	body	dosha	Planet
Crown Chakra Sahasara	Sun			Sattva	Anandmaya Kosha	Causal Body Karan Sharira	Vaat	Sun
Third Eye Ajna	Sun & Moon	Ascendent	All 5 elements converge	Sattva	Vigyanmaya Kosha	Astral Body Sukshma Sharira	Pitta	Moon
Throat Chakra Vishuddhi	Mercury	2nd House	Space / Ether	Rajas	Manomaya Kosha	Astral Body Sukshma Sharira	Pitta	Moon
Heart Chakra Anahata	Venus	Kaam Trikone 3rd,7th, 11th	Air Gemini Libra Aquarius	Rajas	Pranamaya Kosha	Physical Sthula Sharira	Kaph	Ascendant lord
	Mars	Dharma Trikone 1st, 5th, 9th	Fire Aries Leo Sagittarius	Rajas	Annamaya Kosha	Physical Sthula Sharira	Kaph	Ascendant lord
Sacral Chakra Swadishthana	Jupiter	Moksha Trikone 4th, 8th, 12th	Water Cancer Scorpio Pisces	Tamas	Annamaya Kosha	Physical Sthula Sharira	Kaph	Ascendant lord
Root Chakra Mooldhara	Saturn	Arth Trikone 2nd 6th and 10th	Earth Taurus Virgo Capricorn	Tamas	Annamaya Kosha	Physical Sthula Sharira	Kaph	Ascendant lord

There is a strong connection between the forces of the planets and the human energy system. This relationship helps us understand how remedies are believed to work and affect our lives. These remedies aim to balance, heal and enhance both our physical and energetic bodies by harmonizing planetary influences and chakra energies.

Planets and Personal Influence

According to astrological beliefs, every thought, action and event in our life is influenced by one of the nine planets. These planetary energies are not just abstract ideas; they have a direct effect on our physical body and our energy system. This includes the seven chakras, which are energy centers in the body that play a key role in our well-being.

Inner and Outer Zodiac

The zodiac can be divided into two spheres of influence:

1. **Inner Zodiac**: This represents our internal world - the thoughts, emotions and personal experiences that shape our mindset and life choices.
2. **Outer Zodiac**: This sphere relates to how we interact with the external world, including relationships, work and the environment around us.

Both the inner and outer zodiacs are influenced by the planets. The planets' movements and their associated energies affect both our internal and external experiences.

Chakras: The Body's Energy Centers

The body has seven major chakras, which are energy centers that align along the spine. Each chakra is linked to specific planets and zodiac signs, meaning that planetary energies can impact these chakras directly. Here's a breakdown:

1. **Root Chakra (Muladhara)**: Associated with **Saturn**, this chakra governs basic survival instincts, security and stability.
2. **Sacral Chakra (Svadhisthana)**: Linked with **Jupiter**, this chakra influences creativity, sensuality and emotional connections.
3. **Solar Plexus Chakra (Manipura)**: Governed by **Mars**, it controls personal power, self-confidence and willpower.
4. **Heart Chakra (Anahata)**: Associated with **Venus**, it represents love, compassion and relationships.

5. **Throat Chakra (Vishuddha)**: Governed by **Mercury**, this chakra influences communication, self-expression and truth.
6. **Third Eye Chakra (Ajna)**: Linked with both **Sun** and **Moon**, it controls intuition, perception and mental clarity.
7. **Crown Chakra (Sahasrara)**: Associated with **Sun**, it governs spiritual connection, consciousness and enlightenment.

The Three Gunas: Fundamental Energies of the Universe

The universe is believed to be governed by three primary qualities, or **Gunad** - which influence all of existence, including our actions, thoughts and emotions:

1. **Sattva**: Represents purity, wisdom and balance.
2. **Rajas**: Embodies energy, activity and passion.
3. **Tamas**: Symbolizes darkness, inertia and ignorance.

Everything in life is affected by these three energies and they interact with the planets and chakras to shape our experiences and actions.

Remedies: Balancing Planets and Personal Energies

Given the interconnectedness between planetary forces, chakras and the Gunas, remedies are used to balance these energies and restore harmony. Remedies are designed to:

1. **Balance Planetary Influences**: By aligning the energies of planets with the individual's body, remedies aim to reduce negative influences or amplify beneficial ones.
2. **Activate and Harmonize Chakras**: Remedies work to activate blocked or underactive chakras and promote their smooth functioning to enhance personal growth and well-being.
3. **Optimize the Three Gunas**: Remedies help balance the energies of Sattva, Rajas and Tamas, ensuring that we are in harmony with both the inner and outer worlds.

By using these remedies, individuals can help create a more balanced and harmonious flow of energy in their lives. These remedies not only aim to fix issues but also support spiritual growth and inner peace. Understanding how planets, chakras and the Gunas work together helps to explain why certain remedies are recommended for different life challenges.

Mindset Matters: Keys to Happiness and Perspective in an Imperfect World

These principles touch on important aspects of mindset and perspective in life:

1. Life will never be perfect.
This acknowledges the inherent imperfection in existence. It reminds us not to chase an unattainable ideal of perfection, but rather to accept and work with life's inevitable challenges and flaws. This outlook can help reduce frustration and unrealistic expectations.

2. Happiness is a choice" and "Happiness is a decision.
These statements, essentially saying the same thing, emphasize our agency in cultivating happiness. They suggest that happiness isn't solely dependent on external circumstances, but significantly influenced by our internal attitudes and choices. This empowers individuals to actively pursue and create their own happiness rather than passively waiting for it.

3. When you change the way you look at things, the things you look at change.
This quote, attributed to Dr. Wayne Dyer, highlights the power of perspective. It suggests that our perception shapes our reality. By altering our viewpoint or attitude towards situations, we can fundamentally change how we experience and interact with the world around us. This principle encourages flexibility in thinking and emphasizes the impact of our mental approach on our lived experience.

These ideas collectively promote a proactive, mindful approach to life. They encourage taking responsibility for one's happiness, maintaining realistic expectations and leveraging the power of perspective to navigate life's complexities. These principles can serve as valuable guideposts for personal growth and emotional well-being.

Planet - Remedies

Remedies for Sun

Practical & Astrological Remedies for Sun

- Respect your father and all father figures.
- Daily Sunbathing (20 minutes, preferably early morning, not between 12pm to 4pm).
- Perform Surya Namaskar at Sunrise.
- Wear coarse and thick clothes like denim.
- Wear dark red or orange-colored clothes.
- Eat bitter foods.
- Consume royal food, 5-star meals, dry fruits and coffee.
- Plant big trees.
- Visit temples, government offices, large buildings and towers.
- Offer a red lotus flower.
- Offer jaggery to monkeys on Sunday.
- Donate jaggery on Sunday.
- Feed cows with jaggery on Sunday.
- Recite Aditya Hriday Strotam.
- Recite the Gayatri Mantra.
- Light a lamp (Diya) in the temple.
- Combustion Remedy: Offer water to the Sun.
- Maintain outward pomp and show.
- Douse kitchen fire by sprinkling a few drops of milk on it.
- Bury 7 square copper pieces on Sunday between 8-10 am.
- Take sugar or a sweet treat, or sip a little water before performing any auspicious task.
- Put a morsel of bread into the fire before eating to ensure domestic happiness.
- Donate to blind people.
- Avoid forming relationships during the daytime.
- Feed brown ants with flour.
- Offer 800 gm wheat and 800 gm jaggery for 8 days starting from Sunday in the temple.
- Keep 5 radishes beside your bed at night and donate them the next morning.

Remedies for the Moon

Practical and Astrological Remedies for the Moon

- Respect your mother and all motherly figures.
- Drink 3 liters of water every day.
- Wear new clothes.
- Wear white-colored clothes.
- Use white-colored items.
- Eat salty-flavored foods.
- Consume milk, milk products, sweets made from milk, rice, water, kheer and paneer.
- Plant rubber trees, trees with sap or oil, green poppy, Shankhapushpi (Convolvulus pluricaulis), Khus (Vetiveria zizanioides), Indian Trumpet flower (Oroxylum indicum), Lotus (Nelumbo nucifera), Bamboo (Bambusa arundinacea), Cucumber (Cucumis sativus) and Palash.
- Offer a lily flower.
- Visit watery places such as lakes, ponds, rivers, oceans, water bodies, hospitals, hotels and beaches.
- Offer milk to the Moon during the full moon.
- Distribute kheer on Amavasya.
- Offer raw milk on Shiva Linga every Monday.
- Perform Rudrabhishek, especially during the Sawan month.
- Wear silver jewelry.
- Drink water in a silver vessel.
- Wear white clothes on Mondays.
- Offer white flowers to Shiva Linga.
- Keep a silver bowl filled with water by the bedside at night.
- Take a bath with turmeric and sandalwood powder on Mondays.
- Keep a piece of camphor in a silver box near the bed at night.
- Recite **Chandra Gayatri Mantra** 108 times daily: ॐ क्षीर-पुत्राय विद्महे अमृत-तत्त्वाय धीमहि तन्नो सोमः प्रचोदयात् ॥
- Bury sugar or masoor dal.
- Bury silver and milk in the foundation of the house.
- Seek mother's blessings.
- Donate rice, silver, or milk at a daughter's birth for wealth.
- Donate wheat, copper, or jaggery at a son's birth.

- Offer milk or water to a thirsty traveler.
- Donate milk, sugar, rice, or silver.
- Avoid drinking milk at night.
- Donate milk in memory of ancestors.
- Keep water from the well of a cremation ground.
- Store river water for 10 years.
- Dip a thin needle of gold in milk or water 11 times and take that milk or water.
- Fill rainwater in a silver vessel and keep.
- Consume milk or water in a silver vessel.
- Throw money in a river while traveling.
- Take silver and rice from your mother and keep it carefully in a white cloth.
- Bury saunf (fennel) in the earth for the well-being of children.
- Build a house after the age of 30.
- Place silver nails on all four sides of the bed.
- Keep a red handkerchief.
- Keep old rice in a silver vessel.
- Offer water and milk to all guests.
- Avoid trading in milk and milk products.
- Perform **Jal Pravah** in running water, along with mishri (sugar candy) and rice in a white cloth on Monday.
- Keep a rabbit as a pet.
- Donate water facilities at a hospital or cremation ground.

Remedies for Mars

Practical and Astrological Remedies for Mars

- Do not fight with siblings.
- Wear a variety of clothes.
- Wear bright red clothes on Tuesday.
- Eat pungent-smelling foods.
- Eat spicy, fried, red chili, hot food, tea and acidic food.
- Plant strong, thorny trees like red sandalwood (Pterocarpus santalinus), khair, red coral (Corallium rubrum), pomegranate (Punica granatum), garlic (Allium sativum), ber (Ziziphus mauritiana) and red gram (Cajanus cajan).
- Offer red flowers.
- Use red color in anything.
- Spend time in the kitchen, factories, fire places, machines, army areas, or battle grounds to activate Mars energies.
- Worship Lord Hanuman.
- Worship Lord Kartikeya.
- Read **Hanuman Chalisa** every day.
- Recite **Sankat Mochan Hanumanashtak** & **Bajrang Baan**.
- Perform **Hanuman Shringar** on Tuesday.
- Offer **Hanuman Chola** and perform **Jalpravah**.
- Donate blood.
- Donate red masoor (lentils) on Tuesday.
- Wear red clothes on Tuesday.
- Keep a copper vessel filled with water near your bed.
- Take a bath with sesame seeds and red sandalwood powder on Tuesdays.
- Wear a tilak or bindi every day.
- Light a ghee lamp in front of Lord Hanuman on Tuesdays.
- Recite **Mangal Gayatri Mantra** 108 times: ॐ अंगारकाय विदमहे शक्ति-हस्ताय धीमहि तन्नो भौमः प्रचोदयात् ॥
- Clean your teeth with water in the morning.
- Take mud from under the root of a banyan tree, mix it with sugared milk and apply a dot on your navel and forehead.
- Bury an earthen pot filled with honey in a deserted place or cremation ground.

- Bury a silver square piece in the foundation of the house.
- Keep and donate copper or jaggery.
- Feed birds with sweet bread.
- Keep ivory at home for auspiciousness.
- Perform **Kanya Poojan**.
- Donate to widows at a widow's ashram.
- Give sweets or tandoori roti to dogs or birds for 43 days.
- Sprinkle a few drops of water on a hot tawa before making chapatis.
- Offer sweet milk (with honey or sugar) to others.
- Always take sweet bread (meethi poori).
- Worship Hanuman Ji every day.
- Let **Rewari** and **Batashe** float in water.
- Avoid anger and be gentle in behavior.
- Keep deer skin and ivory at home.
- Put an iron nail on the south side door.
- Wash 400 gm rice in raw milk and perform **Jal Pravah** for 7 Tuesdays.
- Perform **Jal Pravah** with 400 gm **Rewari** for 7 Tuesdays.
- Keep a square piece of silver with you.
- Clean your teeth with **fitkari** (alum).
- Distribute **chaach** (buttermilk).
- Donate milk, rice and silver to six unmarried females.
- Keep doing construction in your house (make and break).
- Distribute namkeen (salted snacks) instead of sweets at childbirth.
- Feed your younger sister with sweets and start any work after feeding her.
- Keep solid silver at home.
- Keep a solid silver ball in your pocket.
- Gift red clothes to your bua (father's sister) and sister.
- Offer 800 gm or 8 kg **Rewari** or **Batashe** in flowing water.
- Wear a silver chain around your neck.
- For domestic peace, the couple should wear red clothes, fill a copper vessel with rice, apply chandan (sandalwood paste) and offer it in a Hanuman temple.
- Avoid having a tandoor at home, as it is harmful for the females of the house.
- Offer 8 sweet rotis (flatbreads) baked from one side to dogs.

- Offer sweets to widows and take their blessings.
- Eat at least one meal in the kitchen.
- Fill an earthen pot with **deshi khand** (raw sugar) and bury it in a cremation ground or deserted place.
- Keep a red-colored handkerchief.
- Offer **sindoor** (vermillion) in a Hanuman temple.

Remedies for Mercury

Practical and Astrological Remedies for Mercury

- Drink plenty of water.
- Wear green clothes.
- Engage in gardening.
- Wear clean and immaculate clothes.
- Eat a variety of flavors in your diet.
- Eat green and leafy vegetables.
- Plant fruitless trees, green gram (Vigna radiata), durva grass (Cynodon dactylon), amla (Phyllanthus emblica), paan (betel leaf), brahmi (Bacopa monnieri), tulsi (Ocimum tenuiflorum) and apamarga.
- Visit business areas, marketplaces, forests, parks with trees and greenery, playgrounds, bookstores, libraries and communication places like telephone exchanges and call centers.
- Eat green chili.
- Donate books and stationery items to underprivileged kids.
- Worship Lord Ganesha on Wednesday.
- Donate moong dal (green gram).
- Offer green gram dal or green vegetables to Lord Vishnu on Wednesdays.
- Take a bath with green gram dal and turmeric powder.
- Recite the Vishnu Sahasranamam.
- Offer green-colored sweets like peda or laddu to Lord Ganesha.
- Offer green-colored rice or moong dal khichdi to Lord Vishnu on Wednesdays.
- Keep a green-colored handkerchief in your pocket.
- Donate books to libraries.
- Donate green clothes to the kinnar (transgender community).
- Feed pigeons green moong dal.

Budh Gayatri Mantra Recite 108 times: ॐ चन्द्रपुत्राय विदमहे रोहिणी प्रियाय धीमहि तन्नोबुध: प्रचोदयात

- **House No 3** (Communication, Courage, Effort): Avoid taking green pulses like moong dal and avoid the color green.

- Wash moong dal at night and feed sparrows and animals in the morning for 43 days.
- Wash leaves of palash or dhak tree with milk, bury them in a pit in a deserted place, cover them with black stone and mud. Do not bring back the pot containing milk.
- Burn 3 yellow-colored cowries and throw the ash into a river, jungle, or deserted place.
- Worship girls who have not attained puberty before performing any auspicious work or going out of the house.
- **House 8**: Piercing the middle of the nose with silver and wearing a nose pin for 93 days.
- Keep rainwater or milk on the roof.
- Bury a small earthen pot filled with honey and sugar in a deserted place a few days before and after a birthday.
- Fill a copper pot with moong dal and gently throw it into running water.
- Bury a piece of silver beneath the foundation of the house.
- Donate mushrooms for a good career.
- Keep a red iron ball at home.
- Keep silver, saffron, or gold with you.
- Avoid the color green.
- **House 12**: Wear a yellow thread, apply a kesar (saffron) tilak and perform nose piercing.
- Put an unused pitcher in flowing water and let it float.
- Avoid the color green.
- Avoid eating and trading in non-vegetarian food and eggs.
- Keep saunf (fennel seeds) beside your bed at night.
- Stay away from the color green.
- Perform nose piercing and wear silver jewelry.
- Keep water at bedside and offer it to a peepal tree the next morning.
- Soak moong dal overnight, then feed it to animals in the morning.
- Wear a gold or silver chain.
- Wear a brass coin with a hole in a thread.
- Eat saffron for 43 days and apply saffron tilak.
- Fill water in a green bottle and bury it in a deserted place or cremation ground.
- Fill whole moong dal in an earthen pot and offer it in running water.

- Keep mushrooms in an earthen pot and place it in the temple.
- Wash teeth with **fitkari** (alum).
- Do not keep a parrot as a pet.
- Feed crows from your food.

Remedies for Venus

Practical and Astrological Remedies for Venus

- Respect your partner or spouse.
- Maintain good character.
- Wear designer, bright-colored, brocade-style, or decorated clothes.
- Wear white and a variety of clothes.
- Eat sour-flavored foods.
- Consume presentable foods such as juice, cold drinks, rice, biryani, pulao, Chinese food and microwave meals.
- Plant flowering trees such as gular, Venus (Shukra), henna (Lawsonia inermis), jasmine, sandalwood (Santalum spicatum), lotus, white-flowered jasmine and mango (Mangifera indica).
- Visit places of pleasure like amusement parks, theatres, restaurants, malls and salons.
- Spend time at beauty parlors, salons and focus on personal grooming, such as applying makeup.
- Wear perfume.
- Help poor people with their marriage.
- Worship Goddess Lakshmi.
- Offer green chaff (chara) to cows at a gaushala (cow shelter) on Friday.
- Feed or perform seva for a black cow.
- Feed people with lassi or vanilla ice cream on Fridays.
- Wear gemstones like **Diamond** on Fridays.
- Use **Opal** crystals.

Shukra Gayatri Mantra Recite 108 times: ॐ भृगुवंशजाताय विद्यामहे श्वेतवाहनाय धीमहि तन्न: शुक्रः प्रचोदयात॥

- Donate 7 cereals or barley (jaun) for 43 days.
- Keep a silver brick or give one to your daughter at the time of her marriage. It should not be sold.
- Wash private parts with milk, antiseptic, or sauf (fennel seed) water instead of plain water.
- Bury a silver square piece at the root of a neem tree.
- Bury a blue flower in a deserted place in the evening for your spouse's health.

- **Male**: Perform **Kanyadaan** (giving a daughter in marriage).
- **Female**: Perform **Gau Daan** (donating a cow).
- Donate grains (anaaj) for illness.
- Avoid eating jaggery (Gud).
- Take a bath with curd.
- Feed a cow 2 kg of yellowed potatoes mixed with turmeric (haldi).
- Donate 2 kg of ghee in a temple.
- Bury a silver box (dabbi) near a pond in clay soil (chikni mitti).
- Make a hole in an **Adu ki guthali** (a dried fruit), fill it with surma (kohl) and bury it in barren land or a grassy area.
- Put milk, rice and silver in water.
- For the good health of your spouse (female), donate jwar (sorghum) in a temple equal to one-tenth of your spouse's weight.
- Donate 800 gm or 8 kg of jimikand (elephant foot yam) or carrots on Friday at a temple.
- Throw flowers or brass coins into a drain for 100 days.
- Donate almonds in a temple.
- Donate cotton or curd.
- If suffering from skin disease, donate or throw Saturn-related items (such as fish oil) into running water.

Remedies for Jupiter

Practical and Astrological Remedies for Jupiter

- Respect your Guru, Teacher and mentors.
- Wear yellow clothing.
- Eat sweet-flavored foods.
- Wear ordinary clothes.
- Eat wheat-based foods, sweets made from wheat, desi ghee, besan (gram flour), chana dal (split chickpeas) and haldi (turmeric).
- Visit banks, courts, universities, stock markets, temples and monasteries.
- Plant fruitful trees such as Peepal, Banana (Musa paradisiaca), Indian Bael (Aegle marmelos), Holy Basil (Ocimum sanctum), Ashwagandha (Withania somnifera) and Saffron (Crocus sativus).
- **Brihaspati Gayatri Mantra**
  Recite 108 times on Thursday:
  ॐ गुरुदेवाय विद्महे परब्रह्माय धीमहि तन्नो गुरु: प्रचोदयात ||
- Water the Peepal tree every day.
- Plant a Peepal tree on Thursday and nurture it - see it grow.
- Donate yellow clothes, chana dal and money to a priest in the temple.
- Take a bath with turmeric in the water.
- Keep a fast on Ekadashi or at least avoid eating rice.
- Offer yellow flowers like marigold and sunflower in the temple.
- Apply saffron or turmeric tilak.
- Blow out your nose and keep it clean.
- Throw a copper coin into running water for 43 days for better luck.
- Tie chana dal in yellow cloth and donate it in the temple.
- Do not remove clothes in public.
- Donate 600 gm of chana dal for 6 days in the temple for good health.
- Plant a Peepal tree in a cremation ground.
- Remove temples from your house.
- Always keep your nose clean.
- Respect sadhus, saints and priests.
- Avoid telling lies and maintain good conduct.

Remedies for Saturn

Practical and Astrological Remedies for Saturn

- Be disciplined in life and follow a structured timetable.
- Be humble towards servants and subordinates.
- Take responsibility and follow your duties.
- Wear black clothes.
- Eat astringent foods (kasaila).
- Wear old and rugged clothes.
- Eat stale food, raw pulses, black pepper and food from cheap places (dhabas).
- Visit dirty places, slums, prisons, cemeteries, abandoned houses and ruins.
- Plant useless or ugly trees such as Shami plant, black sesame, castor oil plant (Ricinus communis) and blue-flowered morning glory (Ipomoea indica).

Shani Gayatri Mantras
Recite 108 times every Saturday:
ॐ काकध्वजाय विद्महे खड्गहस्ताय धीमहि तन्नो मन्दः प्रचोदयात
ॐ सूर्यपुत्राय विद्महे मृत्युरूपाय धीमहि तन्न: सौरि: प्रचोदयात ॥

- Visit the Shani temple on Saturdays and Amavasya (new moon) for 9 Amavasya days.
- Offer black sesame seeds, black cloth and blue flowers to a Saturn yantra or idol and recite the Saturn mantra "Om Shanishcharaya Namah" 108 times daily.
- Worship Lord Hanuman on Saturdays by reciting Hanuman Chalisa or performing **Sunderkand Path**.
- Keep or feed a black dog.
- Donate or throw almonds, iron rings, or iron plates into fire.
- Bury surma (kohl) for 43 days for good health and a progressive career.
- Donate black lentils (udad dal).
- Visit a Shiva temple barefoot and feed the snake on the Shivalinga.
- Do not drink milk at night.
- During illness, donate items connected with Saturn, such as iron articles, mustard oil, or throw a few drops of mustard oil and wine.
- Feed the snake on Shivalinga with milk.
- Help a poor person, especially a laborer.

- Throw a few drops of milk into a well for monetary well-being.
- Take a few almonds to a place of worship, donate half and bring the other half back home. After 43 days, donate them to the poor at the temple.
- Bury an earthen pot filled with mustard oil in the earth under river water on a dark night, when the moon is not visible.
- Throw coconut or almonds in a river or donate them at a place of worship.
- Keep a square piece of silver with you.
- Take a bath with black sesame seeds (til).
- Keep an earthen pitcher filled with water as a 'Kumbh' while doing auspicious work.
- Throw a few drops of wine or mustard oil on the ground at sunrise for health, wealth and marital happiness.
- Bury black surma in the ground.
- Donate a tawa (griddle) or angithi (hearth) to a sadhu.
- For good health, offer milk at the Bargad tree and do a tilak from wet soil.
- Visit the temple barefoot for 43 days and seek forgiveness for your mistakes.
- Pet 3 black-and-white dogs.
- Feed milk to snakes.
- Put milk and rice in a well.
- Feed fishes with rice.
- Donate almonds equal to 1/10th of your weight in the temple, bring back half and keep them in your home for 1 year. After 1 year, throw them in running water.
- Throw a coconut with water in a flowing river.
- During illness, fill mustard oil in a vessel, see your face in it and bury it under still water.
- Feed a black cow.
- Avoid alcohol and non-vegetarian food.
- Feeding blind people will help.
- Drop watery things associated with Saturn into the river.

Remedies for Rahu

Practical and Astrological Remedies for Rahu

- Rahu is associated with sudden events, passion, technology, foreign connections and attachment.
- Eating non-vegetarian food and consuming alcohol.
- Visiting bars, wine shops and similar establishments.
- Wear gemstones like **Gomed** (Hessonite) on **Saturday**.
- Visit the Bhairon temple on **Wednesday** or **Saturday**.
- Throw black and white fishes in a flowing river on **Wednesday evening**.
- All remedies performed on **Amavasya** (new moon) and **Wednesday** are particularly effective.

Rahu Gayatri Mantra
Recite 108 times:
ॐ शिरोरुपाय विद्महे अमृतेशाय धीमहि तन्नो राहू: प्रचोदयात्।

- Plant black mustard (Brassica nigra), Dhatura (Datura stramonium), Manduka Parni (Centella asiatica), Kala Sarpa (Vernonia anthelmintica), Apamarga (Achyranthes aspera) and Colocynth (Citrullus colocynthis).
- Keep a silver square piece, donate rice and milk for peace of mind.
- Donate Udad Dal (black lentils), Massur Dal (red lentils), or offer monetary help to the poor.
- Throw **Jaun (barley)** in running water.
- Keep **Jaun** under your pillow at night and donate it to the poor in the morning.
- Throw coal into flowing water.
- Wash **Jaun** with cow urine, wrap it in a red-colored cloth and keep it.
- Keep an elephant figure made of silver.
- To nullify Rahu's poison, perform the marriage ceremony again with the same spouse.
- Keep a black marble or small lead ball.
- Keep a black dog.
- For Rahu in the 7th house, give a piece of silver at the time of marriage as **Kanyadaan** (gift to the bride) and the recipient should keep it and never sell or give it away.

- Throw a coconut into running water, rotating it anticlockwise 7 times overhead.
- Keep a silver pot with a lid, fill it with water and place a piece of silver inside; never let the water dry; change the water when necessary.
- Keep silver square pieces for 43 days.
- Keep a bag of sugar or saunf (fennel) in the bedroom.
- Take meals in the kitchen.
- Do not wear black or blue clothes.
- Wear silver jewelry.
- Throw a coconut in flowing water.
- Offer Jaun and milk in flowing water, in proportion to body weight.
- Keep **Billi ki Jer** (cat's umbilical cord) in wheat-colored cloth and place it in the money box.
- Offer **Sukha Dhania** (dry coriander) or almonds in flowing water.
- Keep 3-5 radishes at the bedside and donate them in the temple for 11 days.
- Keep a black glass ball with you.
- Offer blue flowers to the Saraswati idol.
- Keep a brown dog as a pet (black dogs belong to Saturn).
- Keep saunf (fennel) and desi khand (raw sugar) at the bedside.
- Keep **Khote Sikke** (fake coins) in the temple for 43 days.
- Feed blind people.
- Always give something to beggars.
- Eat one meal in the kitchen.
- Give a portion of your earnings to your daughter.

Remedies for Ketu

Practical and Astrological Remedies for Ketu

- Ketu is associated with Moksha, liberation, asceticism and detachment.
- Avoid eating tandoori items, tikka, smoky foods and smoking.
- Worship Lord Ganesha.
- Donate blankets to the poor.
- Feed dogs.

Ketu Gayatri Mantra
Recite 108 times on **Tuesday**:
ॐ पद्मपुत्राय विद्महे अमृताय धीमहि तन्नो केतुः प्रचोदयात्॥

- Jupiter remedies can also help to ward off the ill effects of Ketu.
- Bury a piece of a black and white blanket in a cremation ground or deserted place.
- Wear gold jewelry.
- Bury a silver vessel with honey in a deserted place before the age of 48.
- Keep a dog as a pet.
- Dip your thumb in milk and then suck it.
- Wear a white thread or silver ring on the thumb of the toe.
- Apply **Kesar (saffron)** tilak every day or use yellow chandan (sandalwood paste).
- Jupiter remedies will also be helpful.
- Wear gold jewelry.
- Drink milk mixed with gold powder.
- Perform **Pitron ka Shraadh** (ritual for ancestors).
- Mix saffron in milk and drink it.
- Perform **ear piercing** and wear gold jewelry for at least 96 days.
- Keep **11 radishes** at the bedside of a woman in the house and donate them in the temple the next day for 43 days.

Protection Against Tantric Attacks

Understanding Tantra:

Tantra is a system or method used for achieving specific goals, often involving energy manipulation. Unlike **mantras** (which use words) and **yantras** (which use shapes and numbers), Tantra primarily works through **matter** - specifically through the physical body and material elements.

Main Points to Understand Tantra:

Foundation of Tantra:

Tantra works directly with matter, including the physical body, energy and the material world. This is different from **mantras**, which rely on words, or **yantras**, which use symbols and shapes.Tantra involves using these tools, but the primary focus is the **physical world and body**.

Effectiveness and Danger:

Tantra is often described as **concrete** and **effective** because it directly influences the body and the environment. However, it is also considered **more dangerous** than mantras or yantras.

Example: Tantra is like a sharp blade - t can be used quickly and effectively, but if used carelessly, it can cause harm, just like accidentally cutting your own finger.

Tantra Kriya:

When someone **disturbs or unbalances** the energy of another person - whether physically, mentally, emotionally, or even at an environmental level - that action is called **Tantra Kriya**. This disturbance occurs at a **subtle** level because energies are not visible. These disturbances affect the person's health, mind, emotions and even their surroundings, such as their home, vehicle, or relationships.

Types of Negative Tantra:

There are various forms of Tantra Kriya used for harmful purposes. These include **Uchchatan** (removal), **Maran** (death) and **Abhichar** (harmful magic). Other practices like **Vashikaran** (control), **Vidveshan** (creating discord) and **Bandhan** (binding) are also part of these techniques.These practices are used to manipulate or harm others by disturbing their energies.

Positive Use of Tantra:

Tantra is not inherently bad. It was created by **Lord Shiva** and **Ravana** was a great expert in Tantra.

Positive Tantra can be used to bring about **good changes** in a person's life. By entering someone's **mind or subtle body**, Tantra can heal bad habits, reduce fears and tensions and transform negative emotions like hatred into love.

Example: Tantra can improve someone's emotional well-being, intellect, physical health and behavior.

Potential for Both Good and Bad:

The **power of Tantra** depends on the practitioner. It can either **heal** and **improve** someone's life or **harm** and **destroy** them, depending on how it is used.

Example: A person can be **cured** and regain good health with Tantra, or they can be **made sick**, **disabled**, or even **killed** by its misuse.

Practical Experience:

Tantra is not something that can be mastered by reading theory alone. True expertise comes through **practical experience** and **practice**. Just knowing about it is not enough to effectively use its power.

Aura: The Energy Field Around Us

Every living being, including **trees, animals** and humans, has a unique **aura** surrounding them. The aura is an invisible energy field that cannot be seen with the naked eye. It represents a protective shield around a person, animal, or object and acts as a **sphere of influence**. This aura is crucial for protection against external **subtle energies** and negative forces.

- **Negative Energy Protection**: Any **negative energy** or **powers** sent towards a person cannot affect them until they pass through their aura. If the person's aura is **stronger** than the negative energy, the energy will **bounce back** towards the sender. This is because the aura acts as a **protective shield**.
- **Backfire of Tantra**: If someone uses **Tantric attacks** to harm another and the **target's aura** is stronger, the energy sent will **return** to the sender. However, the sender's **own aura** cannot stop their own energy, causing them to suffer from the backfire, which can lead to illness or misfortune. This is called the **backfire of Tantra Kriya**.

How to Strengthen Your Aura

Strengthening the aura is one of the best ways to protect yourself from **negative energies** and **Tantric attacks**. A **strong aura** acts as a **protective shield** against harmful energies and influences. There are several ways to strengthen your aura:

1. **Mantra Power**: Regular chanting of specific mantras can cleanse and strengthen the aura.
2. **Medicines**: Certain herbal remedies can boost the body's energy and aura.
3. **Yantras**: Wearing yantras (sacred symbols) can also help protect and strengthen your aura.
4. **Blessings of Siddhas**: Spiritual blessings from **siddhas** or enlightened beings can enhance your aura's power.

While it's not hard to strengthen your aura, it's **difficult to maintain** it without careful attention. Your **thoughts, feelings** and **actions** play a significant role in keeping your aura strong. A **weak aura** is ineffective and vulnerable to negative energies, which can cause health issues and make you susceptible to **Tantric attacks**.

What Weakens Your Aura?

A weak aura is a significant vulnerability. Certain behaviors and emotions can weaken your aura, leaving you open to negative influences. These include:

1. **Negative Emotions and Thoughts**:
   - **Despair, insecurity** and **fear**
   - **Anger, jealousy** and **criticism**
   - **Sinful actions** or **wrongdoing**
   - **Greed, lust** and **addiction**
2. These negative emotions create a weakened energy field that reduces your aura's protective ability. If you frequently experience these emotions or act in harmful ways, your aura will become increasingly fragile.
3. **Lack of Harmony**:
   - If there is **no harmony** between your **mind** and **intellect**, or between your **thoughts** and **actions**, your aura becomes weaker.
   - For example, if you constantly ignore the positive urges of your mind or engage in actions that contradict your thoughts, it will create dissonance and make your aura vulnerable.

The Impact of Negative Thoughts

When you hold **negative thoughts**, such as hatred, jealousy, or anger, these emotions create **negative energy** that affects your own aura. For example:

- **Example**: If you get angry with someone and **speak ill** of them or hold **jealous feelings**, even if that person is not physically present, your **negative energy** is still sent out into the world. If that person has a **stronger aura**, the negative energy won't affect them, but it will return to you, damaging your own aura.

This is because **negative energy** comes from your own aura. When it **bounces back**, it creates holes in your aura and weakens your protective shield.

- **Backfire Effect**: If you **send out hatred or evil thoughts** towards someone, these thoughts can bounce back if they encounter a **strong aura** and this backfire damages your own energy field.

Consequences of Weakening Your Aura

A weakened aura doesn't just leave you vulnerable to external attacks. Over time, **negative thoughts** and emotions can affect even the **molecules** in your body, causing physical and emotional harm. For example:

- **Health Problems**: Continuous negative thinking can lead to **stress, mental disorders** and even **physical ailments** like digestive issues, headaches, or immune system problems.
- **Misfortune**: A weak aura can invite misfortune, bad luck and unnecessary challenges into your life.

How to Protect and Strengthen Your Aura

1. **Positive Thinking**: Replace negative emotions with positive thoughts. **Gratitude, peace** and **compassion** increase your aura's strength.
2. **Self-discipline**: Engage in practices that help you stay **balanced, calm** and **focused**.
3. **Good Deeds**: Practicing **good deeds, justice** and **integrity** boosts your self-confidence and strengthens your aura.

Additional Practices to Strengthen Aura

1. **Meditation**: Regular meditation helps align your mind, body and soul, creating a strong aura.

2. **Mantras**: Chanting specific mantras like **"Om Namah Shivaya"** or **"Gayatri Mantra"** regularly purifies the energy around you.
3. **Physical Health**: Engage in physical activities, eat healthy and maintain a balanced lifestyle to keep your energy vibrant.
4. **Good Relationships**: Foster positive relationships, as toxic relationships can weaken your aura.
5. **Aura Cleansing**: Regularly **cleanse** your surroundings and protect yourself spiritually by using mantras, rituals, or even protective symbols like **yantras**.

Ways to Strengthen Your Aura

To protect and strengthen your **aura**, it's essential to stay away from actions and thoughts that weaken it. Trying to strengthen your aura while continuing harmful habits is like trying to fill a tank with water when it has holes – the water (or protective energy) won't stay inside. Here are some methods that can help strengthen your aura:

1. The Grace of a Sadguru or Siddha Purush

- **Spiritual Guidance**: The blessings of a **Sadguru** (spiritual teacher) or **Siddha Purush** (enlightened being) can play a significant role in strengthening your aura. These divine figures can purify and elevate your energy.
- **Limitations**: However, receiving this grace isn't always in our control - t depends on divine will or good fortune.
- **Note**: This is the most powerful form of aura strengthening, but it requires sincere devotion and alignment with the spiritual guide.

2. Penance, Meditation and Positive Thinking

- **Meditation**: Regular **meditation** helps clear the mind and create a calm, positive energy that strengthens the aura.

- **Penance**: Engaging in **penance** (self-discipline and purification) is a way to cleanse your body and mind, allowing your aura to be stronger.
- **Positive Thinking**: Positive thoughts and emotions create a shield of energy around you, helping your aura stay vibrant and strong.
- **Time and Discipline**: This method requires patience, time, concentration and self-restraint. Negative thoughts must be avoided and inner purification must take place.

3. Mantra Prayog (Mantras, Kavach, Talisman)

- **Mantras**: Chanting powerful **mantras** or using **kavach** (protective prayers or symbols) can strengthen your aura.
- **Talisman**: Wearing a **talisman** or **yantra** (sacred symbol) can provide protection and boost your energy.
- **Self-practice**: If you perform these practices yourself, they require time, focus and hard work. However, these methods show **temporary** results unless done correctly and consistently.
- **Professional Guidance**: If you receive a talisman or mantra from an expert (someone knowledgeable and experienced), it will be more effective, but without proper discipline, the effect may be short-lived.

4. Use of Medicine

- **Herbal Remedies**: Certain **herbs** and medicines can boost your physical energy, which in turn strengthens your aura.
- **Timeframe**: This method can show results within **two to four months**.
- **Limitations**: While it is an easier method compared to others, the effect of medicine is limited. It helps temporarily, but its benefits decrease over time and it cannot replace spiritual or mental discipline.

Immediate Protection Tips

Besides the above long-term methods, there are some quick and simple ways to **immediately** provide protection to your aura:

- **Wear Protective Symbols**: Wear protective symbols, like **yantras** or **gems**, that are known for enhancing your aura's strength.
- **Use Salt**: Bathing in **saltwater** or applying salt around your home can help absorb negative energy and protect your aura.
- **Use Aromatic Herbs**: **Frankincense**, **camphor** and **guggul** are powerful for purifying the atmosphere and strengthening the aura.

Precautions to Avoid Weakening the Aura

To maintain a strong and healthy aura, it is crucial to avoid things that weaken it. Here are some behaviors and actions to steer clear of:

- **Negative Emotions**: Constant **anger, jealousy, fear** and **hatred** weaken the aura and attract negative energies.
- **Bad Lifestyle**: Addiction, **wrongdoings** and **sinful actions** significantly damage the aura.
- **Inconsistent Actions**: Lack of coordination between **thoughts** and **actions** also weakens the energy field. If your actions do not align with your higher thoughts, it causes disruption in your energy flow.

First Method: The Importance of a Sadguru

Getting a Sadguru (Spiritual Teacher) is considered to be a matter of **luck** and **divine grace**. The role of the Guru is extremely important because a true **Guru** provides guidance, wisdom and a connection to the higher spiritual realms. Here's how the concept works:

Knowing the Guru:

It's said that one must **"know the Guru"** to benefit from their teachings. If you don't understand your Guru's essence, the guidance will not be effective.The famous saying **"filter the water after drinking it"** implies that the disciple should properly understand and internalize the wisdom given by the Guru.

Choosing Your Guru:

Your Ishta (deity) can become your Guru. You don't necessarily need to follow a physical person; the divine figure or spiritual figure you connect with deeply can act as your guide. A **Sadguru** can be someone who resonates deeply with you, whether **alive or not**. The **Guru's guidance** is more about the **true feelings** and the **dedication** of the disciple, rather than the physical presence.

Surrendering Ego:

The key to benefiting from a Guru's guidance is to **surrender your ego** and approach the Guru with **humility** and **dedication**. If you truly accept the Guru as your center, you are on the path to spiritual growth. **True surrender** is when you trust the Guru completely and follow their teachings without doubt. Without surrender, even if the **Sadguru**, **God**, or **Siddha** is physically present, the disciple will not receive the full benefit of their guidance.

Ego and Doubt:

If the disciple's **ego** is not surrendered, they will doubt the Guru's teachings and this skepticism prevents them from receiving the true benefits.

The **story of Krishna's Vishwaroop (Universal Form)** in the court of **Dhritarashtra** illustrates this. **Pure souls** like **Bhishma** and **Drona** were able to recognize Krishna's divine form, but others like **Duryodhan** and **Shakuni** dismissed it as mere illusion or magic.

Moral: **Pure hearts** can experience the true essence of the Guru or divine guidance, while those with **ego** or **doubt** cannot benefit from the same.

Second method

The Power of the Mind and Meditation

The **mind** has a unique ability to shape our reality. Whatever we think deeply and repeatedly, it starts becoming true in our lives. In simple terms, **thoughts shape our reality** - as the mind grows, so does the body and overall well-being. Negative thoughts can lead to **disease** and **illness**, but by shifting to **positive thinking**, health and wellness can emerge, healing both the mind and body.

The Connection Between Mind and Body:

Think of it like applying pressure on one end of a rope: The pressure gradually moves all the way to the other end. **Positive thinking** works the same way - t gradually influences the whole body and mind. **Meditation** and **penance** are the tools used to **transform** negative thinking and improve one's well-being.

Understanding Penance:

Penance is not about extreme acts like standing on one leg or lying on embers. It's about **changing your habits** - giving up bad habits, negative thinking and vices and practicing **self-restraint**. **Penance** is a **cleaning process**. It's about **purifying** the soul, mind, body, intellect and senses. This purification prepares you to connect with the higher spiritual energy through **meditation**.

The Importance of a Clean Vessel:

Imagine a vessel - f it is clean and empty, it can hold new, pure substances. But if the vessel is dirty or full of **impurities**, anything you pour into it will get **spoiled** or **spill out**. Similarly, a purified mind is ready to **absorb divine energy**, while an impure mind cannot connect with higher energies.

Supernatural Powers and Mind Purification:

Divine powers and **spiritual energy** can only be attained after purging the mind from **illusions**, **disorder**, **lust** and **bad qualities**. If we don't do this, we risk being overwhelmed, as seen in many cases where people try to practice **Tantra** or other spiritual practices without proper purification.

Example: Trying to handle a high-voltage current with equipment not designed for it will cause the fuse to blow. Similarly, if we are not prepared spiritually, the power we seek can overwhelm and harm us.

The Role of Meditation and Imagination:

When we **close our eyes**, we turn inward, away from the distractions of the outside world. However, many people fear the **darkness inside** because they are not familiar with their inner selves. This fear prevents us from connecting with our **true nature**.

Concentration is essential. We need to focus the **mind, intellect, senses** and **life force** to become completely **positive**. Imagine yourself as **radiant, soulful, free** and **powerful**. This process of **imagination** (not mere desire) will lead to real change and growth.

The Power of Imagination:

The mind's **imagination** is more powerful than knowledge. For example, negative thoughts or fears can cause a person to be afraid even if they know it's irrational. This is the **power of imagination** - a person can feel physically unwell just because they **imagine** being sick and this fear can manifest in reality.

Example: A person sleeping peacefully may not be harmed by a rat bite, but if they wake up and imagine being bitten by a snake, they may die out of fear. The mind's ability to **create** and **believe** shapes reality.

This is why **meditation** becomes essential - by planting **good thoughts** and **positive imaginations** in our minds, we can enhance **self-confidence** and bring about positive changes in our life.

Third Method: Using Mantras, Kavachs, Yantras and Other Spiritual Tools for Protection

To protect yourself from negative energies, **black magic** and other harmful forces, it is essential to create a protective shield around you. One powerful way to do this is through the use of **mantras, stotras, kavachs, yantras** and **talismans**. These spiritual tools, when practiced with discipline and purity, can safeguard you from various dangers. Below are some effective methods to strengthen your aura and protect yourself:

1. Mantras and Worship for Protection:

Several sacred mantras and worship practices can help shield you from negative influences, fears and obstacles. They provide **spiritual protection** from **black magic**, **evil spirits** and even from death itself:

- **Devi Atharvashirsha**: A powerful text for protection.
- **Mahamrityunjaya Mantra**: This mantra is known for removing obstacles and protecting against death.
- **Rudrabhishek with sugarcane juice**: A ritual that invokes Lord Shiva's blessings for protection.
- **Hanumanbahuk**: Regular recitation can protect from troubles and fears.
- **Shatchandi**, **Sundarkand**, **Gayatri Kavach**, **Durga Kavach**, **Narasimha Kavach**: These mantras and worship rituals are highly effective in removing obstacles and shielding from negative energies.

Important Note: These practices must be done with **complete discipline, cleanliness** and **focus**. The effectiveness of mantras and yantras can be diminished if performed with impure thoughts or in an unclean state. For best results, seek guidance from a learned **Acharya** (spiritual teacher).

2. Lalita Sahasranama and Sharabeshwar Sadhana:

- **Lalita Sahasranama**: Reciting this 1,000-name praise of the Divine Mother daily provides protection from enemies and black magic.
- **Sharabeshwar Sadhana**: Performing regular sadhana of **Sharabeshwar** protects from all types of dangers, including the effects of black magic. Chant **Sharab Gayatri** 11 times a day:
  - "ॐ शवेशाय विद्महे, पक्षिराजय धीमहि तन्नो रुद्रः प्रचोदयात्"
  - This mantra helps repel negative forces and shields you from harm, including backfiring of black magic.

3. Protection through Sarpagandha and Jatamansi:

- **Mantra**: Chant "ॐ ऐं ह्रीं क्लीं चामुण्डायै विच्चै" (Om Aim Hreem Kleem Chamundaye Viccha) 21 times daily during **Navratri**.
- Consecrate the roots of **Sarpagandha** and **Jatamansi** for 10 days until **Dussehra**, then wear them in a clean cloth around your neck. This shields you from black magic and all harmful influences.

Important Note: Ensure that this process is done with pure thoughts and complete focus. The subtle effects of these practices can be ruined by any impurity, whether in the mind or in the surroundings.

4. Using Sacred Soil from Banyan Trees:

- Collect soil from the **roots of a Banyan tree** in a sacred place or from a field plowed by oxen, mix it with **turmeric powder** and store it in a **silver or copper container**.
- Chant the following mantras:
    - "ॐ रुद्राय नमः", "ॐ ह्रीं हनुमंताय नमः", or "ॐ ह्रीं दुं दुर्गायै नमः"
- Perform this practice during **Navratri**, **Diwali**, or **Dhanteras**. Mix the soil in a little **raw cow's milk** or **vermilion** and apply it as a tilak on the **Hanuman idol** every day. This provides protection from **black magic** and **supernatural forces** and keeps your home safe.

5. Chanting 'Kshaum' Mantra for Protection:

- The **Kshaum Mantra** of **Narasimha** is known for its power to protect from **black magic**:
    - "ह्रीं क्षौं ह्रीं ॐ क्षौं ॐ" (Hreem Kshom Hreem Om Kshom Om).
- Chant this mantra daily, either 10 times, 1008 times, or using a **rosary** (108 times). This mantra strengthens your spiritual shield and keeps both you and your home safe from negative energies.

6. Shiva's Protection and the Power of the 'Ram' Mantra:

- **Lord Shiva** is the master of all negative forces. To invoke his protection:

- o Close your eyes, call Shiva into your heart and recite the **Ram mantra** repeatedly:
    - "Ram".
  - o Chant it for **2-5 minutes daily**, concentrating deeply. This practice purifies your mind and **expands your aura**, bringing peace, fearlessness and **good fortune**.
- Since **Hanuman** is also an incarnation of Shiva, chanting the **Ram mantra** in his honor is also beneficial, provided you maintain **self-discipline** and **purity**.

7. Shri Yantra for Protection:

- Keep a **consecrated Shri Yantra** in your home. Regularly perform its **puja** and meditate on its central point. This powerful symbol provides protection from all troubles, **black magic** and **negative influences**.
- Wear a **Rudraksha** or **Betel Nut** talisman, sanctified with 1008 mantras of your Ishta (chosen deity), in a **silver capsule** for further protection.

Important Note: Practitioners of **Shri Yantra** must avoid **alcohol**, **anger**, **greed** and **laziness**. The environment should be clean and negative behaviors should be refrained from.

8. Coconut Kavach for Energy Protection:

- During **Navratri** or **Basant Panchami**, take a **small coconut**, wrap it in **silver wire** and consecrate it as a **kavach** (protective shield).
- Apply a **saffron** or **ashtagandha tilak** on it daily while meditating. This shields your energy and keeps it balanced.
- Chant **51 rosaries of** "ॐ ऐं नमः" (**Om Aim Namah**) to strengthen your aura and communication abilities. Over time, this practice helps improve your ability to express yourself effectively and strengthens your self-confidence.

Fourth Method: Strengthening and Improving Your Aura with Remedies

To improve and strengthen your aura, you can use natural remedies and spiritual practices. This method helps in enhancing **health**, **positivity** and **immunity** while keeping negative influences and black magic at bay. Below is a detailed guide that includes herbal remedies, dietary practices, spiritual rituals and personal habits that can help you improve your aura:

1. Herbal Remedies and Supplements:

- **Cinnamon Powder with Honey**: Lick cinnamon **powder** mixed with honey daily. This boosts **brain function**, improves **body strength**, increases **immunity** and strengthens your **aura**.
- **Ashwagandha**: Take **ashwagandha powder** mixed with **sugar candy** or **milk** daily. This helps in building **physical strength**, improving immunity and enhancing the aura.

2. Healthy Juices for a Strong Aura:

- Drink **50 ml of amla juice** and **basil (tulsi) juice** on an **empty stomach** every morning. After **15 minutes**, drink the same amount of **aloe vera juice** or **giloy juice** and **neem leaf juice**. These drinks help improve **blood flow**, detoxify the body and prevent the accumulation of **cholesterol** and other harmful substances. They also enhance your **aura** and protect against diseases.

3. Tulsi (Basil) Rituals and Pranayama:

- **Walk around a basil (tulsi) plant** or perform **pranayama** near it. Watering the plant and applying **tilak of soil** from the plant on your forehead daily increases the brightness and positivity in your aura.
- Keeping a **basil leaf** under your tongue helps reduce mistakes in speaking and diminishes the impact of **bad habits** (such as **tobacco** use). This practice strengthens the mind and clears **negative thoughts**.

4. Consuming Healing Herbs and Spices:

- Regularly consume **betel juice, liquorice, honey, fennel, cardamom** and **sugar candy**. These ingredients keep the **body, mind** and **throat** healthy, clear **phlegm**, improve **digestion** and **boost energy**. They reduce **laziness** and **negative thoughts**, gradually improving your **aura**.

5. Cleansing Rituals for the Aura:

- **Bathing in salty water** or in **sacred rivers** like the **Ganges** helps remove **bad thoughts** and **negative energy**, improving your aura.
- **Sitting with feet dipped** in salty water for **5-10 minutes** also helps cleanse your energy field and refresh your aura.

6. Drinking Sacred Water for Health and Aura:

- **Conch water**: Fill a **conch shell** with water at night and drink it in the morning to improve health and enhance **consciousness, memory** and **peace**.
- **Drinking cow urine, Madhupark** and **Charanamrit** is another way to boost health and purify the aura over time. These substances help cleanse the mind and remove **negative thoughts**.

7. Sun Salutation and Daily Practices for Aura Strengthening:

- **Look at the rising sun** every morning to absorb positive energy. Perform **Surya Namaskar** and **Pranayama** to energize your body and strengthen your aura.
- **Touch the feet of elders, clean your shoes** and apply **tilak** with **ashtagandha** on your forehead to increase **positivity** and **good luck**. These practices improve your aura and remove **negativity**.

8. Clapping to Increase Energy:

- **Clapping continuously** for **2-5 minutes** in the morning increases **good energy** and **aura**, lasting for **3-8 hours**. This practice is a quick way to boost **positivity** and feel energized.

9. Small Habits for Long-Term Improvement:

- **Speak less** and avoid unnecessary conversation. When you speak, do so with **love**, **respect** and **softness**.
- **Drink water while sitting**, ideally from a **silver glass**. Drinking slowly and with intention enhances the absorption of positive energy.
- **Wear shoes less often** and **use leather products sparingly**. Maintain cleanliness in your footwear and hygiene, as it contributes to overall **spiritual cleanliness**.

10. Fast and Feed for Spiritual Growth:

- **Fasting once a week** or eating only **fruits**, **milk**, or **water** on fasting days helps detoxify the body, improve clarity and boost **spiritual energy**.
- **Feeding a poor person** on the fasting day or at any time increases **spiritual merit** and purifies your aura.

11. Time with Nature for Aura Healing:

- **Spend time with nature** - whether it's walking on **grass**, sitting under a tree, or playing with a pet. Spending **30 minutes to an hour** daily with **plants, animals** and **birds** enhances the **positivity** and **vitality** in your aura.

12. Sacred Rituals for Energy and Aura Protection:

- **Write your name** or the name of your **deity** 21 times in a **diary** with a **red pen**. This practice brings good changes and boosts **self-confidence** and your aura.
- **Feed at least two people** daily, such as a **cow, crow, dog, sadhu,** or **guest**. Charity brings **blessings** and creates a protective **wall of positivity** around you.

13. Special Offerings for Protection from Enemies:

- **Offer Sindoor, Kajal, Sesame oil** and **Dahi-vade** to **Bhairav Baba** on **Saturdays** and **Sundays** to keep away enemies and difficulties.
- Wrap a **yellow cotton thread** around a **Peepal tree** on Thursdays and offer **jaggery** and **gram prasad** for **11 Thursdays** to protect yourself from enemies and troubles.

14. Sacred Energy Practices:

- **Betel leaf and basil juice** mixed with raw milk is a powerful tool to improve your **attraction** and **positivity** on any given day. It helps you make a **positive impression** and adds more good energy to your aura.

15. Home Environment and Energy Flow:

- Ensure **light** and **air** flow into the home from the **east** for better health and **luck**. This boosts **progress**, increases positive energy and removes **bad luck**.
- Use **guggul**, **camphor**, or **frankincense** daily to purify the home and your surroundings. **Regularly clean** areas like **lofts**, **storage** and **garages** and draw a **lime line** around negative items to contain harmful energy.

16. Protecting the Home and Aura:

- Take **11 Gomti Chakras**, place them in a **silver box** and add a layer of **vermilion**. This practice reduces **bad energy** and **harmful elements** from your home, bringing **prosperity** and **positivity**.

17. Mustard Oil and Peepal Tree Rituals for Cleansing:

- **Rub mustard oil** on all the **nails** of your **hands** and **feet** and on the **heels** and **soles** (24 places). Do this while reciting the **Gayatri Mantra** daily, except on Sundays.

- Also, offer **36 drops** of mustard oil to the **Peepal tree** daily and apply a tilak with that oil to remove **misfortune, negativity** and **debt** over time.

18. Using Papaya or Apple Seeds for Aura Strength:

- **Wear papaya or apple seeds** sewn in a thin **yellow cloth** around your neck to gradually improve your aura over time.

19. Betel Leaf Remedy for Aura Purification:

- **Write your name** on a **betel leaf** with **gorochana** and immerse it in **running water** on **Mondays** and **Thursdays**. This removes **bad effects** from your aura and increases **self-confidence**.

20. Additional Benefits of Sphatik Shivling or Shri Yantra:

- Keeping a **Sphatik Shivling** or **Shri Yantra** near your pillow at night helps maintain **positive energy** and purify your aura while you sleep.

Test Method for Measuring Aura:

You can check the strength and health of your aura using a simple test. This method helps you understand if your aura is positive or if there is any negative energy present. Follow these steps:

1. **Stand Facing the Sunlight**: Position yourself facing the **opposite direction of the sunlight**.
2. **Spread Your Hands**: Extend both your hands and look at the **sky** 5 to 10 feet away from you.
3. **Look for Shining Particles**: In this position, you will notice **small shining particles** floating in the air. These are reflections of your **energy** or **aura**.
4. **Rub Your Palms**: Rub both of your **palms rapidly 21 times**. This creates energy in your hands.
5. **Bring Your Hands Close**: Now, slowly bring your hands closer together. **Feel the space between your palms**. Your hands will stop at a certain distance and this distance is the **limit of your energy** or **aura**.

- ○ **If the hands stop at a certain point**, it indicates that your aura is balanced and stable.
- ○ **If the hands move towards each other** without stopping, it means there is **negative energy** in your aura.

Wealth and Good Luck Mantra - Simple Use

These mantras are very useful. According to your birth sign, the money mantra given below should be repeated 11 or 108 times daily. (If your birth sign is not known, then choose the mantra according to your name and sign).

- **Aries / Scorpio:**

Mantra:"ॐ ऐं क्लीं सौः।" **"Om Aim Kleem Sauh"**
Aries: Chant with a rosary of Rudraksha.
Scorpio: Chant with a rosary of white sandalwood.

- **Taurus / Libra:**

Mantra: "ॐ ह्रीं क्लीं श्रीं " **"Om Hreem Kleem Shreem"**
Taurus and Libra: Chant with a rosary of crystals.

- **Gemini:**

Mantra: "ॐ क्लीं ऐं सौः" **"Om Kleem Aim Sauh"**
Gemini: Chant with a rosary of Tulsi.

- **Cancer:**

Mantra: "ॐ ऐं क्लीं श्रीं" **"Om Aim Trilo Shreem"**
Cancer: Chant with a rosary of pearls or white sandalwood.

- **Leo:**

Mantra: "ॐ ह्रीं श्रीं सौः" **"Om Hloum Shreem Sauh"**
Leo: Chant with red sandalwood or Tulsi beads.

- **Virgo:**

Mantra: "ॐ श्रीं ऐं सौः" **"Om Shreem Aim Sauh"**
Virgo: Chant with Vaijayanti beads or Tulsi beads.

- **Sagittarius / Pisces:**

Mantra: "ॐ ह्रीं क्लीं सौः" **"Om Hloum Kleem Sauh"**
Sagittarius: Chant with a rosary of turmeric.
Pisces: Chant with a rosary of Tulsi or red sandalwood.

- **Capricorn:**

Mantra: "ॐ ऐं क्लीं ह्रीं श्रीं सौः" **"Om Aim Kleem Hreem Shreem Sauh"**
Capricorn: Chant with a rosary of Rudraksha.

- **Aquarius:**

Mantra: "ॐ ह्रीं ऐं क्लीं श्रीं" **"Om Hreem Aim Kleem Shreem"**
Aquarius: Chant with a rosary of black agate or Rudraksha.

Devotion to Zodiac God

According to your birth sign, the following God of Money should be worshiped daily for financial gain (those who do not know their birth sign should do it according to their name sign).

For Aries/Scorpio:
Deity: Special worship of Ganesha

Ganesh Mantra:
Aries: "ॐ गण गणपतये नमः"। **"Om Gan Ganapataye Namah."**

Scorpio: "ॐ वक्रतुण्डाय हुं।" **"Om Vakratundaya Hoom."**
(Chant with turmeric rosary)

For Taurus/Libra:
Deity: Worship of Maa Durga (Kushmanda Devi)
Durga Mantra:

Taurus: "ॐ दुं दुर्गायै नमः।" **"Om Dun Durgaaye Namah."**

Libra: "ॐ ऐं ह्रीं क्लीं चामुण्डायै विच्चै।"
"Om Aim Hreem Kleem Chamundayai Vicchai."

Or chant the mantra of Goddess Kushmanda. (With sandalwood rosary or red hakeek rosary)

For Gemini/Virgo:
Deity: Worship Lord Kuber.

Kuber Mantra:
Gemini: Mantra: "ॐ यक्षराज कुबेराय नमः।" **"Om Yaksharaj Kuberaya Namah."** (Chant with Kamalgatta or sandalwood and yellow hakeek rosary.)

Virgo: Mantra: "ॐ देव धनाध्यक्षाय नमः।" **"Om Dev Dhanadhyakshaya Namah."** (Chant with Kamalgatta or sandalwood and yellow hakik rosary.)

For Sagittarius/ Pisces:
God: Worship Dattatreya Ji.

Dattatreya Mantra:

Sagittarius: Mantra: "ॐ द्रां दत्तात्रेयाय नमः।" "Om Dram Dattatreya Namah." (Chant with Tulsi rosary.)

Pisces: Mantra: "ॐ द्रां दत्तात्रेयाय नमः।" "Om Dram Dattatreya Namah." (Chant with white sandalwood rosary.)

For Cancer:
God: Worship Lord Shiva or Rudra Puja.
Shiva / Rudra Mantra
Mantra: "ॐ नमः शिवाय।" "Om Namah Shivaya."
Mantra: "ॐ रुद्राय नमः।" "Om Rudraya Namah."
(Recite with a garland of Rudraksha.)

For Leo:
God: Worship Lord Vishnu or Sun God Worship.
Vishnu / Surya Mantra
Mantra: "ॐ नमो नारायणाय।" "Om Namo Narayanaya."
Mantra: "ॐ ह्रीं धृणि: सूर्यादित्योम।" "Om Hreem Dhrini Suryadityom."
(Recite with a garland of Tulsi or sandalwood.)

For Capricorn/Aquarius:
Deity: Worship Hanuman ji or worship Shanidev ji.
Hanuman / Shani Mantra
Capricorn:
Mantra: "ॐ हं हनुमते नमः।" "Om Hum Hanuman Namah."
Mantra: "ॐ शं शनैश्चराय नमः।" "Om Sham Shanicharyaya Namah."
(Recite with Rudraksha.)

Aquarius:
Mantra: "ॐ हं हनुमते नमः।" "Om Hum Hanuman Namah."
Mantra: "ॐ शं शनैश्चराय नमः।" "Om Sham Shanicharyaya Namah."
(Recite with a garland of black Haqiq or Rudraksha.)

For Sagittarius/ Pisces
Dattatreya Mantra
Sagittarius:
Mantra: "ॐ द्रां दत्तात्रेयाय नमः।" **"Om Dran Dattatreya Namah."**
(Chant with Tulsi rosary.)

Pisces:
Mantra: "ॐ द्रां दत्तात्रेयाय नमः।" **"Om Dran Dattatreya Namah."**
(Chant with white sandalwood rosary.)

Mantra for Daily Monetary Gains

Mantra

"ऐं क्लीं हूँ वद वद वाग्वादिनी स्वाहा।"

"aiṃ klīṃ hūṃ vad vad vāgvādinī svāhā."

Method of chanting
- Sit in Padmasana.
- Chant in the three evenings of morning, noon and evening.
- Chant 10 times each and do it regularly for 6 months.
- You will get daily monetary gains.

Use of rosary
- Use white sandalwood rosary.
- Use crystal rosary.

Direction of sitting
- Sit facing north.

Mantras for Debt Relief and Wealth Attainment

For debt relief, money benefits:

Mantra

श्रीद: श्रीश: श्रीनिवास: श्रियः पति: ।
श्रीपरम: श्रीनिकेतन श्रीधराय नम: ।।

"śrīdaḥ śrīśaḥ śrīnivāsaḥ śriyaḥ patiḥ | śrīparamaḥ śrīniketana śrīdhārāya namaḥ ||"

Method of chanting
- Recite 10 times in the Pushya constellation (Gurupushya/Ravipushya is best) falling in the northern fortnight.
- Then chant once daily.

- This Mahamantra quoted from 'Agni Purana' is very effective and brings quick debt relief and abundant wealth.

Debt removal Ganesh Mantra:

Mantra
"ॐ गौं गणेश छिन्धिवरेण्यं हुं नमः फट ।"

"Om Gaum Ganesha Chhindhivarenyam Hum Namah Phat."

This mantra is said by Shiva to Parvati in 'Krishnayamal Tantra' and is an amazing debt-removal mantra. It has been experienced countless times.

Method of chanting

- Chant at least 21000 times. This will bring sudden monetary gains.
- Chant 125000 (one and a quarter lakh) times with meditation and dedication. This will fulfill all your desires.
- Chant facing north.

If 'Rinharta/Daridryanashak Ganesh Stotra' is also recited in the morning and evening, the benefits will be faster and in greater quantity.

Annapurna Mantra for Wealth and Prosperity:

Mantra

"ॐ श्रीं ह्रीं क्लीं नमः भगवती महेश्वरी अन्नपूर्णा स्वाहा क्लीं श्रीं ह्रीं ॐ"

"Om Shreem Hreem Kleem Namah Bhagavati Maaheshwari Annapoornna Swahaa Kleem Shreem Hreem Om"

This mantra increases wealth and prosperity in the house and provides prosperity. Due to this there is never a shortage of food in the house.

Method of Chanting

- The number of chanting of this mantra is two lakhs.
- The mantra is effective, but the process is a bit long.
- Chant daily at least 10 times on a rosary of red hakik or crystal while sitting on a red cloth/seat or on a white cloth/seat.
- After completion of two lakh mantras:
    - Perform havan of kheer, dal, ghee and jaggery with 20,000 mantras.
    - Perform tarpan in a river/pond with 2000 mantras.
    - Perform Abhishek on the idol of the goddess with 200 mantras.
    - Feed 20 Brahmins and donate to 2 poor Brahmins.
- After this, keep chanting 21 mantras daily.

Be patient during the sadhana period and have full faith and trust while chanting the mantra.

Anushthan Mantra for Daily Wealth Gain and Prosperity

1. Mantra for wealth and peace

Mantra

"ॐ ह्रीं कमले कमलालये प्रसीद श्रीं ह्रीं श्रीं महालक्ष्म्यै नमः"

"Om Hreem Kamale Kamalalaye Praseeda Shreem Hreem Shreem Mahalakshmyai Namah."

This mantra is very effective for those who do not get wealth despite enough honest efforts and are always worried due to lack of money.

Method of chanting
- Chant the mantra 11 times daily.
- Sit on a red/white seat in front of the idol/statue of Lakshmi/Lakshmi sitting on Garuda/Lakshmi sitting with Ganesha (not standing) facing north with Shree Mantra/Vishnu Sahasranama.
- Chant the mantra on a garland of lotus seeds.

Benefits: Chanting this mantra soon relieves you from the worry of money and you start getting money according to your hard work and your financial condition remains stable.

2. Mantra to keep your financial condition stable

This mantra is very effective for those people whose financial condition is unstable or money does not stay in the house.

Mantra

"ॐ ह्रीं क्लीं महालक्ष्म्यै नमः"

"Om Hreem Kleem Mahalakshmyai Namah."

Method of chanting
- Chant the mantra 10 times daily.

3. Vaibhav Lakshmi Mantra

Mantra
- "ॐ श्रीं ह्रीं क्लीं श्रीं आगच्छागच्छ मम् मन्दिरेतिष्ठ तिष्ठ स्वाहा"
  "Om Shreem Hreem Kleem Shreem Aagachchaagachcha Mam Mandire Tishtha Tishtha Swahaa"

Method of Chanting
- If both Sun and Moon are in Venus's sign Libra, then every Friday night in stable Lagna:
- Sit on a white seat facing north in front of Lakshmi Ji's picture with Shree Mantra.
- After reciting 'Shri Sukta', chant the above mantra 10 times.
- The rosary should be of Sphatik or Red Hakik.
- Thereafter chant this mantra once daily.Chanting this mantra brings Lakshmi's blessings and increases wealth.

Precaution

Sadhaks of Vaibhav Lakshmi should avoid the following:
- Desire
- Impurity
- Anger
- Laziness
- Neglecting wife

4. Mantra for debt relief

Mantra

"ॐ वक्रतुण्डाय हुम्"

"Om Vakratundaya Hum."

Method of chanting
- Sit under a Peepal tree and chant the mantra 21/51/108 times daily.

- Recite 'Gajendramoksha Stotra' once in the morning and evening.

This sadhna opens the path to debt relief within three months and debt relief is achieved within one year.

5. Bhagwati Bhaveshwari Annapurna Mantra

Mantra

"नमः भगवती भवेश्वरी अन्नपूर्ण स्वाहा क्लीं श्रीं ह्रीं ऐं ॐ"

"Namah Bhagwati Bhaveshwari Annapurna Swaha Kleem Shreem Hreem Aim Om"

Method of chanting
- Sit on a red cloth/asan or on a white cloth/asan and chant at least 10 rosaries daily on a rosary of red agate or crystal.
- After completing two lakhs:
    - Perform Havan with sesame seeds, puffed rice, lentils, peel or particles of red rice and ghee with tenth (20,000) mantras.
    - Standing in water up to the navel/heart, perform Tarpan with tenth (2000) mantras.
    - Perform Abhishek on the Devi idol with tenth (200) mantras.
    - Then feed tenth (20) of it to Brahmins and donate tenth (2) of it to poor Brahmins.
    - This way, this mantra becomes Siddha.
    - It increases wealth, prosperity and blessings.
    - Afterwards, its 21 mantras should be chanted regularly.

Be patient during the sadhana period.

6. Padmavati Mantra for monetary gains

Mantra

"ॐ नमो भगवते श्री पार्श्वनाथाय भक्तिपरेण धरणेन्द्रेण प्रिय देवी श्री पद्मावती मम वांछित लक्ष्मी कुरु कुरु स्वाहा"

"Om Namo Bhagavate Shree Parshvanathaya Bhaktiparen Dharnendraen Priya Devi Shree Padmavati Mam Vanchit Lakshmi Kuru Kuru Swaha"

Method of Chanting
- Sit on a yellow seat.
- Wear yellow clothes.
- Sit facing north.
- Offer yellow flowers for Goddess Padmavati on a copper Sriyantra.
- Chant this mantra 5 times daily.

7. Advancement and prosperity in business in Jain Sadhana

Mantra

"ॐ ह्रीं श्रीं क्लीं श्री पार्श्वनाथाय नमः पद्मावती सहिताय नमः धरणेन्द्र पूजिताय नमः मम महालक्ष्मी देहि देहि फट् स्वाहा।"

"Oṁ hṛiṁ śrīṁ klīṁ Śrī Parsvānāthaya namaḥ Padmavatī sahitaya namaḥ Dharanendra pūjitaya namaḥ Dehi dehi dehi phat svaha."

Method of Chanting

- Recite 5 rosary of this mantra daily.
- Recite this mantra to get advancement and prosperity in business.

8. Tulsi Mantra

Mantra

"ॐ श्रीं ह्रीं क्लीं ऐं वृन्दावन्यै स्वाहा।"

"Om Shreem Hreem Kleem Aim Vrindavanye Swaha."

Benefits
- Getting happiness, wealth, peace and prosperity in the house
- Blessings, wealth and grains

- Relief from disease and grief
- Getting a bride and groom/child etc.

Method of chanting
- Plant 5 Tulsi trees in the courtyard.
- On an auspicious day, auspicious time, install a Shaligram in a Tulsi plant.
- Worship with incense and lamp.
- Chant 10 rosaries of the above mantra.
- Recite the names of Tulsi 11/21/51 times.

'ॐ वृन्दा वृन्दावनी विश्वपूजिता विश्वपावनी। पुण्यसारा नन्दिनी च तुलसी कृष्णजीवनी॥'

'Om Vrinda Vrindavani Vishwapoojita Vishwapaavani. Punyasara Nandini Cha Tulsi Krishnajeevani.'
- Offer water to Tulsi and circumambulate it.
- Light a lamp of Desi Ghee near Tulsi every morning and evening.
- Keep reciting one rosary (at least) of the above mantra and 11 names of Tulsi.
- The effect starts showing soon.

9. Sabar Mantra (साबर मंत्र)

Mantra

"ग्लोड प्लाड धिन् धिन् सुंड धेबिसीन विकृट रहा ब्लैण्ड हबतायै, ॐ महारुद्राय नमः।"

"Gloḍ Plāḍ Dhīn Dhīn Suṇḍ Dhebīsīn Vikṛṭ Rahā Blaiṇḍ Habatāyai, Om Mahārudrāya Namaḥ."

Receipt of funds
- This mantra is very special for getting money very quickly.
- Recite it for 11 days or maximum 21 days.
- Recite it only in case of a special problem.
- Do not do it due to greed, impatience, ambition, dissatisfaction, desire.
- Otherwise, adverse effects can also be possible.

Method of chanting

- Start from any auspicious day.
- Recite it every night at around 12 o'clock.
- Recite this mantra 11 times.
- Soak lotus seed in desi ghee and offer 108 mantras.
- Recite it at a fixed time.
- It opens the way to wealth within a week.

10. Mahalakshmi Mantra and Hakik Experiment

Mantra

"ॐ ऐं ह्रीं श्रीं श्रियै नमो भगवति मम् समृद्धौ ज्वल ज्वल मां सर्व सम्पदं देहि देहि मम् अलक्ष्मीं नाशय हुं फट् स्वाहा।"

"Om Aiṁ Hrīṁ Shrīṁ Shriyai Namo Bhagavati Mam Samṛddhau Jvala Jvala Māṁ Sarva Sampadaṁ Dehi Dehi Mam Alakṣmīṁ Nāśaya Huṁ Phaṭ Svāhā."

Method
- Do it on the night of Diwali.
- Place 27 Hakiks on a red cloth in front of Lakshmi's picture or keep it in the left fist.
- Chant the above mantra on a red Hakik/coral rosary with the right hand.
- Do it from Nishithkaal (around 2 o'clock at night) to sunrise.
- Keep these 27 proven Hakiks safely in the morning.
- By keeping them in the safe, one gets blessings and blessings of Lakshmi.

Benefits:
- By burying 21 in the house, one keeps getting abundant wealth.
- By remembering any important work/desire, if 11 Hakiks are offered in the temple, that wish/work gets fulfilled.
- By keeping them in the cash box in the shop, business increases.
- Keeping one of these with you helps you get your work done/get money.

- If needed, you can also give these to your loved ones or a needy person and benefit them.

11. Gunja use for Lakshmi

Mantra

"ॐ श्रीं ह्रीं श्रीं कमले कमलालये प्रसीद प्रसीद श्रीं ह्रीं श्रीं ॐ महालक्ष्म्यै नमः।"

"Om Shreem Hreem Shreem Kamale Kamalalaye Praseed Praseed Shreem Hreem Shreem Om Mahalakshmyai Namah."

Method
- Perform on Diwali night in stable Lagna.
- Keep white and black Gunjas in a copper or silver vessel in front of Lakshmi idol on a yellow cloth.
- Facing North-West, light ghee lamp and incense, chant the following mantra 1008 times (10 rosaries) on a garland of lotus seeds.
- Then recite Shri Sukta/Kanakdhara Stotra.
- In the morning keep the Gunja seeds in the safe/treasury or cash box/wallet etc.
- There will be no shortage of money, there will be blessings.
- You can also give it to a needy person.

12. For Wealth and Material happiness

Those who do not have time for rosary, mantra chanting, worship/asan etc., or are unable to chant at one place every day.

For them, while walking, getting up, sitting or working, one should keep on reciting or chanting the following chaupaayi as many times as possible without rosary and chanting:

जे सकाम नर सुनहिं जे गावहिं।
सुख संपति नानाविधि पावहिं।।
सुरदुर्लभ कर जग माहीं।
अंत काल रघुबर पुर जाहीं।।

Je sakām nar sunahiṁ je gāvahiṁ.
Sukh sampati nānāvidhi pāvahiṁ.
Suradur labh kar jag māhīṁ.
Anta kāla Raghubar pur jāhiṁ.

Or

For Vishnu devotee, chant the mantra
'ॐ नमो नारायणाय।'
'Om Namo Narayanaya.'

For Shiva devotee, chant the mantra
'ॐ शम्भवाय नमः।'
'Om Shambhavay Namah.'

For Goddess devotee, chant the mantra
'ॐ श्रीं ह्रीं क्लीं ऐं कमलवासिन्यै नमः।'
'Om Shreem Hreem Kleem Aim Kamalavasinye Namah.'

13. Simple money-giving mantra

- Those who do not want to get into too much trouble, but also do not have a great desire for money.
- But there is a shortage of money.
- They should chant the mantra

  'ॐ विष्णवे नमः।'
  'Om Vishnuve Namah' 5 times (use Vaijayanti mala/Tulsi mala.
- Sit on a yellow mat facing east).
- It becomes effective after chanting it ten thousand times.
- Work does not stop due to money.
- After every ten thousand chants, money keeps coming in - it is experienced.

14. Recession Removal Mantra

- If the shop or business is going through recession despite honest efforts, then worship Lakshmi-Vishnu together.

- Put a picture of Lakshmi pressing the feet of Sheshashayi Vishnu and chant the mantra

'ॐ लक्ष्मी चारु कुचंद्वंद्वं कुंकुमांकित यक्ष से।'

'Om Lakshmi Charu Kuchandwandvam Kumkumankita Yaksha Se'

with a garland (of Tulsi/Sandalwood) in front of it every day.

- While opening the shop or establishment or office, recite this mantra 11/21 times while lighting the Puja lamp.
- The recession will definitely go away in a few days and you will start getting profits.

15. Lakshmi Mantra to destroy poverty

- During Navaratri, place a silver Sriyantra or Lakshmi Yantra on a copper plate filled with whole rice.
- Offer rose/lotus on it for 9 days along with incense sticks and lamps.
- Chant 21/51 rosaries of

'ॐ धं ह्रीं श्रीं रतिप्रियै स्वाहा'

'Om Dham Hreem Shreem Ratipriyai Swaha'

mantra daily (with a crystal rosary) and perform havan with one rosary of the same mantra.

- After nine days, keep chanting 11 rosaries and performing havan of 21 mantras daily.
- When one and a quarter lakh rupees are attained, poverty goes away forever and auspicious Lakshmi is attained.
- After that, keep chanting one rosary daily.
- The rice from the plate should be kept in the cash box/safe/wallet later. Or you can also give it to the needy.

16. Simple practice to destroy poverty

- During Navratri, sit on a white mat facing north and recite 'Shri Sukta' or 'Kanakdhara' in front of Lakshmi's idol/picture/Shriyantra.
- And chant

'ॐ श्रीं नमः।'

'Om Shreem Namah'

mantra 11 times on a crystal rosary.
- After Navratri, keep chanting this mantra at least once every day.
- This does not let work stop due to lack of money.
- It makes the financial situation better than before.

17. Kuber Mantra for abundant profits

- Those who want to earn special/more wealth or want to get abundant profits, then on Dhanteras (or Diwali or Navratri can also be used.)
- Install 'Kuber Yantra' in the north direction and chant 51/108 rounds of

'ॐ श्रीं ॐ ह्रीं श्रीं क्लीं श्रीं क्लीं ॐ वित्तेश्वराय नमः'

'Om Shreem Om Hreem Shreem Kleem Shreem Kleem Om Viteshwaraya Namah'

mantra on a pearl/white hakik/crystal rosary (if done on Diwali/Dhanteras. If done during Navratri, chant 10 rounds daily for 9 days).
- After this, keep chanting 5 rounds daily.
- After chanting 25 lakh times, it shows miraculous benefits.
- Abundant profits, splendor and wealth are attained.

18. Dhanagaam Ritual

- This ritual is of 16 days from Ganesh Chaturthi to Radhashtami.

- Then it is completed after the second instalment from Radhashtami for 16 days.

- In the first installment for 16 days (from Ganesh Chaturthi) chant the mantra

'ॐ गं गणपतये नमः।'

'Om Gan Ganpataye Namah'

11/21 times on turmeric rosary in front of Ganesha idol (on yellow seat) by lighting a ghee lamp.

- Then from Radhashtami chant the mantra

'ॐ श्रीं ह्रीं श्रीं कमला कमलालये प्रसीद प्रसीद श्रीं ह्रीं श्रीं महालक्ष्म्यै नमः।'

'Om Shreem Hreem Shreem Kamalala Kamalalaye Praseed Praseed Shreem Hreem Shreem Mahalakshmyai Namah'

11 times on crystal rosary in front of the picture of Lakshmi joined by elephant on red/white seat.

- Both husband and wife will do this.
- Give up food and consume milk, makhana, fruits, water chestnut/buckwheat flour and keep feeding the cow.
- On the sixteenth day serve 3 plates of food.
- Give one to Lakshmi Ji (give it to a cow the next day) and the remaining two should be eaten by the husband and wife.
- Facing north, the husband and wife should say loudly 3 times -

'हे माँ लक्ष्मी आओ'

'O Mother Lakshmi come'.

- After this ritual, keep chanting 8 rounds of the mantra

'ॐ श्रीं नमः।

'Om Shreem Namah'

throughout the year.
- Wealth, prosperity and blessings remain throughout the year.
- And marital happiness and family happiness also increase.

19. Shiva Mantra for wealth

Some of the mantras related to wealth problems suitable for Shiva devotees are as follows:

- For happiness and prosperity,

'ॐ महते नमः।'

'Om Mahate Namah.

- For advancement in business,

'ॐ नियमाय नमः।'

'Om Niyamaya Namah.

- For blessings and auspicious wealth,

'ॐ शम्भवाय नमः।'

'Om Shambhavaya Namah.

- For the happiness of the vehicle,

'ॐ बीजवाहनाय नमः।'

'Om Bijavahanaya Namah.

- For family happiness,

'ॐ महाबीजाय नमः।'

'Om Mahabeejaya Namah.

- To run work/business,

'ॐ सर्वकर्मणे नमः।'

'Om Sarvakarmane Namah'

- Recite all the mantras 11 rosary on Rudraksha rosary daily.
- The total number of chants is 125,000.
- Keep your face in the northeast.
- After chanting, anoint water/milk on Shivling.

20. Lakshmi Gayatri for wealth

- When Guru Shukra is not setting/retrograde, Gods are not asleep, Sutak etc. are not in effect, then start it from Ashtami of Shukla Paksha or from Rohini Nakshatra Monday/Friday.
- On a garland of lotus seeds/crystal/white sandalwood, facing north, on a red/white seat in front of the picture of Lakshmi along with Vishnu, recite 'श्रीसूक्त' **'Shri Sukta'** and chant just one rosary:

'ॐ श्रीं महालक्ष्म्यै च विद्महे, विष्णु पत्न्यै च धीमहि, तन्नो लक्ष्मी प्रचोदयात्।'

'Om Shreem Mahalakshmyai cha vidmahe, Vishnu patnyai cha dheemahi, tanno Lakshmi prachodayat.'

- Keep a ghee lamp lit during the chanting time.
- Do not chant it during vacant days or during Sutak. Do chant it in Rohini Nakshatra.
- This mantra shows sufficient effect with daily chanting of one rosary.
- But in its sadhana, one should especially stay away from laziness, quarrels, intoxication, anger, meat-alcohol, impurity/impurity (although it is best to apply the above conditions in all types of Lakshmi sadhanas. But in Gayatri sadhana or Gayatri Mukt

Lakshmi sadhana, the above actions are especially prohibited.

21. Use of Dhanteras

- On Dhanteras, light 13 lamps of pure ghee near the safe (in the evening).
- Worship Kubera.

Recite the mantra

'ॐ यक्षराज कुबेराय देवधनाध्यक्षाय नमः।'

'Om Yaksharaj Kuberaay Devdhanadhyakshaay Namah'

11/21/51 times.

- This ensures prosperity of wealth throughout the year.
- Light a ghee lamp in front of the Kubera Yantra idol every day and keep reciting the above mantra 11/21/51 times.

22. For immense wealth

- Recite 5/10 times Kuber's mantra

'ॐ श्रीं ॐ श्रीं ह्लीं ॐ श्रीं ह्लीं क्लीं वित्तेश्वराय नमः।'

'Om Shreem Om Shreem Hleem Om Shreem Hleem Kleem Vitteshwaraya Namah.'

under the Bel tree.

- Then perform havan with honey, ghee, sesame seeds, cloves, seven colours and mango wood and offer 51/108 oblations with the above mantra.

- Or offer 108 oblations with the mantra

'ॐ वैश्रवणाय नमः।'

'Om Vaishravanaya Namah'

and offer yellow flowers to Kuber and Lakshmi.

- Start this experiment from Dhanteras/Diwali/Dussehra.
- Do it regularly for at least one year and see the miracle.

23. For wealth gain in the house

- At home, perform Havan with 100 mantras in front of 'Ashtalakshmi Yantra' with the mantra

'ॐ नमः धनदायै स्वाहा' '

Om Namah Dhandayai Svaha'

throughout the year.

- Recite 8 beads of the mantra throughout the year (at least).

'ॐ श्रीं ह्लीं क्लीं महालक्ष्म्यै नमः।'

'Om Srim Hlim Klim Mahalakshmyai Namah.

- Or Recite 11 rows of the mantra daily, in front of the life-giving 'श्री यंत्र' 'Sri Yantra', say

'ॐ श्रीं ह्लीं श्रीं महालक्ष्म्यै श्रीं ह्लीं श्रीं नमः।'

'Om Srim Hlim Srim Mahalakshmyai Srim Hlim Srim Namah.

24. For Money Gains

ॐ सरस्वती ईश्वरी भगवती माता क्रां क्लीं श्रीं श्रीं मम धनं देहि फट स्वाहा ॥

Om Saraswati Ishwari Bhagwati Mata Kram Kleem Shreem Shreem Mam Dhanam Dehi Phat Swaha ||

- Chant this Mantra for 43 days 108 times daily
- Use Rudraksha beads rosary for chanting
- Do not miss any day if missed repeat again for 43 days
- Keeping a figure in mind for money will be beneficial.

25. Use of Peacock Feathers for Versatile Benefits
- For the planet that is troubling you, count backwards from 9 from Sun to Ketu and take that many peacock feathers.
- Clean those feathers with Gangajal (especially the sticks).
- Then tie a thread of the color of that planet on their sticks.
- Place them in a plate with 8 whole betel nuts, recite the mantra of that planet and chant it 21 times adding 'जाग्रय स्थापय स्वाहा' **'Jaagray Sthapay Swaha'** at the end.
- Sprinkle Gangajal on them with every mantra.
- Then offer the item of that planet as bhog.
- Consecrate those feathers in this way. (Like for Moon - 'ॐ सों सोमाय नमः जाग्रय स्थापय स्वाहा' **'Om Som Somay Namah Jagray Sthapay Swaha'**).

Benefits
- Keeping them in the treasury increases wealth and brings prosperity.
- Placing them on the main door removes Vastu defects.
- Placing them on the study table increases concentration, intelligence and knowledge.
- Keeping them near the head of the patient gives him health and protection.
- Keeping them in the living room increases good luck and peace.
- Keeping them near you removes planetary obstacles/pain.
- If fanned with them, negativity goes away.

- If kept near the head while sleeping at night, fear and nightmares are destroyed.
- If placed on the walls, positivity increases and lizards do not come.

9 Planets: Mantras, Colors and Offering items

- **Sun: Mantra -**

ॐ ह्रीं घृणिः सूर्याय नमः

Om Hreem Ghriniah Suryay Namah

Color - Orange
Offering - Plum/Wheat
Peacock Feathers - 9

- **Moon: Mantra -**

ॐ सों सोमाय नमः

Om Som Somay Namah

Color - White
Offering - Litchi/Rice
Peacock Feathers - 8

- **Mars: Mantra -**

ॐ अं अंगारकाय नमः

Om Am Angarkaya Namah

Color - Red
Offering - Plum/Honey/Vermillion
Peacock Feathers - 7

- **Mercury: Mantra -**

ॐ बुं बुधाय नमः

Om Bum Budhay Namah

Color - Green
Offering - Moong/Guava

Peacock Feathers - 6

- **Jupiter: Mantra -**

ॐ बृहस्पतये नमः

Om Brihaspataye Namah

Color - Yellow
Offering - Banana/Gram/Turmeric
Peacock Feathers - 5

- **Venus: Mantra -**

ॐ शुं शुक्राय नमः

Om Shum Shukraya Namah

Color - Bright White
Offering - Curd/Makhana/Amla
Peacock Feathers - 4

- **Saturn: Mantra -**

ॐ शं शनैश्चराय नमः

Om Sham Shanaishcharaya Namah

Color - Blue/Black
Gift - Jamun/Urad
Peacock Feathers - 3

- **Rahu: Mantra -**

ॐ रां राहवे नमः

Om Ram Rahve Namah

Color - Blue/Brown
Gift - Radish/Dhatura/Lentil

Peacock Feathers - 2

- **Ketu: Mantra -**

ॐ कें केतवाये नमः

Om Kem Ketave Namah

Color - Sky Blue/Grey
Gift - Sesame Seeds/Oleon/Lemon
Peacock Feather - 1

Special Ganesh Mantra

There is a very good and effective mantra for Ganesh worshippers to get wealth, happiness and good fortune:

ॐ हस्तिमुखाय लम्बोदराय उच्छिष्ट महात्मने।
आं क्रीं ह्रीं क्लीं ह्रीं हूं घे घे उच्छिष्टाय स्वाहा॥

Om Hastimukhaya Lambodaray Uchchhishta Mahatmane. Aum Kreem Hreem Kleem Hreem Hoon Ghe Ghe Uchchhishtay Swaaha.

This mantra is for the worship of Ganesha and is considered effective for getting wealth, happiness and good fortune. Chant it 1.25 lakh times after Nyasa, Peetha Puja, Avaran Puja etc. Offer ghee with 1008 mantras. Again do tarpan-marjan with 108 mantras and feed ten Brahmins, then it is proved. After it is proved, lack, poverty, pain, obstacle, sorrow, misfortune etc. cannot trouble you throughout life.

Special Kali Mantra

There is a very effective and best mantra for the worshippers of Kali to get wealth, prosperity and good fortune:

ॐ ह्रीं ह्रीं हूं हूं क्रीं क्रीं क्रीं दक्षिणे कालिके क्रीं क्रीं क्रीं हूं हूं ह्रीं ह्रीं

Om Hreem Hreem Hoon Hoon Kreem Kreem Kreem Dakshine Kalike Kreem Kreem Kreem Hoon Hoon Hreem Hreem

This mantra is considered effective for the worshippers of Kali to get wealth, prosperity and good fortune. There are some Tamasik uses of this mantra too, but they are not possible for ordinary people. Therefore, the simple and Satvik method is to make it Siddh by doing 1.25 lakh Japa, Dashansh Havan, Dashansh Tarpan and Dashansh Brahmin Bhojan after Nyasa etc. This is the Tantric Mantra of Kali which gives all the Siddhis.

Do it in front of the picture of Kali. Special Those who do the Sadhna of Kali should stay away from acts like anger towards women, harsh words, beating or hurting them etc. for their own benefit.

Special Surya Mantra

For Surya-worshippers, the infallible mantra that destroys both poverty and disease and increases fame and longevity is:

ॐ ह्रीं घृणिः सूर्य आदित्यः श्रीं

Om Hreem Ghrinih Surya Adityah Shreem

Chant this mantra 21 times daily in front of the rising sun, facing east, under a Bel tree. Although its total number of chants is 10 lakhs. But it has been observed in experience that it starts showing its effect in 3 to 6 months. Sattvic Sadhaks have accepted that they experience its effect in just one and a half months.

Tantric Hanuman Mantra:
The unique mantra that grants wealth, happiness, power, protection, protection and all kinds of desires to the worshippers of Hanuman is:

'हौं हस्त्रैं ख्फ्रें हसां हस्खौं सौं हनुमते नमः'

'Haum Hastrain Khphren Hasāṃ Haskhauṃ Sauṃ Hanumate Namaḥ.'

Use and benefits:

Chanting this mantra 9 times every night for 10 days frees one from the fear of the king and the enemy. On chanting it 1.25 lakh times, wealth, happiness, health and strength increase. It becomes Siddha by chanting it 9 lakh times. After Siddhi, just drinking the water consecrated with this mantra protects one from diseases and weapons. The practitioner does not have any fear of ghosts and enemies etc.

Warning:
It is mandatory for the devotees of Hanuman Ji to stay away from intoxication, lust and anger and maintain purity and sanctity.

Worth remembering:
All types of Mantra Sadhna require unity of place, action, time and person. Regularity, patience, restraint and concentration are essential. Chanting at least 1.25 lakh mantras is essential for achieving the fruit. It is safest for the Sadhak to have Satvik food, behavior, thoughts and actions. One should be especially cautious in Tantric Mantras.

Simple Home Remedies and Totake for Wealth and Good Luck

Mango Root Remedy (Vishakha Nakshatra, Sunday):

> **Action**: On a Sunday, during **Vishakha Nakshatra**, take the **root of a mango tree** and place it in the **grain store**.

> **Purpose**: This remedy is believed to **prevent the shortage of food grains**. By doing this, you can ensure that there will be a steady supply of grains in your household.

Peepal Banda Remedy (Bharani Nakshatra, Sunday):

> **Action**: On a Sunday, during **Bharani Nakshatra**, take a **banda** of **peepal leaves** and keep it in the **grain store**.

> **Purpose**: This practice is said to **increase food grains**. If tied on the hand, it can also help in **curing eye diseases** and **removing ghost possession**. It serves as a remedy for both material and physical ailments.

Shwetark Root Remedy (Ravi Pushya Yoga):

> **Action**: During **Ravi Pushya Yoga**, take the **root of Shwetark (white arka)** and rub it with **turmeric**. Keep this mixture in the **puja room** or in the **cash box**.

> **Purpose**: This remedy is said to **bring prosperity** and **financial gains** by invoking positive energies associated with wealth.

Durgashtottara Shatanam Stotra Remedy (Shatabhishan Nakshatra, Amavasya):

> **Action**: On a **Tuesday**, when **Shatabhishan Nakshatra** and **Amavasya** (new moon) occur together, write verses **2 to 15** of the **Durgashtottara Shatanam Stotra** (starting with "Om Sati Sadhvi..."

and ending with "Pratyaksha Brahmavadini") using a **red ink pen** on a **clean, new piece of paper** or **register** for at least **one hour**. If time is limited, you can write it **108, 51, or 21 times**.

Post-Writing Action: After writing, distribute **jaggery** and **gram** as offerings.

Purpose: This ritual is believed to bring **wealth, happiness, good health, a loving spouse and children**, along with the **blessings of Maa Durga**. The paper or register used for writing should be **disposed of** by throwing it into a river after the ritual is completed.

Gunja Seeds Consecration (Diwali Night):

Action: On the night of **Diwali**, consecrate **white and black gunja seeds** with the **Lakshmi mantra** and place them in the house.

Purpose: This practice is believed to attract **prosperity** and **wealth** into your home.

Old Shoes and Slippers Ritual (Diwali on Saturday):

Action: If Diwali falls on a **Saturday**, wear **old shoes or slippers** and walk in the morning before sunrise or in the evening after sunset. At the first intersection, take off your shoes and return **barefoot, without looking back**.

Purpose: This ritual is said to **remove misfortune** and **poverty**. If Diwali does not fall on a Saturday, perform this on the **first Saturday after Diwali**.

Mustard Oil Lamp (Peepal Tree Ritual on Diwali):

Action: On **Diwali**, before sunrise or after sunset, light a **four-sided mustard oil lamp** (made from flour) under a **Peepal tree** and return without looking back. Continue lighting the lamp **every Saturday**.

Purpose: This ritual is believed to **remove misfortune and poverty** and bring **prosperity** into your life.

Damru and Conch Sound (Post-Laxmi Puja on Diwali):

Action: After worshipping **Maa Lakshmi** on **Diwali**, play the **damru** (drum) and **conch shell** in all rooms of the house. Also, throw a handful of **black sesame seeds** over the head of all family members seven times, then throw the seeds **outside the house in the west direction**.

Purpose: This practice is believed to ensure **prosperity**, **health** and **well-being** for all family members.

Bhaiduj Rice Ritual:

Action: On **Bhaiduj**, while remembering **Maa Lakshmi**, drop a handful of **clean Basmati rice** into **flowing clean water**. Continue doing this **every Monday**.

Purpose: This ritual brings **wealth**, **prosperity**, **happiness**, **peace** and **good health**.

Navratri Ritual for Money (Ninth Day):

Action: On the **ninth day of Navratri**, mix **clay**, **vermilion** and **turmeric** and write the words "Pam Dam Lam" on **11 Ashoka/Banyan/Bel leaves** using a **pomegranate pen**. Throw these leaves in the **river**.

Purpose: Doing this **every Friday Navami** will bring and retain **money** and **prosperity**.

Shop Prosperity Remedy:

Action: If a shop is facing **decline in business**, place a **crystal pyramid** on the **counter** or hang it in the shop. Tie **asafoetida** with a thread and also wash a

new Peepal leaf daily, placing it in the shop (remove it in the evening).

Purpose: This remedy is said to **boost business** and bring prosperity to the shop.

Shivling Ritual for Financial Gains:

Action: Bring a **Shivling** made of **crystal or mercury** at home. Offer **half a spoon of milk** and **5-7 black sesame seeds** daily on the Shivling and apply **a drop of honey** with your **ring finger**.

Purpose: This ritual is believed to open **financial pathways**, bring **money inflow** and **relieve debts**. (Dispose of the offered milk-water in a pot, but avoid using a **Tulsi pot**).

Offering Aak Flowers for Business, Marriage, or Child Issues:

Action: Offer **red or white aak flowers** daily on **Shivling** or **Durga** for at least **6 months**.

Purpose: This remedy is believed to bring **positive changes** in business, marriage and child-related problems. It helps in resolving **obstacles** in these areas.

Apamarg or Sarpagandh Root Remedy for Evil Eye Protection:

Action: During **Gurupushya Yoga**, take the **root of Apamarg** or **Sarpagandh** and tie it with a **white thread**, then hang it near the **main door** of the house, shop, or office.

Purpose: This remedy protects the space from the **evil eye** and negative energies. The root should be hung in such a way that it **moves with the wind**, but does not touch the wall or door.

Henna Plant for Vastu and Prosperity:

Action: Plant a **henna plant** in the house or keep henna in the house. If wealth is decreasing due to changing houses, keep the **root of henna** taken during **Gurupushya**, **Ravipushya**, or **Sarvarthasiddhi Yoga** in the **place of worship**.

Purpose: The **henna plant** helps **remove Vastu defects** and brings **prosperity** to the home.

Tulsi and Other Plants for Prosperity and Harmony:

Tulsi: Planting **Tulsi** in the **northeast direction** increases **prosperity** and **prestige**.

Sunflower: Planting **sunflower** in the **east** increases **position** and **respect**.

Aak: Planting **white Aak** in the **east** brings **peace** and **happiness** to the house.

Marigold: Planting **marigold** in the **northeast/north** increases **love** and sweetness in relationships.

Amla: Planting **Amla** in the **southeast/north** brings **prosperity**.

Coriander: Planting **coriander** in the **south** prevents the **evil eye**.

Peepal: Plant a **Peepal tree** in a **pot in the west** and donate it to the temple when it grows to remove **poverty** and **misfortune**.

Five Tulsi plants: Planting **five Tulsi** in the house helps control **Vastu defects**.

Potato or Money Plant: Planting **potato plants** or **money plants** brings **prosperity**.

Selling Goods in the Shop:

Action: If goods in the shop are not selling, keep them in the **northwest direction** of the shop.

Alternatively, tie **nutmeg** and **betel nut** consecrated with the **Nirvana mantra** in a bundle and keep it with the goods during **Navratri**.

Purpose: This will help the goods to **sell quickly**.

Loan Repayment Remedy:

Action: Pour **jaggery** continuously into the **drain** for **43 days**. After this, continue pouring jaggery every **Tuesday**.

Purpose: This ritual helps in **repaying loans** and resolving financial issues.

Recovering a Loan from Someone:

Action: If someone is not returning the loan, remember them and offer a **coconut** to **Bhairav Baba** on **Saturday**, praying for the return of the money.

Purpose: After performing this ritual for **5 Saturdays**, the person is expected to **return the loan** or agree to repay it.

Getting a Loan Returned:

Action: If someone close to you is not returning the loan or you hesitate to ask, **remember** the person and **pray to Bhairav Baba** for the return of the money. Additionally, **pour some alcohol in the drain** on **Saturday**.

Purpose: This remedy is believed to help recover the loan and improve the chances of receiving the owed money.

Permanent Property or House:

> **Action**: On **Diwali/Navratri**, wear the **root of Anantmool** on a **red/white thread** around your neck after chanting **1008 Mangal Mantras**. Also, **donate bricks** 3-4 times a year on **Tuesdays** to a **temple**, **school**, or **labourer's house**.

> **Purpose**: This ritual is believed to remove **obstacles** in acquiring **permanent property** or a **house**.

Managing Finances:

> **Action**: Keep your **money** with **wife** or **mother** and only take the amount you need for daily expenses. **Ask for money** from them daily as per your need.

> **Purpose**: This practice is believed to bring **prosperity in money**.

Dealing with Financial Loss in Business:

> **Action**: If you face financial losses in business due to your partner, **light a jasmine lamp** in the **south direction** every **Tuesday**.

> **Purpose**: This is said to help resolve financial troubles in partnerships.

Overcoming Extravagance:

> **Action**: Wear a **silver Swastika** around your neck to curb **extravagance**. Additionally, tie the **root of Sarpagandh** in a **white thread** and hang it in your **kitchen** or **puja room** in a way that it does not touch the wall when it moves.

> **Purpose**: This helps prevent **excessive spending** and fosters **financial discipline**.

Preventing Debt:

Action: For those who often fall into **debt**, get **copper nails** hammered in the **four legs of your bed**.

Purpose: This remedy is believed to prevent financial issues and help **manage debt**.

Happiness and Good Fortune:

Action: **Anoint the Shivling of Sphatik** with **raw milk** daily and apply **white sandalwood** to bring **happiness** and **good fortune**.

Purpose: This remedy is believed to promote **prosperity** and overall well-being.

Removing Poverty on Somvati Amavasya:

Action: On **Somvati Amavasya**, perform **108 parikramas** around **Tulsi**.

Purpose: This is considered one of the simplest ways to **remove poverty** and bring **prosperity**.

Wealth and Prosperity on Diwali/Makar Sankranti/Baisakhi:

Action: Take a handful of **paddy husks, Basmati rice, whole moong, wheat, black mustard, black sesame** and **barley**, tie them in a cloth and keep them in the house during **Diwali, Makar Sankranti**, or **Baisakhi**.

Purpose: This remedy helps in gaining **happiness, peace, blessings** and combats **negative planetary influences**.

Enhancing Wealth and Prosperity:

Action: Place **Ganesha**, a **wall clock, mirror, money plant, clean drinking water**, or a **picture of fish or ship** in the **north direction**.

Purpose: These items are believed to attract **wealth** and **prosperity**.

Debt Relief with Mustard Oil:

Action: Apply **mustard oil** on **20 nails of hands and feet** and on both soles and heels daily, while reciting the **Gayatri Mantra** (except Sundays).

Purpose: This remedy is effective in **getting rid of debt** within a year, especially during **Sadhesati of Saturn**.

Positive Energy with Dakshinavarti Shankh:

Action: Keep a **Dakshinavarti Shankh** (conch shell) in the house, filled with water and sprinkle it daily. Also, ring **brass or bronze bells** in the evening and light a **ghee lamp**.

Purpose: This is believed to bring **happiness** and **prosperity** to the home.

Job/Business Improvement:

Action: If you face problems in your job, livelihood, or business, **change the color of your clothes**. Wear colors different from your usual ones.

Purpose: This change is said to bring **positive energy** and resolve obstacles in **career**.

Removing Vastu Defects:

Action: Paint the **main door** in **cherry color** and place a **Ganpati Yantra** in front of it or hang a **black horseshoe** upside down. Also, offer **coconuts** to **Bhairav** for **11 Saturdays**.

Purpose: This is believed to clear **Vastu defects** and **remove obstacles**.

Overcoming Delayed Household Work:

Action: Start distributing **sugar candy** or **batasha** every **Tuesday**.

Purpose: This remedy helps in overcoming **delays** in household work.

Preventing Money from Leaving:

Action: Keep **gold and white ratti grains** tied in **yellow cloth** and always carry them with you.

Purpose: This remedy helps in **retaining wealth** and prevents **money from slipping away**.

Job Transfer Issues:

Action: To get transferred to a desired location, **float four lemons** (without stains) in the **Yamuna River** during **Pushya Nakshatra**.

Purpose: This ritual helps in getting **transferred** successfully.

Financial Crisis Relief:

Action: Offer **mung beans** to **Lord Ganesha** and distribute them among the poor. Start on **Wednesday/Chaturthi Tithi** and continue for **43 days**.

Purpose: This remedy is believed to resolve financial problems and attract **prosperity**.

Protection from Evil Eye:

Action: Keep **whole salt** in an **earthen pot** at home.

Purpose: This protects the house from the **evil eye** and maintains **prosperity**.

Success in Business:

> **Action**: A **combination of orange and white** is favorable for **success** in business. Avoid wearing **black**, **blue**, or **dark purple** combinations.

> **Purpose**: These colors are believed to attract **success** and remove obstacles in business.

Wealth and Prosperity:

> **Action**: Keep **raw soil** in the house for **wealth**, **happiness** and **prosperity**. If you cannot keep it in the courtyard, place it in **pots**.

> **Purpose**: Raw soil is considered auspicious for **financial well-being**. Alternatively, bring **soil from a field ploughed by a bull** on Dhanteras/Navratri.

Job and Prestige:

> **Action**: Wear the **root of a vine** with a **Bombay cap** on both sides around your neck on a **Sunday** using a **white thread** and offer water to the rising **sun**.

> **Purpose**: This enhances **job prospects** and **prestige**.

Financial Loss After Marriage:

> **Action**: If your husband faces **financial losses** after marriage, the cause may be **Mangal Dosha**. **Mix vermilion in jasmine oil**, offer it to **Lord Ganesha** and distribute **red sweets** to laborers or **batashas** on **Tuesday**.

> **Purpose**: This remedy is believed to overcome **financial issues** caused by Mangal Dosha.

Stability in Job:

> **Action**: Keep **dhatura seeds** in your pocket when going to work. Also, offer **milk** to **Shivling** and apply **honey** with the **ring finger**.

> **Purpose**: These practices are believed to **stabilize** your **job** and remove obstacles.

Struggling in Business:

> **Action**: If you face **business losses** or financial struggles, wear a **silver ring** on the **little finger** and a **copper ring** on the **ring finger**.

> **Purpose**: This remedy helps with **financial stability** and **wealth retention**.

Removing Financial Blockages:

> **Action**: If you are facing a **financial blockage**, keep a **crystal Shivling** at home, offering **milk** and **black sesame seeds** daily and apply **honey** with the **ring finger**.

> **Purpose**: This ritual is believed to help remove **obstacles** and improve **monetary flow**.

Debt Recovery:

> **Action**: To get a loan repaid, remember the person for **21 days** and offer a **whole betel nut** to **Lord Ganesha/Hanuman** while praying for the return of the money.

> **Purpose**: This is believed to ensure the repayment of loans within **21 days**.

Home Vastu Adjustments:

> **Action**: **Close extra doors** in the house, especially if there are more than two, as money does not stay in

such homes. Repair any **holes** in the **main door** or **roof**.

Purpose: These Vastu remedies are believed to bring **financial stability** and **prosperity**.

Difficulties After Moving to a New Home:

Action: **Name the house** according to the **birth sign/ascendant** or the **fourth house sign** of the house owner to improve circumstances.

Purpose: This remedy is believed to solve problems associated with **Grihapravesh** and bring **peace**.

Preventing Financial Losses:

Action: If facing **losses** from business or financial dealings, place a **silver Swastika** around your neck.

Purpose: Wearing the **silver Swastika** helps bring **stability** and **financial growth**.

Money Retention:

Action: To ensure that **money stays** with you, keep **gold** and **white ratti grains** tied in a **yellow cloth**.

Purpose: This is believed to enhance **money retention** and prevent money from **leaving**.

Overcoming Job/Business Losses:

Action: If facing **recession** or losses in **business**, burn whole wood (without breaking) to make **coal** and throw it into the river.

Purpose: This helps to **overcome financial crises** and improves **business flow**.

Improving Wealth Flow:

Action: On **Diwali**, distribute **5 almonds** to children and give them to your **father/grandfather** with milk.

Purpose: This increases the chances of receiving **wealth** and **prosperity**.

Monthly Prosperity Boost:

Action: On every **monthly Shivratri**, offer **milk** on the **mercury Shivling** to invite **monetary gains**.

Purpose: This ritual leads to **wealth accumulation** and **debt relief**.

Overcoming Job/Business Obstacles:

Action: **Offer yellow potatoes** with **turmeric** to a **cow** on **Thursdays**, or feed **yellow rice** on **Fridays**.

Purpose: This ritual helps in **overcoming business obstacles** and boosts **profit**.

Financial Gain with Vastu Corrections:

Action: If you face **losses** after moving into a house, correct any **Vastu defects** by following proper Vastu principles.

Purpose: This remedy aims to ensure **stability** in wealth and **financial gain**.

Dharma, Devotion, Grace of God, Perfection, Fulfillment of Wishes - Mantras (Simple Uses)

Ashtakshari Mantra -

- ॐ नमो नारायणाय।
- Om Namo Narayanaya.

Dwadashakshari Mantra -

- ॐ नमो भगवते वासुदेवाय
- Om Namah Sri Vasudevaya

Vishnu Mantra -

- ॐ विष्णवे नमः।
- Om Vishnuve Namah.

Krishna Mantra -

- श्री कृष्णः शरणं मम।
- Shri Krishnah Sharanam Mam.

- ॐ क्लीं कृष्णाय गोपीजन वल्लभाय स्वाहा।
- Om Kleem Krishnaya Gopijan Vallabhaya Swaha.

- ॐ क्लीं कृष्णाय राधा वल्लभाय नमः।
- Om Kleem Krishnaya Radha Vallabhaya Namah.

- ॐ क्लीं कृष्णाय नमः।
- Om Kleem Krishnaya Namah.

Rama Mantra -

- ॐ रां रामाय नमः।
- Om Ram Ramaya Namah.

- ॐ जानकी वल्लभाय नमः।
- Om Janaki Vallabhaya Namah.

- ॐ सीता रामाय नमः।

- Om Sita Ramaya Namah.

- ॐ शरणागत वत्सलाय नमः।
- Om Sharanaagata Vatsalaya Namah.

Ganesha Mantra -

- ॐ गं गणपतये नमः।
- Om Gam Ganpataye Namah.

- ॐ वक्रतुण्डाय हुं।
- Om Vakratundaya Hum.

- ॐ श्रीं ग्लौं गं गणपतये वर वरद सर्वजनं मे वशमानय स्वाहा।
- Om Shri Glaun Gan Ganpataye Var Varad Sarvjanam Me Vashmanaya Swaha.

- ॐ विघ्नहर्त्रे नमः।
- Om Vignahartre Namah.

Kartikeya Mantra -

- 'ॐ तां त्राम्रचूडाय नमः।
- Om Tam Tramrachudaya Namah.

- ॐ उमापुत्राय कार्तिकेयाय नमः।
- Om Umaputraya Kartikeya Namah.

- ॐ देवसेनाय नमस्तुभ्यम्।
- Om Devasenaaya Namah.

Vārāha Avatar Mantra -

- ॐ नमः श्री वाराहाय धरण्युद्धारणाय स्वाहा।
- Om Namah Sri Vārāhaya Dharanyuddharanāya Swāhā.

Narasimha Mantra -

- ॐ क्ष्रौं नमो भगवते नृसिंहाय।
- Om Ksraun Namo Bhagavate Narasimha.

Krishna Vishnu -

- श्रीकृष्ण गोविन्द हरे मुरारे, हे नाथ नारायण वासुदेव।
- Sri Krishna Govinda Hare Murare, O Nath Narayana Vasudeva.

Ram Krishna -

- हरे राम हरे राम राम राम हरे हरे।
  हरे कृष्ण हरे कृष्ण कृष्ण कृष्ण हरे हरे।।
- Hare Ram Hare Ram Ram Ram Hare Hare.
  Hare Krishna Hare Krishna Hare Krishna Hare Hare.

Hanuman -

- ॐ ह्रीं हनुमते रामदूताय नमः।
- Om Hreem Hanumate Ramdutaya Namah.

- ॐ हं हनुमंताय नमः।
- Om Ham Hanumataya Namah.

- ॐ नमो भगवते आंजनेयाय महाबलाय स्वाहा।
- Om Namo Bhagavate Anjaneyaya Mahabalaya Swaha.

Durga Narvani Mantra -

- ॐ ऐं ह्रीं क्लीं चामुण्डायै विच्चै।
- Om Aim Hreem Kleem Chamundaye Viccha
-

Durga Beej Mantra -

- ॐ दुं दुर्गायै नमः।
- Om Dum Durgayai Namah.

Maya Beej Mantra -

- ॐ ह्रीं नमः।
- Om Hreem Namah.

Kali Mantra -

- क्रीं कालिके स्वाहा।
- Kreem Kalike Swaha.

- क्रीं क्रीं क्रीं हूं हूं ह्रीं ह्रीं दक्षिणे कालिके स्वाहा।
- Kreem Kreem Kreem Hum Hum Hreem Hreem Dakshine Kalike Swaha.

Parvati Mantra -

- ॐ पार्वत्यै नमः।
- Om Parvatyai Namah.

- ॐ पां पार्वतीभ्यां नमः।
- Om Pam Parvatibhyam Namah.

Lakshmi Mantra -

- ॐ श्रीं श्रीयै नमः।
- Om Shreem Shriyai Namah.

- ॐ श्रीं ह्रीं क्लीं महालक्ष्म्यै नमः।
- Om Shreem Hreem Kleem Mahalakshmyai Namah.

- ॐ महालक्ष्म्यै नमः।
- Om Mahalakshmyai Namah.

- ॐ कमलवासिन्यै नमः।
- Om Kamalvasinyai Namah.

Saraswati Mantra -

- ॐ ऐं सरस्वत्यै नमः।
- Om Aim Saraswatyai Namah.

- ॐ वाग्देव्यै नमः।
- Om Vagdevyai Namah.

- ॐ क्लीं हूं ऋद्वद् वादवादिनी स्वाहा।

- Om Kleem Hum Trat Vad Vadini Swaha.

Kubera Mantra -

- ॐ वैश्रवणाय स्वाहा।
- Om Vaishravanaya Svaha.

- ॐ यक्षराज कुबेराय देवधनाध्यक्षाय नमः।
- Om Yaksharaj Kuberaaya Devadhanadhyaakshaya Namah.

- ॐ निधिपतये नरवाहनाय नमः।
- Om Nidhipataye Narvahanaya Namah.

Shiv Mantra -

- ॐ नमः शिवाय।
- Om Namah Shivaya

Panchakshari Mantra -

- ॐ जूं सः।
- Om Jum Sah.

Laghu Mrityunjaya/Triyakshari Mantra -

- ॐ हौं जूं सः जूं हौं ॐ।
- Om Hau Joom Sah Joom Hau Om.

Laghu Mrityunjaya Beej Mantra -

- ॐ हौं जूं सः मां पालय पालय सः जूं ॐ।
- Om Hau Joom Sah Mam Pala Pala Sah Joom Hau Om.

Maha Mrityunjaya Mantra -

- ॐ त्र्यम्बकं यजामहे सुगन्धिं पुष्टिवर्धनम्।
- उर्वारुकमिव बन्धनान्मृत्योर्मुक्षीय माऽमृतात्॥

- Om Tryambakam Yajamahe Sugandhim Pushtivardhanam|
- Urvarukamiva Bandhanan Mrityor Mukshiya Ma Amritat.

Mrityunjaya Mantra -

- ॐ ह्रीं ॐ जूं ॐ सः ॐ भूः ॐ भुवः ॐ स्वः। ॐ त्र्यम्बकं यजामहे सुगन्धिं पुष्टिवर्धनम्। उर्वारुकमिव बन्धनान्मृत्योर्मुक्षीय माऽमृतात्॥ ॐ स्वः ॐ भुवः ॐ भूः ॐ सः ॐ जूं ॐ ह्रौं॥
- Om Hreem Om Joom Om Sah Om Bhu Om Bhuvah Om Swah. Om Tryambakam Yajamahe Sugandhim Pushtivardhanam, Urvarukamiva Bandhanan Mrityor Mukshiya Ma Amritat. Om Swah Om Bhuvah Om Bhu Om Sah Om Joom Om Hau Om

Mrityusanjivini Mantra -

- ॐ नमः शिवाय मृत्युञ्जय महादेवाय नमस्तुते।
- Om Namah Shivaya Mrityunjaya Mahadevaya Namastute

Stuti Mantra / Prayer Mantra / Hymn of Praise

Gayatri Mantra -

- ॐ भूर्भुवः स्वः तत्सवितुर्वरेण्यं भर्गो देवस्य धीमहि धियो यो नः प्रचोदयात्।
- Om Bhur Bhuva Swaha, Tat Savitur Varenyam, Bhargo Devasya Dhimahi, Dhiyo Yo Nah Pracodayat.

Dattatreya Mantra -

- ॐ द्रां दत्तात्रेयाय नमः।
- Om Dram Dattatreyaaya Namaha.

Agni Mantra -

- ॐ अग्नये नमः।/ ॐ सप्तजिह्वाये नमः।
- Om Agnaye Namaha. / Om Saptajihvaye Namaha.

Vayu Mantra -

- ॐ वायवे नमः।/ ॐ यं वायुदेवाय नमः।
- Om Vayave Namaha. / Om Yam Vayudevaya Namaha.

Varuna Mantra -

- ॐ वं वरुणाय नमः। / ॐ नीलपुरुषाय नमः।
- Om Vam Varunaya Namaha. / Om Nilapurushaya Namaha.

Akasha Mantra -

- ॐ खं ब्रह्म।/ ॐ महाशून्याय नमः।
- Om Kham Brahm. / Om Mahashunyaya Namaha.

Prithvi Mantra -

- ॐ पृथिवी देव्यै नमः।/ ॐ भुं भूम्यै नमः।

- Om Prithvi Devyai Namaha. / Om Bhur Bhomyai Namaha.

Tulsi Mantra -

- ॐ तुलस्यै नमः। / ॐ कृष्णजीवनीभ्यां नमः।
- Om Tulasyai Namaha. / Om Krishna Jivani Bhayam Namaha.

Bhairava Mantra -

- ॐ भैरवाय नमः। ॐ कालभैरवाय नमः। 'ॐ बटुकभैरवाय नमः।'/ 'ॐ महाभैरवाय नमः।' 'ॐ आपद्धारणाय नमः।'
- Om Bhairavaya Namaha. / Om Kalabhairavaya Namaha. / Om Batuk Bhairavaya Namaha. / Om Mahabhairavaya Namaha. / Om Apaddharanaya Namaha.

Nav Grah Mantras

Surya Mantra (Mantras for Sun)

Mool Mantra:
- ॐ ह्रीं घृणिः सूर्यादित्योम्।
- Om Hreem Ghrinih Suryadityom

Beej Mantra
- ॐ सूं सूर्याय नमः
- Om Sum Sūryāya Namaḥ

Tantric Mantra:
- ॐ ह्रां ह्रीं ह्रौं सः सूर्याय नमः।
- Om Hraam Hreem Hraum Sah Suryaya Namaha

Mental Chanting:
- श्री वल्लभशरणं ममः।
- Shri Vallabh Sharanam Mama

Simple Mantra:
- ॐ सूर्याय नमः।
- Om Suryaya Namaha

Maha Mantra:

- जपाकुसुम संकाशं काश्यपेयं महदद्युतिम्।
  तमोरिंसर्वपापघ्नं प्रणतोऽस्मि दिवाकरम्॥1॥
- Japakusuma   Sankasham   Kashyapeyam
  Mahadadyutim
  Tamorim   Sarvapapaghnam   Pranatosmi
  Divakaram ॥1॥

Surya Gayatri
- ॐ आदित्याय विदमहे प्रभाकराय धीमहि तन्नः सूर्य प्रचोदयात्
- Om Ādityāya Vidmahe Prabhākarāya Dhīmahi Tannaḥ Sūrya Prachodayāt

Chandra Mantra (Mantras for Moon)

Mool Mantra:

* ॐ सों सोमाय नमः।
* Om Som Somaya Namaha

Beej Mantra
* ॐ चम् चन्द्राय नमः |
* Om Cham Chandrāya Namah

Tantric Mantra:
* ॐ श्रां श्रीं श्रौं सः चन्द्रमसे नमः।
* Om Shraam Shreem Shraum Sah Chandramase Namaha

Mental Chanting:
* श्री विठ्ठल शरणं ममः।
* Shri Vitthal Sharanam Mamah

Simple Mantra:
* ॐ सोमाय नमः। (सरल मंत्र)
* Om Somaya Namaha

Maha Mantra:

* दधिशंखतुषाराभं क्षीरोदार्णव संभवम्।
  नमामि शशिनं सोमं शंभोर्मुकुट भूषणम्।
* Dadhishankhatushaarabhm, Ksheerodarnava sambhavam,
  Namami shashinam somam, Shambhor mukut bhushanam.

Chandra Gayatri

* ॐ क्षीर-पुत्राय विद्महे अमृत-तत्वाय धीमहि तन्नो सोमः प्रचोदयात् ॥
* Om Ksheer-Putraaya Vidmahe, Amrit-Tattvaaya Dhimahi,
  Tanno Somah Prachodayat.

Mangal Mantra (Mantras for Mars)

Mool Mantra:
* ॐ अं अंगारकाय नमः।
* Om Ang Angarakaya Namaha

Beej Mantra

- ॐ कुं कुजाय नमः
- Om Kum Kujaya Namah

Tantric Mantra:
- ॐ क्रां क्रीं क्रौं सः भौमाय नमः।
- Om Kraam Kreem Kraum Sah Bhaumaya Namaha

Mental Chanting:
- श्री गोकुलेश शरणं ममः।
- Shri Gokulesh Sharanam Mamah

Simple Mantra:
- ॐ भौमाय नमः।
- Om Bhaumaya Namaha

Maha Mantra:

- धरणीगर्भ संभूतं विद्युत्कांति समप्रभम्।
  कुमारं शक्तिहस्तं तं मंगलं प्रणमाम्यहम्॥
- Dharanīgarbha sambhūtam vidyutkānti samaprabham |
  Kumāram śaktihastam tam maṅgalam praṇamāmyaham ||

Mangal Gayatri

- ॐ अंगारकाय विदमहे शक्ति-हस्ताय धीमहि तन्नो भौमः प्रचोदयात्।
- Om Angārakāya Vidmahe Shakti-Hastāya Dhīmahi Tanno Bhaumaḥ Prachodayāt |

Budh Mantra (Mantras for Mercury)

Mool Mantra/ Beej Mantra :
- ॐ बुं बुधाय नमः।
- Om Bun Budhaya Namaha

Tantric Beej Mantra:

- ॐ ब्रां ब्रीं ब्रौं सः बुधाय नमः।
- Om Braam Breem Braum Sah Budhaya Namaha

Mental Chanting:
- श्री गोविन्द शरणं ममः।
- Shri Govind Sharanam Mamah

Simple Mantra:
- ॐ बुधाय नमः।
- Om Budhaya Namaha

Maha Mantra:

- प्रियंगुकलिकाश्यामं रुपेणाप्रतिमं बुधम्।
  सौम्यं सौम्यगुणोपेतं तं बुधं प्रणमाम्यहम्॥
- Priyangu-kalika-shyāmaṁ rūpeṇāpratimaṁ budham |
  Saumyaṁ saumya-guṇopetaṁ taṁ budham praṇamāmyaham ||

Budha Gayatri

- ॐ चन्द्रपुत्राय विदमहे रोहिणी प्रियाय धीमहि तन्नोबुधः प्रचोदयात् ॥
- Om Chandraputrāya Vidmahe Rohiṇī Priyāya Dhīmahi Tanno Budhah Prachodayāt

Guru Mantra (Mantra for Jupiter)

Mool Mantra/ Beej Mantra :
- ॐ बृं बृहस्पतये नमः।
- Om Brim Brihaspataye Namaha

Tantric Mantra:
- ॐ ग्रां ग्रीं ग्रौं सः गुरवे नमः।
- Om Gram Greem Graum Sah Gurave Namaha

Mental Chanting:
- श्री गिरिधरशरणं ममः।
- Shri Giridhar Sharanam Mamah

Simple Mantra:

- ॐ बृहस्पतये नमः।
- Om Brihaspataye Namaha

Maha Mantra:

- देवानांच ऋषीनांच गुरूं कांचन सन्निभम्।
  बुद्धिभूतं त्रिलोकेशं तं नमामि बृहस्पतिम् ॥
- Devānāmṛṣi-nāṁca gurūṁ kāñcana-sannibham.
  Buddhi-bhūtaṁ tri-lokeśaṁ taṁ namāmi bṛhaspatim.

Brishaspati Gayatri:

- देवानांच ऋषीनांच गुरूं कांचन सन्निभम्।
  बुद्धिभूतं त्रिलोकेशं तं नमामि बृहस्पतिम् ॥
- Devānāmṛṣi-nāṁca gurūṁ kāñcana-sannibham.
  Buddhi-bhūtaṁ tri-lokeśaṁ taṁ namāmi bṛhaspatim.

Shukra Mantra (Mantras for Venus)

Mool / Beej Mantra:

- ॐ शुं शुक्राय नमः।
- Om Shum Shukraya Namaha

Tantrik Mantra:

- ॐ द्रां द्रीं द्रौं सः शुक्राय नमः।
- Om Dram Dreem Droum Sah Shukraya Namaha

Mental Chanting:

- श्री यदुनाथ शरणं ममः।
- Shri Yadunath Sharanam Mamaha

Simple Mantra:

- ॐ शुक्राय नमः।
- Om Shukraya Namaha

Maha Mantra:

- हिमकुंद मृणालाभं दैत्यानां परमं गुरूम्।
  सर्वशास्त्र प्रवक्तारं भार्गवं प्रणमाम्यहम्॥
- Himkund Mrinalabhm Daityanam Param Gurum,
  Sarvashastra Pravaktaram Bhargavam Pranamamyaham.

Shukra Gayatri

- ॐ भृगुवंशजाताय विद्यामहे श्वेतवाहनाय धीमहि तन्न: शुक्र: प्रचोदयात्॥
- ॐ अश्वध्वजाय विद्महे धनुर्हस्ताय धीमहि तन्नः शुक्र: प्रचोदयात्।
- Om Bhṛguvanśajātāya Vidyāmahe Śvetavāhanāya Dhīmahi Tannaḥ Śukraḥ Prachodayāt.
- Om Ashvadhwajāya Vidmahe Dhanurhastāya Dhīmahi Tannaḥ Śukraḥ Prachodayāt.

Shani Mantra (Mantras for Saturn)

Mool/ Beej Mantra:

- ॐ शं शनैश्चराय नमः।
- Om Sham Shanaischaraya Namaha.

Tantrik Mantra:

- ॐ प्रां प्रीं प्रौं सः शनये नमः।
- Om Praam Preem Praum Sah Shanaye Namaha.

Mental Chanting:

- श्री घनश्याम शरणं ममः।
- Shree Ghanashyam Sharanam Mama.

Simple Mantra:

- ॐ शनिदेवाय नमः।
- Om Shanidevaya Namaha.

Maha Mantra:

- नीलांजन समाभासं रविपुत्रं यमाग्रजम्।
  छायामार्तंड संभूतं तं नमामि शनैश्चरम्॥

- Nīlāñjana samābhāsaṃ raviputraṃ yamāgrajam |
  Chāyāmārtaṇḍa sambhūtaṃ taṃ namāmi śanaiścaram ||

Shani Gayatri:

- ॐ काकध्वजाय विद्महे खड्गहस्ताय धीमहि तन्नो मन्दः प्रचोदयात् ||
  ॐ सूर्यपुत्राय विद्महे मृत्युरूपाय धीमहि तन्न: सौरि: प्रचोदयात ||
- Om kākadhvajāya vidmahe khaḍgahastāya dhīmahi tanno mandaḥ pracodayāt ||
  Om sūryaputrāya vidmahe mṛtyurūpāya dhīmahi tannaḥ saurih pracodayāt ||

Rahu Mantra

Mool/ Beej Mantra:
- ॐ रां राहवे नमः |
- Om Raam Rahave Namaha

Tantrik Mantra:
- ॐ भ्रां भ्रीं भ्रौं सः राहवे नमः |
- Om Bhraam Bhreem Bhraum Sah Rahave Namaha.
- ॐ छ्रां छ्रीं छ्रौं सः राहवे नमः |
- Om Chhraam Chhreem Chhraum Sah Rahave Namaha.

Mental Chanting:
- श्री बालकृष्ण शरणं ममः |
- Shree Bala Krishna Sharanam Mama.

Maha Mantra:

- अर्धकायं महावीर्यं चंद्रादित्य विमर्दनम् |
  सिंहिकागर्भसंभूतं तं राहुं प्रणमाम्यहम् ||||
- Ardhakāyaṃ mahāvīryaṃ candrāditya vimardanam |
  Siṃhikāgarbhasambhūtaṃ taṃ rāhuṃ praṇamāmyaham ||||

Rahu Gayatri

- ॐ शिरोरुपाय विद्महे अमृतेशाय धीमहि तन्नो राहू: प्रचोदयात् ॥
- Om shirorupāya vidmahe amṛteśāya dhīmahi tanno rāhuḥ pracodayāt.

Ketu Mantra

Mool/Beej Mantra:
- ॐ कें केतवे नमः।
- Om Kem Ketave Namaha.

Tantrik Mantra:
- ॐ स्त्रां स्त्रीं स्त्रौं सः केतवे नमः।
- Om Straam Streem Straum Sah Ketave Namaha.

- ॐ सां सीं सौं सः केतवे नमः।
- Om Sraam Sreem Sraum Sah Ketave Namaha.

Mental Chanting:
- श्री रघुनाथ शरणं ममः।
- Shree Raghunath Sharanam Mama.

Maha Mantra:

- पलाशपुष्पसंकाशं तारकाग्रह मस्तकम्।
  रौद्ररौद्रात्मकं घोरं तं केतुं प्रणमाम्यहम्॥
- Pālāsapuṣpasaṅkāśaṁ tārakāgraha mastakam.
  Raudraṁ raudrātmakaṁ ghoram taṁ ketuṁ praṇamāmyaham ॥

Ketu Gayatri:

- ॐ पद्मपुत्राय विद्महे अमृताय धीमहि तन्नो केतुः प्रचोदयात्॥
- Om Padmaputraya Vidmahe Amritaya Dhimahi Tanno Ketu Prachodayat ॥

Navagraha Mantra -

- ब्रह्मा मुरारिस्त्रिपुरांतकारी भानुः शशि भूमिसुत बुधश्च।
  गुरुश्च शुक्रः शनिराहुकेतवः कुर्वन्तु सर्वे मम सुप्रभातम्॥

- **Brahma, Murari, Tripurantakari Bhanu, Shashi, Bhoomisuta Budh।**
  Gurushca Shukra, Shanirahuketavah, Kurvantu Sarve Mama Suprabhatam ॥

Simple Home Remedies and Totke

Donate Seven Grains(Sat Anaja):
A mixture of seven grains - urad, moong, wheat, chickpea, barley, rice and kangani - should be donated. Each of these grains holds spiritual significance and donating them helps in gaining blessings for wealth and prosperity. The act of donating is also seen as a way to remove obstacles and improve one's financial situation.

Tilak with Ashtagandha and Incense:
Applying a daily tilak (mark) made of Ashtagandha on the forehead helps increase concentration, spiritual growth and positivity. **Ashtagandha** is a mixture of eight powerful fragrances (agar, kasturi, kumkum, camphor, sandalwood, gorochan, devdar and long pepper). It is believed to enhance one's inner power and create a protective aura. Along with applying the tilak, burning **Ashtagandha incense sticks** during meditation (made of agar, chharila, jatamansi, kapurkachari, guggul, devdar, gau-ghrit and white sandalwood) also helps improve focus and overall well-being. This practice is recommended for those looking to enhance their meditation and inner peace.

Maha Mrityunjaya Havan for Debt Relief:
Performing a **Havan** (fire ritual) using the **Maha Mrityunjaya Mantra** is one of the most powerful remedies for getting rid of debt-related doshas (past life debts). Even offering 21 offerings daily can bring positive changes. Acts of service - such as helping orphans, the sick, lepers, animals, or plants - also help in spiritual growth and devotion and by doing so, one can remove financial blockages. This practice connects you with higher energies and purifies past karmic debts

Lighting Ghee Lamp & Reciting Gayatri Mantras:
Lighting a **ghee lamp** and reciting **108 Gayatri Mantras** followed by 10 recitations of the **Devi Atharvashirsha** daily (especially during the first Navratri to Dashami or during Mangal Ashwini Yoga) helps attract the blessings of Goddess Durga. This practice is said to provide the four primary goals of life - **dharma (righteousness), artha (wealth), kama (desire), moksha (liberation)** - and fulfill all desires. Reciting at least one mantra daily after completing 108 mantras helps maintain

a steady connection with the divine and ensures the continued blessings of the Goddess.

Writing Ishta's Name for Blessings:
Writing your **Ishta's (chosen deity's)** name daily with a **pen made of pomegranate wood** and **ink mixed with Astagandha (eight fragrances)** and Ganga water helps establish a spiritual connection with your deity. This practice should be done without any corrections, at least 51 or 108 times a day in a diary. Once the diary is full, it should be immersed in a river. This act brings blessings, increases positivity and deepens your devotion to the deity, while also strengthening your faith.

Navratri Ritual with Narvaan Mantra:
During the nine days of **Navratri**, write the **Narvaan Mantra** ("हौं हस्र रब्र हसा हस्खौं सौं हनभत नभौं") five times daily on **nine Bhhojpatra** (birch bark) leaves using a pen made of pomegranate wood and ink mixed with Astagandha, sandalwood, saffron, or turmeric. After writing, perform a ritual of lighting incense and lamps. Keeping these leaves with you or in your home, office, or shop provides protection from the evil eye, boosts confidence and wards off negative energies. If you're suffering from an illness or negative thoughts, immerse one of the leaves in water, recite the mantra and drink the water for healing.

Meditation Tips for Better Focus:
To improve your meditation practice, apply a tilak of **Astagandha** on your forehead before sitting down. Burn **incense, camphor and loban (a type of resin)**, or place **4-5 big cinnamon sticks** in front of you. Performing **3 rounds of Pranayama (breathing exercises)** helps clear the mind, improves focus and prepares the body for a deeper meditative state. This practice is especially useful for those looking to meditate effectively, calm the mind and increase concentration.

Getting Rid of a Bad Habit (Coconut Ritual): If you want to break a bad habit, perform a ritual on a Saturday by breaking a coconut three times on your head and offering it to Goddess Kali. This symbolizes the bad habit and by praying to Kali, you are asking her to help you free yourself from it. Over the course of 5 to 11 Saturdays, your desire to continue the habit will reduce and you will begin to find the strength to break it. If necessary, continue this practice for up to 41 or 70 Saturdays for quicker or more stubborn results.

For Brahmins - Gayatri Japa and Rituals: Brahmins should engage in Gayatri Japa (chanting of the Gayatri mantra), Gayatri Kavach (protective mantra armor) and perform a Gayatri Havan (fire ritual). Doing this on Sundays, particularly with **mango wood**, will bring swift results. This strengthens their connection with the divine and enhances spiritual power. Additionally, worshipping Lord Shiva (Shiv Upasana) is also highly beneficial for Brahmins.

For Kshatriyas - Worship Durga, Narasimha, or Hanuman: Kshatriyas, who are traditionally warriors, will see quick results by worshipping powerful deities like **Durga**, **Narasimha**, or **Hanuman**. These deities help them attain strength, protection and success in battles and challenges.

For Vaishyas - Worship Vishnu, Ram, or Krishna: For Vaishyas, who are associated with commerce and business, worshipping **Vishnu**, **Ram**, or **Krishna** is beneficial. These deities bring prosperity, success in business and wealth.

For Shudras - Seek Protection from Kali, Bhairav, or Rudra: Shudras can worship **Kali**, **Bhairav**, or **Rudra** to overcome struggles and challenges in life. These deities provide protection from harm and help in overcoming difficult situations.

Peacock Feathers for Removing Negative Energies: Clean and purify **4-5 peacock feathers** and during **Navratri** (on the 8th, 9th, or 10th day), wrap them in **yellow cloth** and place them in the **north direction**. Recite the mantra 'ॐ ह्रीं बटुकाय ह्रीं' **(Om Hrim Batukaya Hrim)** 10 times. This helps eliminate negative influences in the house, workplace, or any area with **Vastu dosha** (architectural defects). The feathers can also be kept near your study table or pillow to improve focus and remove bad energies.

Shivalingam Ritual for Quick Results: Mix **turmeric, cow dung, flour, sugar, seven grains, ghee, shami/peepal/ber tree ashes, Ganges/Narmada water/cow's urine, black sesame seeds** and **flower petals** to form a **Shivalingam**. Place the 12-finger long Shivalingam in the **north direction**

and perform daily worship. This quickly grants Lord Shiva's blessings, resolving difficult problems in life.

Using Dhoop (Incense) for Fear of Death: To overcome the fear of death, burn **dhoop (incense)** made from **durva grass**. For fertility and progeny issues, use **belpatra** leaves or flowers. To become Shiva-like and to remove past life debts, use **shami leaves** or flowers. For wealth and prosperity, use **lotus flowers**. **Belpatra** is also recommended for success in jobs and government matters. For spiritual growth, **Chandan (sandalwood)** is used and for happiness and peace, **milk** is used in the abhishek (ritual bathing). **Honey** is used during worship for debt removal.

Night-Time Spiritual Practices for Success: Performing **Shiv Puja** or other spiritual practices between **3 hours after sunset to 9 hours later**, especially during the **Abhijit Muhurta (11:45 am to 11:45 pm)**, helps in achieving success in life. These practices bring balance to all aspects of life, including **Dharma (righteousness)**, **Artha (wealth)**, **Kama (desires)** and **Moksha (liberation)**.

Self-Improvement with Peacock Feathers or Datura Seeds: During **Navratri**, place **peacock feathers** or **Datura seeds** in the north direction, sit on a **yellow or white mat** and perform a **havan** by mixing **Jatamansi**, **Guggul** and **Camphor** with **samidha (wood sticks)**. Recite the mantra 'ॐ नमो भगवते रुद्राय शूलपाणये पिशाचाधिपतये आवेशाय कृष्णपिंगलाय फट् स्वाहा' 1008 times. This helps in overcoming mental obstacles, depression, fear, anxiety and negative tendencies, replacing them with confidence, positivity and inspiration.

Reciting Sacred Texts (Shrimad Devi Bhagavat, Ramayana, or Sunderkand): Reciting the entire **Shrimad Devi Bhagavat**, **Ramayana**, or the **108 chapters of the Sunderkand** is an extremely powerful remedy for all kinds of problems. These recitations, if performed without any expectation of material gain or reward, bring divine grace, devotion and help uplift the self. Regular recitation leads to spiritual growth, clears obstacles and brings blessings. By dedicating time and focus to these sacred texts, a person receives guidance and divine protection in their life.

Shravan Month Ritual for Fulfilling Desires: During the **Shravan month**, a special ritual can be performed from **Pratipada** to **Purnima** (from the first day of the month to the full moon). For this, you need to take **Nagkesar flowers** corresponding to the number of the day (one flower on Pratipada, two on Dwitiya and so on up to fifteen flowers on Purnima). Offer prayers and place the flowers on a **Shivling**. Then, face north and recite the **Panchakshari mantra** (the mantra "ॐ नमः शिवाय" or "Om Namah Shivaya") 108 times (or at least 51 times). Afterward, offer **milk** to the Shivling. This ritual is believed to fulfill all desires, bring prosperity and enhance spiritual growth. It is important to avoid tamasic food and behaviors during this ritual for the best results.

Pranayama and Meditation to Calm Restless Mind: If your mind feels restless and distracted during meditation, **Pranayama** (breathing exercises) can help calm it. You can also drink water from a **silver vessel** and apply **white sandalwood paste** on your forehead. Sit on a **Kushasan** (a sacred grass mat) in front of a silver **Ganesha idol**. Recite the mantra 'ॐ विघ्नेश्वराय नमः' (Om Vighneshvaraaya Namah) and the **Ketu mantra** for **5 malas** (108 repetitions per mala) daily. Practicing this regularly will help bring focus and stability to the mind in just a few days.

Lighting Lamps and Using Brass Bells During Worship: During worship, light **5 lamps** using **desi ghee** (clarified butter). **Ring a heavy bell** made of **brass** or **bronze** while reciting the mantra 'ॐ' (Om). You can also perform **Udgeet Pranayama**, which involves taking **3 deep breaths** with a prolonged 'ॐ' sound. Alternatively, perform **8 cycles** of **Pranayama**. Afterward, recite your personal mantra (or, if not possible, recite it while lying down). Filter the water used in the ritual and drink it in small quantities, both in the morning and evening. This practice purifies the mind, body and spirit, bringing spiritual benefits and physical well-being.

Meditation and Tilak of Ashtagandha: When meditating, apply a **tilak** (mark) of **Ashtagandha** on your forehead. This mixture of fragrances (agar, kasturi, kumkum, camphor, sandalwood, gorochan, devdar and long pepper) enhances focus, removes negative energies and brings spiritual purity. Additionally, burn **Agarwood**, **Camphor** and **Loban incense sticks** or place **4-5 sticks of Big Cardamom** in front of you.

Perform **3 Pranayama cycles** to increase concentration and deepen meditation. These practices help you focus better, bringing clarity and peace of mind during your meditation sessions.

Health Mantra

Eye Pain -

'ॐ नमो रामा का धनुष लक्ष्मण का बान। आँख दर्द करे तो लक्ष्मण कुमार की आन।' **"Om Namo Rāmā kā dhanuṣ Lakṣmaṇ kā bān. Ãkh dard kare to Lakṣmaṇ Kumār kī ān."** mantra is believed to provide relief from eye strain and pain. Reciting this mantra is said to eliminate eyestrain and give comfort to the eyes. Additionally, it is recommended to recite this mantra 7 times and then gently press the eyes to relieve any discomfort. This mantra is the **"Sabar Mantra"**.

Eyes Diseases/Disorders -

'ॐ शां शंखिनीम्यां नमः। ' **'Om Shām Śaṅkhinīmyām namaha.'** (Reciting this mantra at least one rosary daily controls eye disorders. Medicines become fruitful. New flower-like disorders are destroyed by reciting the mantra 11 times daily, taking a red flower at sunrise and sprinkling it. Reading 'Netropanishad' is also very beneficial.) 'ॐ यं यमघण्टाम्यां नमः।' **'Om Yam Yamaghaṇṭāmyām namaha.'**

Ear Disorders -

'ॐ द्वां द्वारवासिनीम्यां नमः।' **'Om Dwām Dwāravāsinīmyām namaha.'** (Reciting this mantra with 'Shunya Mudra' (a specific hand gesture) benefits ear pain, hearing difficulties and other ear-related issues. It also makes medicines more effective.

Throat Diseases -

'ॐ चिं चित्रघण्टाम्यां नमः।' **'Om Chim Chitraghṇṭāmyām namaha.'** Reciting this mantra is beneficial for throat-related diseases. Recite at least one rosary daily. It has been found to be particularly effective in cases of throat cancer.

Tooth Diseases -

'ॐ कौं कौमारीम्यां नमः।' **'Om Kaum Kaumārīmyām namaha.'** Reciting this mantra benefits toothache, tooth pain and other tooth-related diseases. For painless tooth extraction in children, give them water sanctified by 108 recitations of this mantra.

Tongue Disorders -

'ॐ सं सर्वमंगलाम्यां नमः।' **'Om Saṁ Sarvamaṅgalāmyām namaha.'** Reciting this mantra is highly beneficial for tongue-related disorders and problems such as stuttering, stammering, etc. Regular recitation of 10-11 rosaries daily can help experience its tangible effects within a few weeks.

Diseases of the Throat and above (EENT) -

'ॐ ऐं ह्रीं क्लीं क्लौं क्लौं अर्हं नमः।' **'Om Aiṁ Hrīṁ Klīṁ Klaūṁ Klaūṁ Arhaṁ namaha.'** Reciting this mantra is beneficial for all diseases above the throat, including disorders of the teeth, ears, nose and eyes. It is advisable to recite this mantra while sitting on a red-colored seat, wearing red clothes, in front of the 'Navadurga Yantra'.

Brain disorders -

'ॐ उं उमादेवीम्यां नमः।' **'Om Uṁ Umādevīmyāṁ namaha.'** Reciting this mantra is beneficial for mental illnesses such as madness, epilepsy, mental instability and hysteria. One can recite this mantra themselves or get it done by a Brahmin priest with a sankalpa.

Abdominal Disorders -

'ॐ शुं शूलधारिणीम्यां नमः।' **'Om Shuṁ Shūladhāriṇīmyāṁ namaha.'** This mantra helps control abdominal pain and all disorders related to the abdomen. It helps alleviate childbirth pain and reduces obesity.

Intestinal Disorders -

'ॐ कां कालरात्रिम्यां नमः।' **'Om Kāṁ Kālarātrimyāṁ namaha.'** This mantra is beneficial for all disorders of the intestines, stomach and also the liver. It is an experienced mantra in all the aforementioned subjects.

Liver disease -

Liver Disease -

'ॐ यकाराय नमः शिवाय।' **'Om Yakārāya namaḥ Śivāya.'** By placing the right hand on the liver and chanting this mantra daily in a high pitch, it helps to remove liver weakness and is beneficial in liver diseases.

Heart Disease -

'ॐ लं ललितादेवीम्यां नमः।' **'Om Laṁ Lalitādevīmyāṁ namaha.'** This mantra helps to remove heart diseases, provides health benefits and increases self-confidence.

Note - Chanting the 'Gayatri mantra' while sitting on a Kushasan (a sacred grass mat) facing the rising sun or standing under a Banyan tree for half to one hour with a loud and clear voice has been found to be extremely effective in heart diseases.

Spinal Cord Disorders -

'ॐ धं धनुर्धारिणीम्यां नमः। ' **'Om Dhaṁ Dhanurdhāriṇīmyāṁ namaha.'** This mantra is beneficial for spinal cord diseases, back pain and other problems like cervical spondylosis. One can chant it themselves or get it done by a Brahmin priest with a sankalpa (a vow or resolution). Chanting it with faith yields amazing results.

Secret Diseases -

'ॐ गुं गुह्येश्वरीम्यां नमः। ' **'Om Guṁ Guhyeśvarīmyāṁ namaha.'** This mantra is beneficial for diseases like diabetes, urinary disorders, leucorrhoea, piles, semen defects, etc. Chant the above mantra with purity and cleanliness after taking a bath.

Bone, Blood, Marrow and Skin Disorders -

'ॐ पां पार्वतीम्यां नमः।' **'Om Pāṁ Pārvatīmyāṁ namaha.'** This mantra is especially beneficial for blood, marrow and bone-related diseases. Skin patients or leprosy patients should chant this mantra as much as possible. It will have a greater and faster impact when combined with medicine. Leprosy patients should chant while sitting under a neem tree and skin patients should chant while sitting in the sun.

Blood Pressure -

'ॐ वं वज्रहस्ताम्यां नमः।' 'Om Vam Vajrahastāmyām namaha.' Chant this mantra with a calm mind in the morning or before sleeping at night. This will help control blood pressure and eliminate all air-related disorders.

Fever Relief -

'ॐ मुं मुकुटेश्वरीम्यां नमः।' 'Om Mum Mukuteśvarīmyām namaha.' This mantra is useful for fever relief, reduces heat and also controls blood acidity or acidity. It is recommended to chant this mantra while holding the root of Calotropis (Ak) or Achyranthes (Apamarg) or ginger in your hand or keeping it under your pillow to get quick benefits.

Grief, Depression, Anger, etc. -

'ॐ शो शोकविनाशिनीम्यां नमः।' 'Om Sho Shokavināśinīmyām namaha.' Chanting this mantra is useful for calming grief, depression, tension, anger, fear, mental disorders and conflicts between husband and wife and for bringing mental peace and normalcy.

Note: If an angry person cannot chant this mantra themselves, their spouse or blood relative can chant it 108 times on a Tuesday, write the person's name along with the mantra on a Bhojpatra leaf using a pomegranate pen and Ashtagandha/White Sandalwood and then soak the leaf in pure honey. This will calm the person's anger and they will become normal. If necessary, repeat the process for 5 or 11 Tuesdays. The effect will be seen from the first attempt itself.

Ghostly or Spiritually related Obstacles -

'ॐ कं कल्याणशोभनाम्यां नमः।' **'Om Kaṁ Kalyāṇaśobhanāmyāṁ namaḥ.'** Chanting this mantra along with using a peacock feather to ward off evil spirits and burning incense sticks made of Lohban, Gugal, Jatamansi, Desi Kapur, Red and White Sandalwood on cow dung with ghee, will bring benefits. Chanting the mantra 108 times daily will bring benefits within 11 to 45 days. If the problem is severe, continue for 3 to 6 months.

Note: In cases of untimely death and planetary obstacles, chanting this mantra with faith, at least 5 rosaries daily, will also bring benefits.

Tuberculosis/Disease of Consumption -

'ॐ पं पद्मावतीम्यां नमः।' **'Om Paṁ Padmāvatīmyāṁ namaha.'** This mantra is beneficial for tuberculosis and phlegm-related diseases. For tuberculosis, chant this mantra 11 times and consecrate a single clove of garlic, then wear a garland of 21 or 51 cloves of garlic consecrated in the same way. Inhale Desi Kapur and take pills made from old jaggery and black pepper, 5-10 times a day. Chant this mantra. When the garland dries up, make a new one and wear it again. This will also bring benefits for asthma.

Chant 'Jwargathari' as regularly as possible yourself or get it recited by some learned person for 21 days, then all the recurring fevers will be cured.

Diabetes -

'ॐ ह्रीं' - 'ऐं श्रीं।' **'Om Hrīṁ'** - **'Aiṁ Śrīṁ'**. Chant this mantra mentally, like pranayama, with inhalation and exhalation. Inhale deeply with the mantra 'ॐ ह्रीं' 'Om Hrīṁ' and exhale with 'ऐं श्रीं।' 'Aiṁ Śrīṁ'. Do this daily 108/111 times, but start with 11 times initially. Then, gradually increase the practice to 21, 51, 81 and so on, up to 108/111 times.

Alternatively - 'ॐ नमो भगवते रुद्राय (हं हं हं)।' **'Om Namo Bhagavate Rudrāya (Haṁ Haṁ Haṁ).'** Chant the first part of this mantra mentally, taking deep breaths and then exhale the second part, which is in parentheses, in three strokes, as if the breath is moving towards the spine, near the navel. Start with 11 times and gradually increase to 21, 51, 81 and so on, up to 108/111 times. Do this both in the morning and evening. The more you do, the more benefits you will get. However, it is recommended to do this at least half an hour before eating or at least three to four hours after eating.

Heart Protection -

'ॐ उद्यन्नद्य मित्रमहः आरोहन्नुत्तरां दिवम्। हृद्रोगं मम सूर्य हरिमाणं च नाशय।' **'Om Udyannadya Mitramahah Ārohannuttarāṁ Divam. Hṛdrogaṁ Mama Sūrya Harimāṇaṁ Ca Nāśaya.' Chant** this mantra 108 times daily, facing the rising sun, with the 'Mrityunjaya Mudra'. It removes heart pain and severe chest pain. It strengthens the heart and keeps it disease-free, preventing heart attacks/heart failure. This is a proven practice. Additionally, reciting the 'Aditya Hridaya Stotra' three times brings rapid benefits.

Breast Problems Relief -

'ॐ मं महादेवीभ्यां नमः।' **'Om Maṁ Mahādevibhyaim Namaha.'** For women, chanting this mantra 7 times daily, using an old cloth of the child and waving it over the breasts, brings relief from breast problems such as pain, lack of milk, or contaminated milk, within 7 days. This practice should be repeated 3 times a day.

Note: Writing this mantra with a pomegranate twig on a Bhojpatra leaf using white sandalwood paste and then chanting 11 rosaries, worshiping with incense and lamp and placing it in a silver amulet and tying it around the child's neck with a red or black thread, removes the child's restlessness and protects them from the evil eye of others, including their mother. Perform this ritual at an auspicious time.

All Fever and Viral Infections -

'ॐ नमो अजयपाल की दुहाई, जो ज्वर रहे तो महादेव की दुहाई फुरो मन्त्र।' **'Om Namo Ajaypal Ki Duhai, Jo Jwar Rahe To Mahadev Ki**

Duhai Phuro Mantra.' With this mantra, chant 7 times and make the patient swallow tulsi leaves with tea or water. Alternatively, take 5-7 tulsi leaves, chant the mantra 51 times and soak them in the patient's water, then make them drink this water throughout the day, or use the mantra to wave over the patient.

Typhoid and other Severe Fevers -

'ॐ भस्मायुधाय विद्महे, एकदंष्ट्राय धीमहि, तन्नो ज्वरः प्रचोदयात्।' **'Om Bhsmayudhaya Vidmahe, Ekadanshtraya Dhimahi, Tanno Jvarah Prachodayat.'** When fever occurs, chant this 'Jvar Gayatri' mantra daily for 7 days, or have a knowledgeable person chant it for 21 days and all recurring severe fevers will be cured.

Headache/Migraine -

'ॐ नमो आदेश गुरु को बाल में कपाल, कपाल में भेजी भेजी में कीड़ा करे पीड़ा, सोने का सलाका रूप हथौड़ा, ईश्वर गढ़े गौरिया तोड़े, इन का शाप श्री महादेव तोड़े, शब्द सांचा, पिण्ड काचा, फुरो मन्त्र ईश्वर वाचा।' **'Om Namo Aadesh Guru Ko Baal Mein Kapal, Kapal Mein Bheji Bheji Mein Kida Kare Pida, Sone Ka Salaaka Roop Hathauda, Ishwar Gadhe Gauriya Tode, In Ka Shaap Shri Mahadev Tode, Shabd Saancha, Pind Kaacha, Phuro Mantra Ishwar Vaacha.'**
Chant this **'Sabar Mantra'** 7 times, sanctify sacred ash/vibhuti and apply it to the forehead. Then, stop the current breath and take 7 breaths through the other nostril, while mentally chanting this mantra.

Ear Ache -

'वनरा गांठि बावरी तो डांटे हनुमान कंठ बिलारी बाघी थनैजी कर्ण मूल सन जाई। श्री रामचन्द्र की बानी पानी पथ होई जाई।' **'Vanara Gaanthi Baawari To Daante Hanumaan Kanth Bilaari Baaghi Thaneji Karn Mool San Jaai. Shri Raamchandra Ki Baani Paani Path Hoee Jaai.'** When experiencing ear ache, assume the 'Shunya Mudra' and chant this mantra 7 times. If you are unable to chant, simply assume the 'Shunya Mudra'; and another person should recite the mantra 7 times and perform the sweep up.

Relief from all types of pain (Back, Stomach, Hands, Feet, Neck, Head, etc.) -

'ॐ मीढुष्टम शिवतम शिवो नः सुमना भव। परमे वृक्षेऽआयुधं निधाय कृत्तिं वसान आचर पिनाकं बिभ्रदागहि।' **'Om Meedhustam Shivatam Shivo Nah Sumana Bhav. Parame Vrikshaayaa Ayudham Nidhaaya Kruttim Vasaan Achar Pinakam Bibhradagahi.'** This is a mantra from the Shukla Yajurveda. Chanting and reciting this mantra regularly brings relief from all kinds of pain in all parts of the body.

Migraine/Headache -

'ॐ नमो। बन में ब्याई बानरी, उछल वृक्ष पै जाए। कूद कूद शाखा नपै, कच्चे बन फल खाए। आधा तोड़े, आधा फोड़, आधा दैय गिराए। हुंकारत हनुमान जी, आधासीसी जाए। **'Om Namo. Ban Mein Byaai Baanaree, Uchhal Vriksh Pai Jaaye. Kood Kood Shaakha Napai, Kachche Ban Phal Khaaye. Aadha Tode, Aadha Phode, Aadha De Giraaye. Hunkaarat Hanumaan Jee, Aadhaaseesee Jaaye.'** When experiencing migraine/headache, chant the above mantra and apply ash to the affected area or read the mantra and put 2 drops of cow's ghee in the nostril. Alternatively, tie a cloth or thread on the hand above the elbow on the opposite side. To prevent this, read the mantra on an empty stomach before sunrise and eat half an apple, then place the other half under a tree or on the roof. Do this for at least 15 consecutive days.

Eye Pain -

'ॐ नमो बने ब्याई बानरी जहां हां हनुमंत'
'Om Namo Bane Byaai Baanaree Jahan Haan Hanumat', When experiencing eye pain, chant this mantra 7 times while moving your hand over your eyes and blowing air.

Eye pain, conjunctivitis and other eye problems will be cured by the power of the guru's mantra, which is the essence of my devotion. The mantra is:'आंखि पीड़ा कषिरी गिहिया थनै लाई चरिठ जाई भस्मन्तन गुरु की शक्ति मेरी भक्ति फुरो मन्त्र ईश्वरो वाचा। नेत्र पीड़ा मेरी भक्ति फुरो मन्त्र ईश्वरो वाचा।' **'Aankhi Pida Kasiri Gihia Thnai Laai Chari Thaai Bhsmantan Guru Ki Shakti Meri Bhakti Furo Mantra Ishwaro Vaacha.'**

Repeating this mantra will bring relief from eye pain, conjunctivitis and other eye problems.

Easy Delivery -

ॐ मुक्तापाशा विपाशाश्च मुक्ताः सूर्येण रश्मय्। मुक्त सर्वभयाद् गर्भ त्राहिहि मारीच स्वाहा।। **'Om Muktaapasha Vipaashashcha Muktaah Suryena Rashmay. Mukta Sarvabhyaad Garbha Traahih Maareech Swaahaa.'** (For an easy and trouble-free delivery, chant this mantra 8 times and sanctify the holy water, then give it to the pregnant woman to drink.

Hydrocele (Scrotal Swelling) -

'ॐ नमो आदेश गुरु को जैसे के लेहु रामचन्द्र कबूत ओई करहु राधा बिनन कबूत पवनपूत हनुमन्त धाउ हर-हर रावन कूट समरावन श्रवई अण्ड खेतहि श्रवई अण्ड-अण्ड विहण्ड खेतहि श्रवई बाज गर्भहि श्रवइ स्त्री षीलहि श्रवइ शाप हर-हर जंबीर हर जंबीर हर हर हर।' **'Om Namo Aadesh Guru Ko Jaise Ke Lehuramachandra Kaboot Oi Karahu Raadha Binan Kaboot Pavanpoot Hanumanth Dhau Har-Har Ravan Koot Samaravan Shravai And Khetahi Shravai And-And Vihand Khetahi Shravai Bajam Garbhahi Shravai Stree Shilahi Shravai Shaap Har-Har Jambheer Har Jambheer Har Har Har.'**
For hydrocele or scrotal swelling, chant this mantra while gently massaging the swollen scrotum with your hand. Drink sanctified water and apply a paste made of soft clay, letting it dry before washing it off after about an hour. This will bring relief from hydrocele.

Scorpion Sting -

'ॐ छः फट् स्वाहा।' **'Om Chah Phat Swaha.'** For scorpion sting, chant this mantra at least 21 times and sanctify the water, then give it to the person to drink. This will reduce the effect of the venom

'आदित्यरथ वेगेन विष्णु बाणबलेन च ताक्ष्य पक्षनिपातेन भूम्या।' **'Aadityarath Vegena Vishnu Baanbalena Cha Taakshry Pakshanipaaten Bhoomyaa.'** With this mantra; use mustard seeds to remove the poison. Then mix lime, honey and turmeric; and apply it to the affected area. This will also reduce the effect of the venom.

Universal Disease and Peace -

'सोमनाथो वैद्यनाथो धन्वन्तरिश्चाश्विनो।'
'Somnatho Vaidyanatho Dhanvantarishchaashvino.'
Anyone suffering from any disease should mentally recite this mantra. This brings quick relief from the disease and provides comfort from the suffering.

'अच्युताय नमः अनन्ताय नमः गोविन्दाय नमः।'
'Achyutaya Namah Anantaya Namah Govindaya Namaha'
Alternatively, mentally recite this mantra during illness. This brings a possibility of getting relief from the disease.

'देहि सौभाग्यमारोग्यं देहि मे परमं सुखम् रूपं देहि जयं देहि यशो देहि द्विषो जहि।' **'Dehi Saubhagyamaarogyam Dehi Me Paramam Sukham Rupam Dehi Jayam Dehi Yasho Dehi Dwisho Jahi.'** This mantra brings health, happiness, beauty, victory, fame and freedom from envy. A person suffering from disease should mentally recite this mantra.

Daily recitation of one rosary of the above mantra is helpful in achieving health. This brings health benefits and helps in staying disease-free.

Health Benefits -

'दैहिक दैविक भौतिक तापा, रामराज नहि काहुहि ब्यापा' **'Daihik Daivik Bhautik Tapaa, Raamaraaj Nahi Kaahuhu Byaapaa'** Daily recitation of this couplet from the Ramayana, as much as possible, is helpful in staying healthy and disease free. This brings health benefits and helps in staying disease free.

Protection from Death and Disease -

'ॐ हौं जूं सः मां पालय-पालय सः जूं हौं ॐ' **'Om Houn Joon Sah Maam Paalay-Paalay Sah Joon Houn Om'** Daily recitation of 11 rosaries of the above mantra protects the reciter from death and complex diseases. If the patient is not capable themselves, then their spouse or blood relative can take a vow and recite. This provides protection from death and disease.

'ॐ अनिमिषाय नमः' **'Om Animishaay Namah'** This mantra can be recited to get relief from blood and heart diseases.

'ॐ स्वयम्भूताय नमः' **'Om Svayambhootaay Namah'** This mantra can be recited 1008 times daily for disease destruction.

For Neck Pain or Heaviness -

'ॐ हूं' **'Om Hoom'**. Those who have neck pain or heaviness should recite the first half of the 'ॐ' mantra while inhaling deeply and the second half 'हूं' while exhaling slowly, at least 51 times daily with seriousness. This will provide relief from neck pain and heaviness. Such people should avoid bending their head while working and stop fearing.

For Eyesight and Eyes -

'ॐ पुण्डरीकाक्षाय नमः' **'Om Pundarikaakshaya Namaha'**. Reciting this mantra daily as much as possible and rubbing both palms together and then gently touching the eyes in between, helps in keeping the eyes healthy, strong and beautiful. Do this with 'Pranamudra'. This will keep the eyesight and eyes healthy.

When suffering from Incurable Diseases or Fear of Death -

'ॐ हौं ॐ जूं ॐ सः ॐ भूः ॐ भुवः ॐ स्वः ॐ त्र्यम्बकं यजामहे सुगन्धिं पुष्टिवर्धनं उर्वारुकमिव बन्धनात् मृत्योर्मुक्षीय माऽमृतात ॐ स्वः ॐ भुवः ॐ भूः ॐ सः ॐ जूं ॐ हौं।'

'Om Houn Om Joon Om Sah Om Bhuh Om Bhuvah Om Swah Om Tryambakam Yajaamahe Sugandhim Pushtivardhanam Urvaarukamiva Bandhanaat Mrityormukshiya Maamritaat Om Swah Om Bhuvah Om Bhuh Om Sah Om Joon Om Houn'. When a person is afflicted with incurable diseases or fear of death, they should recite this mantra daily. After reciting the mantra, say 'ॐ शान्तिः शान्तिः शान्तिः' **'Om Shantih Shantih Shantih'**. It is recommended to recite this mantra at least 11, 5, or 1 rosary on a Rudraksha mala daily. Additionally, one can get a Brahmin priest to perform 125,000 Mritunjaya japas or perform Rudrabhishek with sugarcane juice. Alternatively, one can recite the 'Sundar Kand' for 45 days, at least once a day, in the name of the patient. This will provide relief from incurable diseases and fear of death.

Simple Home Remedies and Totkas for Health

If a **child falls ill frequently,** they should be fed roasted barley and donations should be made in their name. Additionally, 3 grams of cinnamon mixed with one spoon of honey should be given to them regularly. At night, a coin should be kept under their pillow and given to a beggar in the morning. If you are performing any mantra recitation or rituals for the child's health, place a few whole rice grains (akshat) in a conch shell. Later, tie those rice grains in a small pouch and keep it under the child's pillow and the effect will last for a long time. This will improve the child's health.

If a **patient is not recovering from medication**, then make them throw a handful of rice into flowing water. Give a handful of rice to a cow and another handful to an elderly woman.

Those who **do not have children** should tie fennel and rock sugar in a white cloth and flow it in a river for a year. Additionally, they should serve cows, dogs, orphans and plants.

If someone is experiencing **bedwetting, excessive urination, or pain in their legs and back,** they should consume sesame seeds on Thursdays or eat food cooked in sesame oil.

Boil 25 grams of black sesame seeds in half a kilogram of water. Once it reduces to half, drink it on the first and second day of your period to cleanse the uterus. Women should also consume asafoetida regularly.

If **diseases are prevalent in your home or a family member is seriously ill,** bring soil from a field plowed by oxen into your home. It is highly beneficial to bring it on Dhanteras, make a small ball with it and curd and place it in the puja room. Mix a little curd with it and apply a tilak on the forehead of the patient/family member daily. This will provide relief from the disease.

If a **mother is ill or not recovering from medication**, then take raw rice from her hand and distribute it among 8 poor girls (if necessary, repeat this process several times).

If you have **pain in your wrists or elbows**, engage in spiritual discussions or listen to them, or attend satsang. Your complaint will be resolved in a few days. If you have pain in the lower back, stop criticizing or gossiping and your pain will be relieved forever. If the pain returns, grind the root of the Kalihari plant and apply it to your nail. You will get instant relief.

If you frequently experience stomach pain, start giving stomach pain medication to others. You will benefit from it.

If **diseases are not leaving your home,** then once a month, count the total number of family members and the average number of guests who visit your home. Make that many small or large rotis in a tandoor (or on a clay oven if a tandoor is not available) and distribute them among the poor. Also, once a month (preferably on Saturday), throw money into the boundary walls of a crematorium. Whenever you pass by a crematorium, throw money. Whenever you cross a river, throw money into it as well.

If a **patient is not getting cured,** on Thursday, strike a yellow (ripe) pumpkin on his head and keep it inside the boundary wall of the temple. And on Saturday strike a coconut and either break it on the road or keep it under a Peepal tree or in a temple (especially in front of Kali). This will provide relief from the disease.

If the **disease is not being diagnosed** even after using health simple home remedies and tricks; then after hitting the patient's head, pour 325 grams of zinc/tin/lead in water (flowing) without looking; and come back without looking back. The disease will be diagnosed.

If the patient is **also under the influence of Rahu's transit,** then make him touch a small pencil coin and throw it in the drain on Saturday. Or make him donate 5 radishes on Saturday or Wednesday. If the disease is serious or the patient's condition is critical, then once on Saturday, make him donate coins or Sanija equal to his weight to beggars/poor. Then donate a little Sanija every Saturday.

Those who **cannot have children or give birth to weak children** should wash all their body parts with raw milk and wash the private parts with curd daily (especially on Fridays). Then take a bath with fresh or lukewarm water and clean the milk and curd thoroughly. Eat milk-jalebi hot at night and soak the thumbs of the hands in raw milk for some time or rub raw milk on them before going to sleep. Give white food items to a girl on Friday and donate white silk clothes (even a ribbon or handkerchief). Eat makhana kheer on Friday.

If the **child does not start speaking for a long time or has a voice obstruction**, then feed him green chillies with seeds every day. His paternal aunt should talk to him and make him release a bird on Wednesday. If he does not listen, then rub Jaharmohra behind the ears. Lightly massage the soles with raw milk. Massage the head with red oil and make him feed a cow and a dog.

If **due to sorcery, a woman is unable to conceive or there is a miscarriage,** then tie black sesame seeds, asparagus, peepal bark in a fine cloth and tie it on the woman's stomach above the navel (especially in the third-fourth month). Or a pregnant woman should wear white dry ginger and the root of Apamarg around her neck.

Weak children/children who fall sick frequently should wear the root of Indian gooseberry or the root of anantmool on Tuesday (in a red thread) or make an amulet of 11 papaya seeds wrapped in a thin yellow cloth and wear it on Thursday (replace it if it gets damaged).

If **hemoglobin is low,** mix radish juice in pomegranate. Dry spinach and grind it and eat it. Eat flour pudding made with desi ghee and black cardamom by licking it with the index finger every day and offer water to the rising sun and give turmeric-coated rice to the cow. Or give turmeric coated potatoes.

In case of **respiratory allergies,** wear the root of Punarnava around the neck and make 5 black peppers by grinding them in 100 grams of old pure jaggery and suck gram-sized tablets 3-4 times a day. Feed a goat on Wednesday or donate a goat. Serve the goat. Drink goat's milk.

Listening to music is beneficial for health. Listening to Shishir Vadya/Flute gives relief from Vata, listening to stringed instruments/Jaltaranga gives **relief from Pitta and** listening to Percussion instruments/Tabla gives **relief from Kapha.** Listen for 1.5-2 hours in the morning and evening. Listening to 'Sa' gives relief from Kapha, listening to 'Pa' gives relief from Pitta, listening to 'Ma' and 'Re' gives **relief from Vata.** Therefore, the patients of Vata, Pitta or Kapha should listen to these notes.

People **suffering from migraine** should wear the root of Kanain around their neck. Eat hot jalebi and stop screaming in case of pain. Smell camphor/garlic/onion or put 2 drops of onion juice in the nose to get relief. Put a lot of cloves in an apple. When the apple dries up, take out the cloves and keep them aside and suck 2 cloves every day.

If the **child's fever is not coming down,** keep the flowers or leaves of Aak near his pillow. If a little fever/heat persists, wear the root of Aak around the neck. In case of weakness of the eyes or pain in the eyes, apply the milk of Aak leaves on the nails of the big toes daily. Wash your hands thoroughly afterwards, this milk is harmful for the eyes.

In case of a **very sick condition or serious illness,** it is very effective to keep writing your own name on pieces of Bhojpatra using Ashtagandha and pomegranate pen and when you have completed 108 of them, throw them in a holy river. If necessary, do this up to 11 times.

Filling a glass bottle with Gangajal and burying it in the field helps in **getting rid of diseases and improving health.** If the disease is serious and you do not get full relief from this remedy, then donate a black and white blanket to Hanuman Ji's temple on 43 Tuesdays.

In case of a **serious illness or no recovery for a long time or a life threatening situation,** take a saffron coloured thread of the length of the patient from head to toe, tie as many knots in the thread as the age of the patient and put it around his neck/waist. And on Tuesday, make five pedas of flour with a little vermilion(the one used for worship) and lightly roast them on a pan and wrap them in the patient's used (unwashed) clothes and float them in the river at a place where the flow is so strong that it carries them forward. This protects.

Players/runners/wrestlers/strength seekers should apply the soil of the playground/arena on the body (at least on hands-feet/palms/sole and forehead). They should walk/run there barefoot. They should eat honey and on Tuesdays fill almonds with antimony, tie them in a red thread and flow them in running water.

When **you are ill,** offer the sacred thread to Lord Ganesha and chant the Ganesha mantra ten times. The next day tie the sacred thread around your neck or hand (do not let the Moolaadi touch it).

If a **disease is not getting cured for a long tim**e, then on Saturday, throw all the medicines of the patient in the drain and then start taking new medicines from Sunday. If the condition of the patient is very bad, then use the remedy of cow donation as a last resort.

Write the name of the person who is in **danger of accident/death** and that of his mother on 11 betel leaves (smooth side) with saffron, vermilion and kajal mixed together using an incense stick on Saturday afternoon. Write the problem below the name. All the family members should bow to those leaves and float them in flowing water and watch them float. This remedy protects against the possibility of accident/death/murder.

If the **mother is suffering from a serious disease**, then strike a white flower with her and flow it in running water. Do this experiment continuously for 45 days. Or strike a coconut with her and keep dedicating it to Ishta/Kali (at least for 11 days).

If a **scorpion or butterfly has bitten you**, rub the root of Apamarg and apply it there or tie the root of Apamarg there. This will prevent swelling and pain and the sting will also come out. Snakes do not come to the place where Apamarg plants are growing. If you are suffering from labor pain/fever/piles/fear of ghosts, then also tie the root of Apamarg there.

Patients of **premature ejaculation** should bring the red Apamarg plant a day before Mangalpushya or Mangal Ashwani Yoga (on Monday evening). And the next day its root should be uprooted, washed and wiped and tied around the waist. The basil seeds should be swallowed. Or the basil root should be kept in betel leaf and eaten.

On Sunday, in the Ashwini constellation, bring a Peepal tree (first bring it on Saturday). If you rub it in cow urine and make a woman drink it, even a **barren woman will conceive**. Drinking Rudraksha water and Tulsi juice daily also increases the chances of having a child.

If the Peepal branch is brought on Sunday, Revati Nakshatra and tied on the hand of a pregnant woman in the third month, she will give **birth to a son.**

If the root of fig taken in Guru Pushya/Ravi Pushya Yoga is tied on the stomach of a pregnant woman with a yellow thread, **abortion will not happen**. Or tie the root of white aak or root of sarpagandh.

If you have **high blood pressure**, keep water in a copper vessel near your pillow while sleeping. In the morning, put it in the root of a kikar tree and drink half a teaspoon of banana juice. Distributing medicines for this disease among the patients (needy) also gives quick relief. Drink the juice of the stem or wear a pearl Rudraksha rosary made in silver wire, it will be beneficial.

If you have **low blood pressure,** take Tulsi juice in honey and wear a Rudraksha-coral rosary in copper wire. If you have frequent headaches, wear black agate in silver on Saturday in the ring finger. In case of kidney diseases, wear kidney stone in the little finger and in case of diabetes, wear white coral in gold in the ring finger.

Success, Job, Victory and Prestige - Simple Home Remedies and Totkas

In Ravi Pushya Guru Pushya Yoga, by taking the root of Apamarg and rubbing it in the raw milk of a black cow and applying it as a Tilak daily, the **power and influence of a person increases.**

While **travelling or starting a work,** by reciting or remembering 'Tulsi Sita Ram Lakhan Narayan Narayan' and by eating curd and applying a Tilak of sandalwood before leaving, protection and success are achieved. (Raise the foot with the walking sound first).

In Ravi Pushya Guru Pushya Yoga, bring the root of white water lily. Tying it on the right arm brings **victory.** Tying it on the left arm brings **good fortune** to a woman.

In Ravi Pushya Yoga, rubbing the root of white water lily in goat's urine and applying it as a tilak, **impresses people.**

Those who want **good health, leadership and victory** should take bath daily by adding red sandalwood and jatamsi in water and should throw jaggery worth two rupees and batasha worth two rupees in river on Tuesday after reciting'ॐ भौं भौमाय नम:।' 'Om bhoo bhaumay namah' 11 times. This practice brings relief in blood disorders, high blood pressure, skin diseases, itching, bilious fever, typhoid fever, rickets, excessive anger, bleeding nose, piles (bloody) and anemia and Mars in the horoscope is cured.

By mixing black sesame seeds in pure ghee and offering 1008 oblations with 'Ganesh Mantra' for three days (on Wednesday, Thursday, Friday or Chaturthi, Panchami, Shashthi), the officer becomes favourable.

While remembering the wish/work, offer 11 Hakik in the temple. Do this continuously for at least 3 days. This helps in **getting the work done/fulfillment of the wish** and new/closed paths start opening.

By donating one Hakik and one coin (25 paise/8 paise/rupee etc. coin) daily from Diwali for 30 days, the **paths of increase in wealth and profit and success** open.

Sucking betel nut/ clove/ cardamom/ raisin/ shell/ raisin/ almond etc., which were consecrated in Navratri, during exams/ interviews/ competitions etc. **increases the chances of success.**

If **work is not getting done** or is getting spoiled due to **Sade Sati**, then put 5/11 drops of mustard oil in the root of Aak tree every morning and light a four-sided lamp made of flour under Peepal tree in the evening.

If there is trouble due to **Guru's defect,** then rub turmeric on white thread and wrap it 5/7 times on Peepal tree's trunk. If work is getting spoiled due to Rahu's defect, then rub Peepal's bark with white sandalwood in Gangajal and apply Tilak on the forehead.

Bring the fallen feather of a crow from under a Peepal tree on Tuesday/Saturday. Wash and dry it and put it in the vermilion used for worship and keep it in a geometry box etc. and keep it at the place of worship. If it is a **civil case**, wrap it in a white cloth and keep it in your pocket and go to court/hearing. If it is a **criminal case**, wrap it in a black cloth and take it with you. (It is best for those with criminal cases to bring the feather on Tuesday and for those with civil cases on Saturday). If the person is innocent, he will not be harmed. He will win the case.

In case of **business problems,** offering red/white Aak flowers on Shivling/Durga idol daily is beneficial.

If you are **unable to get a job/ lose** it, then tie the root of Apamarg taken in an auspicious time on your arm for a year (at least). If someone has cast an evil eye on your shop/office/factory, then tie the root of Chirchita taken in Ravi Pushya Yoga on the main door. Things improve gradually.

Those who **want position and prestige** should plant Tulsi and Sunflower plants to the east of their house/establishment. And to protect from evil eye, a coriander plant should be planted.

By performing Yagya on mango wood with at least 21 Gayatri Mantras on 21 Sundays at home or by performing Gayatri Yagya for 51 days continuously with 51 Gayatri Mantras, the possibilities of **position, prestige, fame and progress** become very strong and the effect of Vastu Dosh or negative energy is removed.

Wearing betel nut/nutmeg consecrated during Navratras increases self-confidence and chances of victory. (They should be worn after plating them in silver).

If work is not successful or profit is stopped or expenses or illness are afflicted due to **Pitra Dosh/Vastu Dosh,** then on the day of eclipse or Sankranti or Amavasya (Monday is best), wrap a pair of silver snakes, 5 basil leaves, three pairs of whole cloves and 4 black cardamoms on a big Peepal leaf and bury it by digging one foot deep in the ground near the main door of the house. It is very beneficial.

If there is a **problem of unemployment,** then keeping the root/wood of Peepal/Shami in a copper vessel, offering Gunja and Doob, consecrating it with 1008 'Ganesh Mantras' on Chaturthi and keeping/wearing it with you is very beneficial. Do this even if there is a hindrance in studies.

On Diwali, consecrating the root of Anantmool with 1008 Mangal Mantras and wearing it in a red thread removes the **difficulty in acquiring wealth.**

If there is a **decline/loss in business due to the partner**, then on Tuesday light an Akhand Deep (from morning to night) of Jasmine oil in the south of the house - if there is more problem, light an Akhand Deep 5 times from Tuesday morning to Saturday night.

Offering coconut to Bhairav once a month on Saturday and pouring a little lead in the drain and wearing 7.25 Ratti Turquoise in silver around the neck will **prevent your enemies from dominating you.**

If you are **losing your job repeatedly,** then keep Dhatura seeds in your pocket and go to work. Offer one piece each from your food to a cow, crow and dog (or while making rotis in the kitchen, offer the first roti to a cow and the last one to a dog and crow)

If there is a **possibility/fear of losing your job/getting laid off/failure,** then rub the root of the Banyan tree well in Gangajal and apply its Tilak before going to work. If you want, you can also add a little saffron to it.

For **success in exam/interview**, take an orange (not tangerine or seasonal) and peel it in such a way that no part of it remains stuck to the orange (usually the peel remains stuck towards the ends of the slices). Cut the peel into 9 pieces (even if it is not equal, it should not be 10. If it is 10 or more, then leave the previous one and take a new orange). Wrap them in a white cloth handkerchief and take it with you. Smell them once or twice before the exam/interview (smell in between if needed). On the way back, throw the peels under a tree. This is a 90% to 95% successful experiment.

In problems related to **fame, good fortune and government job**, offer Belpatra on Shivling and apply white sandalwood on Shivling, also apply it on your forehead.

If you are **caught in a case despite being honest and innocent**, or if you are troubled by enemies/evil people despite being right, then offer a small axe to Lord Ganesha every Wednesday or Chaturthi. (In small cases offer it on Wednesday and in big cases on Chaturthi). Usually the work gets done in one to four attempts.

If you are **unable to repay the loan despite having good habits and the intention to repay**, then keep a crystal Ganesha in the north of the house. Bathe him with raw milk every day, offer Durva and chant at least one rosary of 'ॐ वक्रतुण्डाय हुं' 'Om Vakratundaya Hum' every day. Soon the paths open up or options start appearing.

If there is a **lot of instability or tension in the job**, then on Wednesday/ Chaturthi wear the root of Ashwagandha, consecrated with 'Ganesh Sahasranama', around the neck in a grey thread.

For **prosperity and blessings in the home,** place a Ganesha idol in the north direction. On the right side of the idol, place a conch (preferably a South-facing conch) and on the left side, place a brass lamp. Light a lamp with desi ghee daily and chant at least one mala of "ॐ गं" (Om Gam). (It is even better if the lamp has five faces or if you use a five-wick lamp.)

If there is a **hindrance in promotion or Sun/Saturn is an obstacle in marriage,** then offer madar flowers/leaves to Ganesha in the evening. And after lighting the lamp, chant one rosary of Ganesha mantra.

Applying one drop of mustard oil on all twenty nails of hands and feet, both soles and heels and chanting Gayatri mantra **frees one from debt in a year.** (Do it daily except Sundays).

If you are facing **problems in job/business**, then change the colour of clothes you usually wear and the type of food you usually eat. You will start seeing a difference in a few days (usually in a week or a month).

The chances of **failure in interview/job are reduced** by keeping dhatura seeds in your pocket and bowing to a jamun/mango tree before going.

If **enemies are troubling you in government job or in life,** then start serving a black cow. Sometimes give gulabjamun/doda barfi/chocolate/black sweets to colleagues.

If the **construction work stops while building a house,** then dig the Brahmasthan a little and bury silver there. If you are facing **government problems,** then bury a 1-inch copper plate in the middle of the plot on Sunday. The problem is solved soon.

If there is **politics against you in the office,** keep a Sphatik Pyramid on your table. Wear Turquoise in silver. Keep flowing black sesame seeds, black pepper, black lentils in water for Saturn.

If there is a **fear of losing reputation or insult/possibility of officer/government getting very angry**, then plant 11 Bael trees and start watering them daily and taking care of them till they become a little strong. You will be protected.

Offering Bael leaves and sesame seeds mixed milk on Shivling, taking some whole rice and a silver item from mother, there will be no quarrel when you **go to meet a quarrelsome/angry person.**

If you are **embroiled in a property dispute**, wear the root of 'Khejri' (in a black thread, around the neck). Flow some mustard seeds in flowing water on Wednesday. And always keep a square piece of silver with you.

To get success in job, rub betel leaf and basil leaves in raw milk and apply its tilak on your forehead in the morning. This strengthens the Sun and the chances of success in job also start getting stronger.

If you are **facing problems in job/workplace/business,** seniors/colleagues are dominating or boss/senior is unnecessarily troubling you, then eat some jaggery and fennel every day before going to work.

By reciting three times 'Aditya Hridya Stotra' or one rosary of 'ॐ ह्रीं घृणिः सूर्यादित्यो।' 'Om Hreem Ghrinih Suryadityo' in front of the rising Sun, gradually **position, reputation, fame and progress** start happening.

If reputation is getting lost, then on Sunday, pour some jaggery in the drain. Feed grains to a cow/bull. Offer water to the rising Sun. Do not accept milk and rice donation from anyone. Do not eat meat and fish. Sometimes throw a copper coin in the river. If the problem is severe, a hand pump must be installed at home. (Make such arrangements that air and light can enter the house from the east).

To increase income/livelihood, do not accept silver for free. Donate milk, silver, rice (it is best if you donate milk with closed eyes). Place Krishna idol and plants in the north of the house, do not let wild pigeons make nests in the house. Keep a silver/mercury Shivling in the house. (Offer milk/water on them). Keep white flowers/crystals on the table. Blow the conch in the house. Wear white clothes more often. Once a month, keep pouring a little lead/coin in the drain.

If the work is not getting done, pour a spoonful of raw cow milk on the root of the fig tree daily (on Thursday and Saturday). Put fig fruits in the bathing water (at night), bathe with it in the morning and bring a flour grinding mill (even if it is small) in the house.

If there is instability in work or things go wrong before they are even done, wear a piece of the root of a very old banyan tree on a Thursday after chanting 10 rounds of 'ॐ नमो नारायणाय' 'Om Namo Narayanaya' on a yellow thread (the older the tree, the greater and faster the effect will be).

If you are **not getting success according to your efforts,** then start donating yellow sweets, yellow lentils, honey tied in a yellow cloth to an elderly person/Brahmin Guru on Thursdays and plant or water a banana tree and worship it.

If the deal for a house is not getting finalized, then keep a red chilli in your pocket while going for the deal. While returning, bury it under a tree. (If there is no Pitra Dosh, then the work will be done).

If the house is embroiled in a legal case or is getting damaged, then in an auspicious muhurat, place a pair of silver Naag-Nagin, raw milk, a pair of cloves and a white flower on a banana leaf and bury it at the Brahmasthan by digging a hand deep.

If the house is not built, tie a sacred thread on a new brick on Diwali and place it on a red cloth during the puja. Worship it daily and chant a rosary of 'Mangal Mantra'. Donate bricks on 4 Tuesdays in a year. Or put a sacred thread on Ganesha idol and tie a knot. And say that the knot will be opened only after the house is built. Offer vermilion to Ganesha daily and chant a rosary of 'Ganesh Mantra' daily. Sometimes keep giving red clothes to paternal **aunt/sister** on Tuesdays and make your child wear a silver ring on the index finger. By this the house gets built or starts getting built within a year and a half.

If you want **positivity in government work/success in government job,** then wear the root of Bael in a white thread on Sunday.

Special Reminders about Changing or Starting a Job

It should be good on the Moon. Only then should one change the work / job / place. (Generally, people affected by Mercury/Mars/Rahu, being very ambitious, impatient and dissatisfied, change jobs/work often and are in a hurry. To control this tendency, they should avoid Vata-enhancing food and Mahadasha, Antardasha and Pratyantardasha. Transiting Rahu should not be in the centre or is not affecting lifestyle. One should sit comfortably and drink plain water in small sips in a silver glass.) One should eat food slowly and comfortably. One should remain silent during meals. And one must keep a vow of silence one day in a week.

If you want to start a new work/business/occupation, keep in mind that the dasha, antar and pratyantar should be auspicious. There should be transiting moon in any of Ashwini, Rohini, Pushya, all three Uttaranakshatra, Hasta, Chitra, Abhijeet and Revati nakshatra. But there should not be Kshayatithi / Kshayanakshatra / Riktaatithi / Amavasya / Ksheenchandra. It should not be Tuesday (Saturday should also be skipped), it should not be Rahukaal. There should be Kumbhlagna. There should be auspicious transit in 2nd, 10th, 11th houses or in Kendra Trikon in the horoscope, but there should not be inauspicious transit in 1st, 8th, 12th houses. None of Lagnesh, Bhagyesh, Dashmesh, Panchmesh should be set. There should be full moon or strong moon but it should not be in 6/8/12th from your birth sign. There should be Tripushkar/Dwipushkar/Sarvarthasiddhi yoga. Then start.

Generally, it is best to avoid changing work/job/place/house during Saturn's Sade Sati/Dhaiya and when Rahu is in the fourth house in Dasha or transit.

Mantra for Education, Knowledge, Wisdom, Self-Confidence

For attainment of wisdom, knowledge -

Whenever you get the opportunity, you should keep remembering this mantra. If you can find time, recite one mala (108) or at least 51 times daily of this mantra in the morning or evening. Gradually, there is a benefit.

बुद्धिं देहि यशो देहि कवित्वं देहि देहि मे। मूढत्वं हर में देविलाहिमाम् शरणागतम् ।।
Buddhim dehi yasho dehi kavitam dehi dehi me. Moodhatvam har me devi lahimam sharanagatam.

If chanting on a garland, chant facing east or in front of a picture/idol of Durga/Kali or Saraswati.

For Quick Acquisition of Knowledge -

गुरु गृह गए पढन रघुराई। अल्पकाल विद्या सब आई ।।
guru griha gaye padhana raghurā'I. alpakāla vidyā sabā ā'I.

When a child starts going to school for the first time, the mother should remember or recite this mantra 11 times daily while the child is going to school. Later, when the child becomes capable, they should recite this mantra at least 11 times while going to school themselves. This will help the child acquire knowledge quickly, without any obstacles and in an excellent manner.

To Increase Intelligence and Speech Power -

On Basant Panchami, wear yellow clothes and sit on a yellow seat. Facing north, place fennel, cardamom, almonds, raisins and a dry coconut in a plate in front of the Saraswati idol. Light incense and a lamp and make them successful by chanting the following mantra 11 times (at least):

'ॐ ह्रीं ऐं ह्रीं ॐ सरस्वत्यै नमः। '
'Om Hreem Aim Hreem Om Saraswatyai Namaha.'

After this, keep chanting this mantra at least once (five times if you can spare the time) throughout the year. Fill the prepared material kept in the plate in a box and place it in front of the idol of Saraswati. If necessary, consume it on occasions of exams etc. (if it is in large quantities, consume it in small quantities every day). This is the best practice of Mantra Tantra for students. It increases intelligence, wisdom, knowledge and talent throughout the year. It makes speech/verbal power, speech style effective and increases self-confidence.

By consuming the material prepared with this mantra during the exam, courage, patience, peace and concentration remain good and it becomes easy to remember the previously studied material.

Repeat this experiment again with new material on the next Basant Panchami. It is well tested. Students must do it.

For Speech Perfection and Removal of Speech Defects -

'ॐ ऐं नमः।'
'Om Aim Namaha'.
Recite the mantra. From Basant Panchami or Navratri or Chaitramasa Pratipada, wear yellow or white clothes and sit on a yellow or white mat. While looking at the picture of Saraswati, or in front of Saraswati's picture, close your eyes, face north, light a ghee lamp, offer yellow/white flowers to Saraswati and start chanting 11 rosaries of this mantra daily on a rosary of white sandalwood or crystal. Chant the rosary more on Basant Panchami and Navratri (21/51). This chanting should be done in a whisper (mumbling) or mentally (in the mind), verbal chanting is not that good. Do it continuously for 3 to 6 years. Although its effects start showing in 6 months to one year. Continuous use for 12 years gives speech perfection.

To Gain Knowledge, Art, Learning and Wisdom -

Chant the mantra'ॐ ह्रीं श्रीं सरस्वत्यै नमः' **'Om Hreem Shreem Saraswatyai Namah'.** Start chanting this mantra in any auspicious time or from Basant Panchami. Chant 11 rosaries daily, sitting on a white seat, facing north with a white sandalwood rosary, in front of the Saraswati idol. Also apply a tilak of saffron and white sandalwood.

By chanting this mantra, one gradually gains knowledge, learning, art, wisdom and peace (power of concentration and patience). The total number of chants is ten lakhs. If you also wear a yantra, then there is special benefit.

Note - If your Moon, Ascendant, Guru or Mercury is affected by Rahu, or the transiting Rahu affects your Ascendant, fourth or fifth house, or there is the Mahadasha of Rahu, then you should change this mantra and chant it.

The new mantra is -'ॐ ह्रीं श्रीं सरस्वत्यै नमः' **'Om Hreem Breem Saraswatyai Namaha'.** Along with this, you should apply a little saffron on your tongue.

For Progress in Education -

Chant the mantra 'ॐ ह्रीं ऐं धीं क्लीं सौं श्रीं सरस्वत्यै नमः' **'Om Hreem Aim Dheem Kleem Soum Shreem Saraswatyai Namah'.** Start chanting this mantra from the first day of Chaitra month (New Year) or Basant Panchami. Chant 21 rosaries daily on a white sandalwood rosary.

One should chant at least one lakh mantras in a year, so one should chant 5 rosaries daily. Also recite 'Neel Saraswati Stotra' or 'Kartikeya Prajnavardhak Stotra' once. This is a very beneficial practice. With this, the seeker soon becomes an excellent scholar.

For Gaining Wisdom and Knowledge -

Sit on a yellow or white mat in front of the joint picture of Saraswati and Ganesh. Sit facing north. Keep your hands in 'Gyan Mudra'. Join the index finger and thumb of both hands and keep the remaining fingers straight. Sit in Padmasana with both hands on the knees in such a way that the palms are facing the sky. Keep the waist and head straight.

Chant the mantra 'ॐ गं' **'Om Gam'** with breathing slowly for 5 to 15 minutes daily. During the practice, fill water in a conch and keep it in front of the picture. After the chanting is complete, drink the water from the conch and wear a tilak of turmeric and saffron on the forehead. (Gradually increase the practice to ½ hour).

For Increasing Self Confidence -

Sit on a kusha seat in front of the rising Sun and chant five rounds of 'ॐ ह्रो हस्।' **'Om Hro Has'** mantra on a rosary of red sandalwood or Tulsi. Or chant one round of 'Gayatri Mantra'. This increases self-confidence very quickly. And gradually fame, prestige, success, victory and health benefits also increase.

If after this you recite 'Aditya Hridya Stotra' three times and offer water to the Sun, then the possibilities of **getting a position, promotion,** livelihood etc. increase. Relations with the officers become good and benefits also increase. Chanting five rounds of 'ॐ रुद्राय नमः।' **'Om Rudraya Namah'** on a Rudraksha rosary in the evening or at night also increases self confidence and fearlessness.

For Memory, Intelligence, Speech -

'ॐ वाग्देव्यै नमः।'
'Om Vagdevyai Namaha.' Sit on a white seat, wear white clothes, apply a white sandalwood tilak on your forehead, face north and sit in front of a picture of Saraswati. Light a lamp with desi ghee or gugal and recite the above mantra at least 5 times a day using a white sandalwood rosary.

Observe a day of silence once a week. By doing so, the **defects of speech** will be removed and memory and intelligence will increase within a year.

For a Bright Voice -

'ॐ खं बृं।' **'Om Kham Brim'**. Chant the above mantra peacefully 5 times every day. After this, apply a mixture of red sandalwood and turmeric on the throat and suck liquorice or licorice.

If you want, then chant at least one rosary of the mantra 'ॐ बुं बुधाय नमः।' **'Om Bum Budhaya Namaha'** and wear the root of Vidhara around the neck. The effect is gradual.

Simple Home Experiments and Totke

During Navaratri, keep 9 pairs of unbroken cloves in a copper/silver vessel in front of Durga idol and make them purified by daily chanting 'ॐ ह्रीं हंसः' 'Om Hreem Hansah' or 'Nirvana Mantra' 11 times.

Later, close these cloves in a box and keep them at the place of worship. On the occasion of **examination, competition, interview, meeting** a special person etc. or on the occasion of **fear/heartache/depressio**n, keep sucking one of these cloves in the mouth. This increases self-confidence, one speaks better and is able to speak more effectively.

If you are f**acing difficulties in acquiring knowledge**, then sit under a Bel tree and chant 'ॐ' **'Om'** for one hour every day. The path opens up quickly.

Chant 'ॐ ह्रीं हंसः' **'Om Hreem Hansah'** or 'Surya Mantra' for 5 minutes while holding the wood/root of bael in hand and looking at the rising sun. **Self-confidence increases** and 'acidity' decreases. If you recite 'Aditya Hridya Stotra' 3 times every day at sunrise while holding bael leaf in hand, your **reputation is protected, increased and you achieve victory.**

To increase the strength of the throat/speaking ability, wear the root of Vidhara on a green thread around the neck on Wednesday. Chant the 'Mercury Mantra' daily and suck a mixture of fennel, cardamom and sugar candy or suck liquorice and sugar candy. Gradually there will be improvement.

Use the peacock feather (the one with 'Jaagray Sthapaay Swaha') given in the chapter on wealth gain to pacify the weakest of your Guru / Mercury / Moon / Panchmesh / Lagnesh / Chaturthesh. Keep the peacock feather awakened by the above mentioned experiment on your study table. You will **benefit in concentration, intelligence and education.**

Keep a Sphatik Shriyantra/Shivling/Pyramid and water on the study table. Put Saraswati's picture and a peacock feather and study facing north **to get good studies.**

On Diwali, place Gunja, Doob, Peepal/Shami wood in a copper vessel in front of Lord Ganesha and consecrate it with 1008

Ganesh Mantras. Keeping them with you helps you **gain knowledge and removes the problem of unemployment.** Keeping them with you is also beneficial in situations like work getting stalled or studies getting interrupted.

If you are **afraid or hesitant about going to college for the first time** because of the thought of ragging or your morale seems to be breaking, then tie the seeds of Datura in a handkerchief or a packet and carry it with you for 5-7 days.

To increase your chances of success in an exam or interview, break an orange peel (whole) into 9 parts (even if not equal) and wrap them in a handkerchief (white) and carry it in your pocket. Smell them 2-4 times before the exam/interview. Afterwards, return and throw the peels under a tree.

If there is a **possibility of failure (in competition/exam etc.) or of losing the job,** then rub the root of the banyan tree well in 2-3 drops of water and apply its Tilak (if Gangajal is available instead of water, use it). This increases self-confidence and also increases the chances of success.

If you are **unable to study or concentrate** due to lack of concentration, then in front of a silver Ganesha idol, on a kusha seat, chant one rosary of 'ॐ विघ्नेश्वराय नमः।' 'Om Vighneshwaraya Namah' and one rosary of 'Ketu Mantra' (daily). You will see a difference soon.

If for some reason/due to **worry about getting good marks**, you are unable to study, then you should consecrate the root of Ashwagandha with 'Ganesh Sahasranama' and wear it around your neck with a grey coloured thread on Wednesday or Chaturthi and drink water from a silver glass or by putting silver in a glass.

Drinking water kept in a conch or water kept in a glass of 4 Mukhi Rudraksha or wearing 4 Mukhi Rudraksha and chanting 'ॐ गं' **'Om Gam'** daily **increases intelligence, concentration, memory power, peace, patience and fearlessness.** Speech and personality are also benefited by long use.

If you are **interested in sports and want to increase your ability as a player/wrestler**, then you must apply the soil of the playground/arena on your hands and feet (at least on the soles and palms) and forehead and at least on one Tuesday of the month, fill almonds (remove the kernels) with antimony and tie them with a red thread and float them in water. You must also consume honey.

Ring a heavy brass/bronze bell near your study table and after ringing it 8-10 times, immerse it in clean water. (Put it in water before its ringing stops so that the water is agitated by its waves). Drink that water. This gives **strength/energy and alertness to the brain and the nerves** of the body and the sound of the bell destroys the negative effects/energy present there.

Take rice in your left fist and sugar in your right fist and recite the Gayatri Mantra 36 times in front of the rising sun. **Self-confidence and morale** start increasing within a week. Later, feed that rice and sugar to a cow / animal / bird etc.

Every day (except on Sundays) pour 36 drops of mustard oil on the roots of a Peepal tree in such a way that it flows down into the soil. Applying a Tilak of the soil soaked in that oil every day also **increases self-confidence and fearlessness.**

Wearing a black thread blessed with the mantra 'ॐ भ्रं कालभैरवाय फट्।' **'Om Bhraam Kalbhairavaay Phat'** 1008 times in front of the idol of Bhairav makes one **assertive.** One gets **fearlessness** and is **protected even when living alone in a foreign country/abroad/hostel etc.**

Writing your name clearly or signing it comfortably with a red pen in a diary/register 51 times every day (do it continuously for 5-6 months, at least) also increases **self-confidence and improves personality** with long practice. (It will also benefit concentration. If you write with full attention and without making any mistakes, then write without crossing out, 51 times is the minimum. You can also write 108 times).

If your **studies or marriage are stopped**, then place a turmeric knot respectfully in the puja and start applying turmeric tilak on your forehead daily. The obstacles will be removed in a few days.

If there is a **lack of self-confidence** due to the low position of the Sun, then wear the root of the oleander tree tied to a white thread around the neck on Sundays. If there is a **problem due to the low position of Jupiter,** then apply a solution of turmeric on the index fingers (of both hands) every night before going to sleep.

If you face **obstacles in acquiring knowledge**, then start offering yellow flowers and yellow sweets to your teacher and Goddess Saraswati and start keeping flowers on your study table. The path will open.

On the **first day when you go to class/work/to learn** something new, eat some sugar before going and take some rice with you. Mentally pray to Goddess Saraswati and donate that rice to someone on the way.

During exams, students should eat curd and sugar candy before leaving home and should first step out of the house with the foot of the nostril from which they are breathing more. It is also auspicious to leave after paying obeisance to Ganesha, Saraswati and mango/jamun tree.

Whenever the child loses interest in studies, make sure to start Surya Sadhna or offering water to the rising sun in the morning. Because in 95% of the cases, he will definitely be affected by Rahu or Saturn or Venus in the transit/Dasha (Sun is their enemy, hence it will reduce their effect).

If Guru is weak/low, the person gets scared of thick books. **If it is retrograde**, there is trouble in studies/self-study. (Problems or obstacles in studies are possible even if Guru is low or weak). If Mercury is retrograde, studies are left incomplete or there is hindrance/problem. Hence, such natives should definitely do remedies for Guru and Mercury. (Anyway, students should always keep their Moon, Guru and Mercury strong).

If you want to progress in art, then chant 'ॐ शुं शुक्राय नमः' 'Om Shun Shukray Namah' on a crystal rosary every day.

Apply white sandalwood on your forehead as a tilak every day. Eat makhana kheer. Eat cardamom and wear a combination of white and orange colors more often.

Those whose mind is very unstable should offer milk, water and then honey daily on the Shiva Linga made of crystal with the ring finger and should wear a garland of crystal and Rudraksha.

If the mind is getting distracted from studies due to Guru (Jupiter), then fill honey in an earthen pot and keep it near the root of Tulsi or keep it on the roof of the house and apply a Tilak of milk and saffron every day or add saffron to milk and drink it. (If saffron is not available, then add a little turmeric)

If the child is not able to concentrate on studies due to attraction towards the opposite sex, then make him wear a silver ring on the thumb and a cut/open gold ring on the index finger. Make him wear a rhinestone and Rudraksha rosary around his neck. Gradually, the difference is seen.

Sitting on a Kusha mat wearing yellow clothes and applying a Tilak of saffron and white sandalwood on the forehead gradually removes the **tendency of being mischievous, hasty and wasting time in useless things.** Due to which the child is able to concentrate better in studies.

If negativity is increasing in the child or he is getting averse to studies due to supernatural / unknown / evil influence, then make him wear the root of Nirgundi or Sarpagandha (not in black thread).

Those who are born at night (after sunset but before sunrise) or in November, October or around an eclipse are generally seen to have a lack of self-confidence or negative attitude in courage. Therefore, they should always chant the 'Gayatri Mantra' in front of the Sun on a rosary of white sandalwood.

To boost the morale of a timid child who is scared of going to school or cries a lot while going to school, he should be fed ashwagandha and sugar candy. Also, before going to bed, rub raw milk on the thumbs of both his hands. Dip the thumbs in milk and let them sit for some time.

Grind nutmeg and sandalwood and apply it as a Tilak every day or sew it in a thin cloth and wear it around the neck. This will **keep the child confident and he will stop being stubborn.** (If the child is very moody or his studies are affected due to mood swings, then sew nutmeg in a white thin cloth and wear it around the neck.)

To gain knowledge or open the mind, wear a Chiti in silver on the index finger on Saturday and for strengthening the mind, wear a solid silver ball around the neck.

If the child does not have the self-confidence due to the weakness of the Sun and does not have the time/capability to worship the Sun, then keep giving him Shyam Tulsi and Rama Tulsi leaves to suck and every second or third day give him pudding made by adding Desi Ghee and black cardamom in the flour, so that he can eat it by licking it with his index finger.

If the child's work is getting spoiled or his relations with teachers are getting spoiled due to speaking too much/speaking without thinking/speaking wrongly/not speaking at the right time, then make him wear a rosary of crystals/a peepal root around his neck. Apply a little saffron on the tongue daily.

If studies are getting affected due to getting angry too much then make a small moon out of silver and hang / keep it on the bed near the head of the child.

If you are not able to study due to laziness, negligence, increased sleepiness because of Saturn, then give 12 almonds in a small bottle/utensil, tie it in a black cloth and give it to someone. Or keep it in your prayer room (then do not open it). Suck small myrobalan and definitely eat cumin and carom seeds.

Applying tilak by mixing saffron in milk before going to sleep and reciting '🕉' 'Om' 31 times (in a slightly long but soft voice) before going to sleep **increases will power.** Children who keep making a time-table but are unable to implement it, should definitely do this for 3-4 months.

'ॐ खकोल्काय स्वाहा' 'Om Khakolkay Swaha': Chanting this 31 times in the morning facing east, in the evening facing west and at night facing north **increases self-confidence** gradually.

If a child does not listen/does not understand even after explaining/is going on the wrong path, tie a coconut with a yellow cloth on his photo and keep it above the photo or next to the photo. Apply Ashtagandha tilak on his forehead. Chant one rosary of 'Guru Mantra' and while looking at the photo, give him a mental order to improve.

Later apply Ashtagandha tilak on the child too. If you have not applied it then apply it while he is sleeping. He will start listening and obeying in 3-4 months. Then if you explain to him with love, he will agree.

Grind Desi Mishri and green cardamom and keep it in a vessel. During Navratri, chant Durga Mantra on it. If you eat a pinch of it every day, your consciousness, **good luck, self-confidence and positivity increase.**

If a child threatens to commit suicide/run away from home in anger, give him water kept in a copper vessel for a few days on an empty stomach in the morning in which fennel, cardamom, betel nut and nutmeg have been kept overnight. Write'ॐ ह्रीं' 'Om Hreem' 21 times daily in your diary using a pomegranate pen using ink made by mixing turmeric, saffron, white sandalwood in Ganga water. Or write the name of your deity or your own name clearly.

If the child's Venus is bad and he is going abroad or to a hostel or away from home for studies and there is a possibility of him getting distracted due to the opposite sex, then make him wear a Sphatik Mala after chanting 10 rounds of Durga/Venus mantras daily for 11 days. He will not get distracted from his goal due to the opposite sex.

If anger suddenly increases/there are quarrels/there is stammering / stuttering / stuttering / slippage of tongue, you start forgetting things after keeping them or you start feeling bored with studies then feed a gourd and a tomato to a cow on 11 Wednesdays.

If there are obstacles in attaining knowledge, then on Thursday/Friday offer 5 betel nuts, 1 coconut and 2/4 white flowers to Saraswati and pray to her. The path opens up soon.

Write your name on a betel leaf with a pomegranate pen and gorochana and flow it in running water on Monday and Thursday. This will not only restore the self-confidence lost during the year, but also **boost your self-confidence and people will start trusting the person** (those who have lost their credibility must do this experiment for one and a half years).

Rub turmeric on a white thread and wrap it seven times with it and wear it on your hand on Thursday (replace it if it gets damaged). Chant Guru Mantra daily. If you don't have friends, **you start making friends and you get good friends.**

If due to speech there are fights / disputes / misunderstandings or reputation is lost/misunderstood/work is spoiled or due to this reason one is not able to get into the 'goodlist' of elders, then on Wednesday five empty and clean pots should be floated in the river. This reduces the speech defect to a great extent and control over speech increases. Also remember that Mercury gets spoiled by giving false arguments or asking meaningless questions.

If a child is very shy/shy/unable to express himself and has low morale, then he should wear dry ginger tied to a black thread around his neck (replace it if it is damaged). Also, it is beneficial to give him coriander water (put dry coriander in water at night and drink it in the morning).

To succeed in knowledgeable subjects like knowledge/education/astrology, make a lump of satanja on Sunday and flow it in running water. Place a lump of turmeric at the feet of Saraswati's idol and offer 4-5 drops of raw milk on that lump and the idol's feet daily for at least 11 days and chant the 'Saraswati Mantra', then sew that lump in a thin white cloth and wear it around your neck and chant the 'Saraswati Mantra' daily.

To succeed in science, tie dry ginger in a black thread on Sunday/Saturday and wear it around your neck (replace it when it dries). Do not drink water in a glass (drink it in a metal glass). Sometimes donate a mirror to an elderly person and sometimes on Saturday silently cover a sleeping beggar/leper/poor person with a blue/black cloth.

To succeed in Mathematics/Commerce, wear the root of Vidhara around your neck on Wednesday in a green thread. Sometimes on Wednesday, float 5 empty pots in a river. On Wednesday, feed birds and goats. Sometimes on Wednesday, buy a bird and set it free or donate a goat. Feed a cow.

For success in art, give potatoes/rice to a cow on Friday. Give white material and white clothes to a girl. Apply white sandalwood tilak. Rub milk (raw) on the thumbs of the hands. And chant 'ॐ शुं शुक्राय नमः।' 'Om Shun Shukraya Namaha.'

Enemies, Fear etc.

Start **getting rid of planetary afflictions and ghost troubles** from Krishna Chaturdashi. Make this mantra perfect by chanting it 5000 times (keep purity, sanctity, restraint and sattvikta in mind during the sadhana period).

'ॐ नमो भगवते नृसिंहाय ज्वालामालिने दीप्तदंष्ट्राय अग्निनेत्राय सर्वरक्षोघ्नाय सर्वभूतविनाशनाय सर्वज्वरविनाशनाय हन हन दह दह पच पच बंध बंध रक्ष रक्ष हुं फट् स्वाहा।'

'Om Namo Bhagavate Nrsimhaya Jvalamaline Diptadamshttraya Agninetraya Sarvarakshoghnaaya Sarvabhutavinashanaaya Sarvajvaravinashanaaya Han Han Dah Dah Pach Pach Bandh Bandh Raksh Raksh Hum Phat Svaha.'

When required, by reciting this mantra 11 times and sprinkling it or by giving water consecrated with it, all the obstacles caused by evil eye, fever, household troubles, ghosts etc. are removed. Even after the mantra is proved, the food, behavior and thoughts should be kept sattvic. So that the siddhi does not get contaminated or weakened or distorted.

To Bring back a Missing / Lost Person -

On Krishna Chaturdashi or Diwali/eclipse, chant the following mantra at least 70 times and make it successful.

'ॐ क्लीं कार्तवीर्योर्जुनो नाम राजा बाहसहस्रवान् । यस्य स्मरणमात्रेण गतं नष्टं लभ्यते ।। ॐ कीर्तवीर्याय नमः 'अमुक' शीघ्र आनय स्वाहा।'
'Om Klim Kartaveeryorjunah Naama Raajaa Baahusahsravaan. Yasya Smaranamaatrena Gatam NashTam Labhyate. Om Kirtaveeryaaya Namah 'Amuk' Sheeghram Aanaya Svaha.'

Write the complete mantra on the clothes worn by the deceased (which should not be washed) with saffron and red sandalwood ink (make it in Pushya Nakshatra) using a pen made of pomegranate. (Write the name of the deceased at the place of 'so and so'). Then press that cloth between two heavy stones (millstones). Do not move it for 21 days. If the deceased is alive, he will return in 21 days or you will get news of him. Afterwards, lift the cloth and feed bread to monkeys and dogs.

Freedom from Fear of Theft -

On the night of Diwali/eclipse, make this mantra effective by chanting it ten times and writing it 108 times.

'तिस्रो भार्याः फिल्लस्य दाहिनी मोहिनी सती । तासां स्मरण मात्रेण चौरो गच्छति निष्फल ।। फिल्लकः फिल्लकः फिल्लकः ।।'
'Tisro Bhaaryaah Phillasya Daahinee Mohinee Satee. Taasaam Smaranamaatrena Choro Gacchati Nishphal. Phillakah Phillakah Phillakah.'

By reciting this mantra 7 times before sleeping at night, there will be no fear of loss due to theft in the house.

Protection from Black Magic -

Take 7 threads of raw cotton spun by a girl below 12 years of age and tie 7 knots on them. Recite the following mantra 7 times while tying each knot

'ॐ प्राच्यां रक्ष प्रतीच्यां च चण्डिके रक्षदक्षिणे। भ्रामणेनाविशूलस्य
उत्तरस्यां तथेश्वरि ।। सौम्यानि यानि रूपाणि त्रैलोक्ये विचरन्ति ते । यानि
चात्यर्थ घोराणि तैरक्षस्मान् तथा भुवम् ।।'

'Om prāchyāṁ rakṣa pratīchyāṁ ca caṇḍike rakṣadakṣiṇe.
bhramṇenāviśūlasya uttarasyāṁ tatheśvari || saumyāni
yāni rūpāṇi trailokye vicaranti te. yāni cātyartha ghōrāṇi
tairakṣasman tathā bhuvam ||'

Then tie this protective thread to the person. This prevents fear
of abortion and black magic. If there is already a hindrance
from black magic/ghost etc. then peace is restored. There is no
need to prove it. This is an effective and successful practice.

Child protection mantra

'खूं खुर्दनं खं हुं फट् स्वाहा।'
'Khun Khurdanam Khan Hun Fat Swaha.'

By mixing mustard, lac, garlic, neem leaves, bamboo peel,
agar, cow ghee and flowers offered to the idol of Lord Shiva
and burning incense on a cow dung cake while chanting the
above mantra at least 21 times, all the doshas like Putana etc.
of the child and the child planets are removed.

Apart from this, taking a bath by mixing the water of the
following things in Gangajal removes the planetary afflictions of
all, young and old: Lajwanti, Koot, Khilave, Kangani, Barley,
Mustard, Deodar, Turmeric, Sarvaushadilodh.

By mixing the water of all these things and taking a bath, the
planetary afflictions of all, are removed.

Miscellaneous Experiments

If you are afraid of scorpions, then take the root of Apamarg, Shukla Gurupushya or Ravipushya and put it in your left ear or keep it near your pillow while sleeping. This will remove the fear of scorpions.

Take the root of a mango on a Sunday and in Anuradha Nakshatra and keep it with you and chant a rosary of Ganesh Mantra. This can help you **find the lost item or find the thief.**

Taking a Peepal Banda and tying it on the hand on Sunday and Bharani Nakshatra can provide **relief from eye diseases and ghost possession**. If the 'Guru Mantra' is chanted and tied on the hand of a pregnant woman in the third month, then a son can be born.

By taking white ark root in Gurupushya yoga, consecrating it with 19000 'guru mantras' and tying it on the left arm, **an unfortunate woman can become fortunate. This experiment can be beneficial for women with widowhood yoga.**

To have a child a woman can take the root of white madaar in Gurupushya Yoga or Ravipushya Yoga, rub it with turmeric and after consecrating it with 'Guru mantra' she can tie it on her waist (above the navel).

By taking the root of Chirchita, 3 fingers long in Magha Nakshatra, consecrating it with the mantra 'ॐ मदन कामदेवाय फट् स्वाहा।' **'Om Madan Kamdevaya Phat Swaha'** and burying it in the courtyard of someone's house, **that person can be controlled.** (The mantra should be made Siddha by chanting it 12 lakh times).

To control a woman -

Consecrate the root of Kali Aparajita by chanting the mantra 'ॐ हं स्वाहा' **'Om Hum Swaha'** 1008 times and put it in betel leaf and feed it to a woman. It is necessary to prove this mantra by chanting it 12 lakh times.

To convert enmity into friendship -

'ॐ दमयन्तीनलाभ्यां च नमस्कार करोम्यहम्। अभिवादी भवेद्व
कलिदोषः प्रशान्तिद् ।।'
'ऐकत्वं भवेदेषा ह्मणानां पृथ्विधाम्। निवेप्ता च जायेत संवादनेन प्रसीद
मे।।'
'Om Damayantinlabhyam Cha Namaskar Karomyaham.
Abhivadi Bhavedva Kalidosh: Prashantid.' 'Ekatvam
Bhavedesha Hmananam Prithvidham. Nivepta Cha Jayet
Samvadanen Prasidh Me.'

Separately, with these two mantras, add ghee to the kheer and
perform Havan. Remembering the face of your enemy, perform
this Havan continuously for at least 61 days. By doing this your
enmity will change into friendship.

To Attract Husband's mind Towards Wife -

If your husband has separated from you, then write the name
of your husband and his mother with saffron and vermilion
using a pomegranate pen or ring finger on his unwashed but
worn clothes.

Spread that cloth and place a 1x1 feet mirror on it. Light a lamp
with a long wick on the mirror in such a way that its shadow
falls on the mirror.

Put both hands on the right and left of the mirror and pray to
God and chant 'Guru Mantra'. With this experiment, your
husband's mind will be attracted towards you.

Wife should take a yellow thread from her head to her feet and
tie as many knots in it as the number of years they have been
married. Then tie this thread to any green vegetable like ridge
gourd, bottle gourd or lady finger and float it in the river.

Or the wife should wake up in the morning and while reciting
the mantra 'ॐ चिन्न चिन्न स्वाहा' **'Om Chinn Chinn Swaha'**, fill
her palm with water and sprinkle it on her face. Collect the
water falling from your face in your palm again, rinse your

mouth with that water while reciting the mantra again and then spit it out. Do this daily for a week, this will open the way for your husband to come back.

To Motivate Husband to Go to Work -

If your husband avoids going to work, take out some blood from your middle finger (2-3 drops are enough) and apply it on your sole. Then walk around the house barefoot. Do this from Tuesday to Saturday or Saturday to Tuesday. This will make your husband feel like going to work.

To avoid black magic -

Keep yellow mustard seeds in the corners of the house, or make an amulet in white cloth and wear it, or bathe the pair of Harada taken in Ravi Pushya Yoga with Panchamrit and keep it on a red cloth in a box filled with vermilion. Or grind the root of Lakshmana and apply its Tilak on your forehead daily. All this will help to protect from black magic.

To Know the Life of a Patient -

Take a photo of the sick person at night. Then place that photo on the table and light 21 candles around it. Place a fruit or vegetable in the middle and put a Peepal leaf on it. If the leaf starts rotating after some time, then the patient will be alive. Do this experiment on Friday in the northwest direction.

To get your Husband his Share in the Property -

If your husband is not getting his share in the property, then on Saturday make 11 flour balls in raw milk. Insert 2 whole cloves in each ball. Then tie them in separate black cloths and make 11 packets. Keep them in your husband's clothes. In two-three months or even sooner, when they get moldy (do not open the bundle, check from outside), then bury them under different trees. This will help your husband get his share in the property.

To Get rid of the Habit of Lying / Stealing -

If the child has got into the habit of lying or stealing, then ask him to donate betel nut, coconut and yellow rice to elders on Saturday and Thursday. Make sure to make the child sit in a temple or near elders. Apply a tilak on his forehead by mixing turmeric, saffron and white sandalwood. Gradually this habit will decrease.

If this solution does not work, then fill a pot with red bricks, keep the child's photo in it and worship it for 11 days. Worship with 'Guru Mantra' or 'Navarn Mantra'.

Then bury this pot in the ground on Tuesday or Saturday. This will also make the child get rid of the habit of stealing. Wearing a Rudraksha bracelet and doing Shramdaan in the temple helps in getting rid of the habit of fighting.

For Foreign Travel -

Placing a copper sun on the eastern wall of the house removes obstacles in air travel.

On Monday, fill a little raw milk in a glass bottle (it is better if the lid is also made of glass) and bury it in the ground/field to create the possibility of going abroad.

Donate honey on Tuesday and tie the root of Anantmool in a red thread and wear it around the neck. In the morning, asking forgiveness from the ground and getting down from the bed strengthens the possibility of returning.

Wearing a black thread that has been sanctified by chanting the mantra 'ॐ श्रं कालभैरवाय फट्' **'Om Shram Kalbhairavaya Phat'** 108 times around the neck will provide protection in a foreign country.

Donating land or wearing a 'Mangal Yantra' will help in settling abroad.

Wearing a 'Chandra Mantra' will help in studying abroad.

Wearing a banana root and a turmeric knot will help in making friends both abroad and in the home country.

Wearing a Sphatik Mala charged by chanting Durga or Shukra Mantra for 11 days reduces the chances of straying from the goal in a foreign country.

If you mix turmeric in a yellow cloth and tie apple seeds in it and wear it around your neck, people will trust you.

Those who fear accidents during travel should perform Rudrabhishek on Trayodashi and wear three Rudrakshas in a red thread.

To protect yourself from the affair of another woman

Place a copper 'Baglamukhi Yantra' on the eastern wall of the house. Sit on a yellow seat in front of it, light a jasmine lamp and recite the mantra of Baglamukhi Devi 36 times. Pray to the Goddess to give wisdom to your husband. If you do this daily, then the house can be settled again within a year.

To avoid conspiracy -

Make an effigy from the soil of a field ploughed by bulls on the first day of Chaitra Navratri, before sunrise while chanting the mantra 'ॐ जयंती मंगला काली भद्रकाली कपालिनी। दुर्गा क्षमा शिवा धात्री स्वाहा स्वधा नमोऽस्तुते।।'
'Om Jayanti Mangala Kali Bhadrakali Kapalini. Durga Kshama Shiva Dhatri Swaha Swadha Namostute.'

Complete the effigy with sunrise and bury it by digging a pit in the house or office, if not possible, bury it in a pot, but do not plant any tree in it. This will prevent any conspiracy or politics against you for the whole year. Do it again next year if needed.

To Pacify an Evil Person -

If a person is very evil or bad and troubles an honest/just but weak person or has taken over his property, then light a lamp with sesame oil for him on Diwali. Collect smoke/soot in that empty lamp. Apply this soot on the picture of that evil person (if there is no picture, write his name) daily and pour spirit/alcohol/medicine in water every Saturday.

For healing -

Keep the cowrie shell, which has been sanctified by chanting 51 rounds of 'ॐ नमो: नारायणाय्' **'Om Namoh Narayanay'** or Lakshmi Mantra, in the cashbox or place of worship in the house. This will bring prosperity and protection. If needed, you can give peace and healing to someone by placing this cowrie on their picture or name.

For Debt Recovery -

If someone has kept your money with you or is not returning it, then chant 108 rounds of Ganesh Mantra in front of Ganesha's idol and tell your problem in his mouse's ear, start on Wednesday or Chaturthi. The work will be done in 14 days, if needed, do it for 41 days.

For Other Problems -

For wish fulfillment, tell your problem in the ear of Nandi in Shivalaya, offer milk on Shivling and chant 11 rounds of Shiv Mantra daily (start from Shukla Paksha Monday, Sawan Monday, Shivratri or Trayodashi).

For marriage, separate the idols of Parvati and Shiva or Radha and Krishna; keep them together only after marriage and chant 11 rounds of Shiva Mantra / Krishna Mantra daily.

To get rid of obstacles, make Lord Ganesh wear a sacred thread and tie a knot in it, untie the knot only after the work is complete, offer a betel nut to Lord Ganesh every day and chant 10 rounds of 'Vighneshwar Mantra' or 'Vakratunda Mantra'.

If you are caught in a false case, take a white cotton thread seven times your height. Mix it with wet turmeric and make it yellow. Wrap this thread around the trunk of a Peepal tree on Thursday. Offer jaggery and gram there for 11 Thursdays and pray for protection. Chant the mantra 'ॐ ह्रीं बटुकाय आपद्धोरणाय

कुरु कुरु बटुकाय ह्रीं।' 'Om Hreem Batukaya Apaddhoraanaya Kuru Kuru Batukaya Hreem' at least 5 times daily in the morning or at night.

Remedies for Planets:

For Saturn one should offer black urad / black sesame or mustard oil, **for Rahu** sindoor/tobacco/blue flower, **for Ketu** white sesame / oleander / lemon or offer milk to cat for Rahu, food to dog for Ketu and food to crow for Saturn.

For Rahu-Ketu use Wednesday-Thursday and for Saturn-Tuesday.

Home Remedies for Marriage and Children

To prevent abortion -
Tying the root or seed of Dhatura on the waist prevents abortion. Women who have repeated abortions should tie this root on their waist.

To subjugate everyone -
If you rub the root of Apamarg taken in Shubh Nakshatra in the milk of a black cow and apply Tilak on it daily, everyone will come under your control.

For a barren woman -
If you rub the Peepal Banda in fresh cow urine on Sunday, Ashwini Nakshatra and give it to a barren woman to drink, she can get a son.

To get a son -
If you tie the Peepal Banda brought on Sunday, Revati Nakshatra to a pregnant woman in the third month, she gets a son.

To increase the good fortune of a woman -
The root of Shwetark taken in Gurupushya Yoga should be tied on the left arm and you should offer Arghya to the rising Sun every day by putting rice in it.

For getting a child

If a woman rubs turmeric on the white madaar root taken in Gurupushya or Ravipushya yoga and ties it around the waist, above the navel, she gets a child (there are no abortions).

For subjugation (Vashikaran)

Vashikaran is done by rubbing the white ark root taken in Ravipushya yoga in goat's urine and applying it as a tilak every day. By taking Manjith, Vacha, Motha, your blood and white ark root in equal quantity, grinding them and applying it as a tilak, everyone comes under your control.

Second method of subjugation

If you grind Gorochan, your urine and white mandar root in equal quantity and apply it as a tilak, then also the person watching gets subdued.

Note:In all these experiments, the roots should be cleaned and worshiped with incense and lamp. Also, it is necessary to chant 1008 Mool Mantras and make them Siddha and burn Guggal incense. This gives more and permanent benefits.

To make the officer favorable
By chanting 1008 Ganesh Mantras, offer black sesame and cow ghee as a sacrifice for three consecutive days. This will make the officer favorable to you.

To subjugate people
Mix white Aparajita juice, Vach, Sahadevi and Bhringraj in Gurupushya Yoga, chant 10 rounds of Ganesh mantras and apply Tilak. This will bring people under your control.

For strong subjugation
Grind the root of Chirchita/Aunga taken in Ravipushya Yoga in Gorochan and apply Tilak daily. This will cause strong Vashikaran.

For semen stasis
By tying the root of red Apamarg taken in Mangalpushya Yoga around the waist before sexual intercourse, semen stasis occurs.

For easy delivery
Tying the root of Apamarg around the waist of a pregnant woman makes the delivery easy and without any pain. If it is tied on a boil, it ripens and bursts quickly.

For subduing someone (Vashikaran)
By chanting 1008 mantras 'ॐ क्लीं कामदेवाय नमः' **'Om Kleem Kamadevay Namah'/Ganesh Mantra** with the desired person's name, bury it in his house. This will bring that person under your control. (Using the mantra 'Om Madan Kamadevaya Phat Swaha' is even better)

Second method of subjugation

Grinding the white Aparajita root taken in Ravipushya/Gurupushya Yoga in Gorochan and applying Tilak also leads to Vashikaran.

To subjugate a woman

Consecrate the black Aparajita root taken in an auspicious constellation by chanting the mantra 'ॐ हं स्वाहा' 'Om Hum Swaha' 1008 times, put it in a betel leaf and feed it to a woman. This will bring the woman under your control. To make the mantras successful, chanting it 12 lakh times is necessary.

For subjugation through looking into eyes

Grind the white Aparajita root taken during lunar eclipse, consecrate it by chanting the mantra 'ॐ क्लीं कामदेवाय नमः' **'Om Kleem Kamadevay Namah'** 1008 times and put it in the eyes to subjugate; whoever looks into your eyes will be subjugated.

Warning: Using subjugation and hypnosis for selfishness or lust fulfillment can be fatal or troublesome. Doing this can spoil a person's mind.

For getting a son or for the progress of the son -

On Diwali, throw 21 Hakiks consecrated with Lakshmi Mantras one by one in the west direction while reciting 'ॐ श्रीं पुत्राय महालक्ष्म्यै नमः' **'Om Shreem Putray Mahalakshmyai Namah'**.

For Surya Dosha

If there is a problem in marriage due to Surya, then wear the root of Bael in a copper cap on Sunday. Also, offer Arghya to the rising Sun with the mantra 'ॐ हीं हंसः' **'Om Hreem Hansah'**.

For repeated abortions

Keep aak wood at the head of the pregnant woman. Also, in Gurupushya yoga, make the root of fig tree perfect by chanting 19000 times Guru mantra or 21000 times Navarn mantra and tie it around the waist.

For problems related to children, marriage or business -

Offer red or white aak flowers to Shivling or Durga Mata.

For Good Luck

In Ravi Pushya Yoga, wash white ark root with Gangajal, rub turmeric on it and keep it in the puja. Offer ghee lamp and laddu and recite 'Ganesh Atharvashirsha' or 'Sankatnashak Ganesh Stotra' daily. This brings good luck to women and removes obstacles for men.

For Ketu Dosh:

If marriage is breaking due to Ketu, then keep the root of Augha/Apamarg tied to the arm for one year.

For marriage problems

In Gurupushya / Ravipushya Yoga, consecrate the root of fig with 19000 Guru Mantras or 21000 Navarn Mantras and wrap it in a yellow thread and wear it around the neck or arm. It is more beneficial to consecrate it during Navratris.

For Mangal Dosh

If there is a problem in marriage due to Mars, then wear the root of Shami on a red thread on Shukra Panchami/Dashami/Purnima.

If marriage does not happen after the age of 30-31 years

Plant an Amla plant in the east direction of the house in Bharani Nakshatra. Make the girl sleep in the north-west direction and the boy sleep in the south-east direction (till marriage).

If the atmosphere of the house deteriorates

Plant 5-7 pots of marigold in the house and plant henna plants outside.

To improve the relationship between husband and wife

Burn 21 pairs of whole cloves with desi ghee on cow dung cakes (9 days in Navratri). Apply ashtagandh tilak on the photo. Chant 'Navaarn Mantra' at least 108 times or wife chant 'Guru Mantra' and husband chant 'Shukra Mantra'.

If you are facing problems related to marriage, child, illness or loss, then put a pinch of turmeric in 5 flour balls and feed it to a cow every Saturday.

If there is a possibility of betrayal from love, marriage, life partner, partner or friends in your horoscope, then you should always keep an old banyan root with you and wear 'Mangalyantra'.

Although, many times wearing 'Mangalyantra' breaks the relationship with friend, partner or lover, but it is necessary to avoid betrayal. Because making a deep relationship with a wrong or deceitful person can cause great harm later on.

If you want to get a life partner or child or you are afraid of death, then keep doing Abhishek with sugarcane juice on Shivling.

And if you are worried about your husband's health, then the wife should offer water to Narmadaeshwar.

If a boy or girl is adamant on marrying someone and his parents do not consider that relationship right, then instead of persuading him, give him some time. During this time, tie the root of a banyan tree with a thread on the photo of the boy or girl. Apply Ashtagandha Tilak on the photo every day and chant 'Guru Mantra' at least 5 or 10 times. Pray to God to bring that boy / girl on the right path. If possible, apply Ashtagandha Tilak to the boy / girl as well. With this experiment, his stubbornness will end in 3-4 months. If needed, you can keep doing it for more time. In some cases, the difference is visible in just one and a half months. This experiment also proves effective for stubborn children.

If a boy or a girl is not getting married, then make some changes in their room. Keep men's items like tie, gloves, bat in the girl's room. And keep women's items like lipstick, bangles, nail polish, mehndi in the boy's room. This small trick can help them get married soon.

If a boy is not getting married

If a boy is not getting married or the girl does not like him, then put a picture of a pair of flowers or birds in his room. Distribute toffees to children for 6 months and gift white food items and white clothes to a girl every Friday. Feed potatoes or rice to a cow.

If a girl is not getting married
If a girl is not getting married or the boy does not like her, then offer Kalgi or Kalngi in Vishnu's temple every Thursday. On Wednesday, offer gram flour laddus to Ganesh ji and distribute them to the children there itself (do not bring them home). Feed yellow lentils or turmeric rice to the cow.

While showing the girl, make her wear pink coloured clothes or those having pink flower designs. In the room where the girl is being shown, put a picture of peony flowers in the west so that the boy's family can see it. But, after the marriage, before the girl's departure, remove that picture from the house and keep it somewhere else or give it to a needy person.

For love between husband and wife
Do not keep scissors, knife, screwdriver, press, heater, TV, dirty utensils, junk, broom, grinding stone, musli, mortar etc. and pictures related to war in the bedroom. Bring a picture of a pair of flowers/birds. (If there is separation/distance between husband/wife, then pink candle should be kept burning in the bedroom at night).

If someone is not getting love in life, or he/she feels neglected, then he/she should install a turquoise Ganesha (can be small too) and worship him/her daily. This will definitely make a difference.

If the distance between children and parents is increasing, then keep a silver Ganesha in the house, make them wear a sacred thread and chant 10 rosaries (at least 1 rosary) of "Ganesh Mantra" in front of him/her daily.

If you are facing problems in your married life or misfortune is increasing due to Rahu or Saturn, then install a slate colored Ganesha on Chaturthi. Consecrate him by reciting 108 Ganesh Chalisas. Worship him by chanting "Ganeshaatharva Shirsha" or "Ganesha Mantra" every day. If slate coloured Ganesha is not available, burn dry wood of mango or jamun to make ash. Bathe Ganesha with this ash and apply Tilak on him with this ash every day. And give up intoxication.

If you are facing problems in your married life due to Mars, then stop eating meat and red chillies (green chillies can be eaten) and cooking them at home. Offer vermilion to Lord Ganesha. Apply turmeric-saffron tilak to Lord Ganesha and yourself and chant a rosary of Ganesha mantra daily.

Neglect of relatives

If no relative asks about you, then definitely donate cotton and curd in the temple.

Discord at home

If there are a lot of fights in the house, then on the Chaturthi of Shukla Paksha every month, offer 108 laddus to Lord Ganesha and distribute them among the poor. Also, keep the idol of Lord Ganesha in front of the main door, with a brass lamp on the left side and a conch on the right side.

Disobedient child

If the child does not listen to you, then apply a tilak of your maang sindoor on his forehead daily. Make him wear a copper bracelet on his right hand and blow on his neck and the back of the head while eating. Or get him to store Surma in a silver box and keep it in the temple. Get him to light a lamp of flour and ghee in the northern direction of the house and apply Ashtagandha Tilak on him daily. If he does not apply it himself, then apply it to him while he is sleeping.

Some tips for pregnancy -

Fair child: A pregnant woman should eat two oranges every afternoon, this will give birth to a fair child.

Healthy and beautiful child: A pregnant woman should eat 25 grams of sugar candy mixed with 100 grams of gourd pulp every day, which will give birth to a healthy and beautiful child.

Easy delivery: Eating a little ball of gourd every day (suck the juice, chew a little and spit it out) makes delivery easy, the need for operation is reduced. (This prevents the fluid of the uterus from drying up.)

Lazy child: The child of a pregnant woman who sleeps during the day is lazy and sleepy.

Mental disorder: The child of a pregnant woman who sleeps with her hands above her head may be insane or suffer from mental disorder.

When the child is born, tie a knot of turmeric in a mauli/kalawa and keep it in the temple of the house. Tie a new knot in it every year on the birthday. Keep doing this until the child turns 36 years old. This keeps the **child healthy and increases good luck and good qualities**.

If work related to marriage or studies stops or problems arise in it, then start applying tilak of turmeric and saffron daily. This will remove the problems and the work will be successful.

If a girl is not ready to get married, then start applying a Tilak of white sandalwood, saffron and turmeric on her forehead. Within six to seven months, she will stop being adamant about not getting married and will agree for marriage.

If the relationship with in-laws is bad or there is a possibility of it getting bad, then stop eating salt and staying barefoot on Fridays. To bring sweetness in mutual relations, do not eat salt on Sunday and do not let your wife stay barefoot. Do not bathe barefoot yourself.

Those who are not getting married (especially girls) should wear a little reddish turmeric around their neck on Thursday and must worship-irrigate-light the banana tree (especially on Thursday). (If possible, also observe a fast on Thursday).

Grinding the root of Kalihar and applying it on the forehead daily during menstruation gives a son. It is also beneficial in **the problem of not having a child.** (Such women must eat asafoetida).

Mix pure saffron, turmeric, camphor oil, Ganga water and write the name of the husband on pieces of Bhojpatra or pure paper with a pomegranate pen (at least 51). Fold them and offer them daily at the feet of Durga/Ishta (no one should touch/open them). Then throw them in the river (**if the husband has fallen in love with another woman).**

If the child starts speaking late (does not speak for long) or does not speak clearly, start feeding him green chillies (especially seeds). And his aunt should start talking more.

If the child does not listen, rub Jaharmohra behind his ears while sleeping. And massage the soles with milk (raw) with a light hand. Massage the head with red oil during the day.

If the relationship with the husband has deteriorated due to someone's actions, then tie a sacred thread on the husband's photo and keep it with coconut and black salt between 11 and 11:30 on Saturday. And chant 5 rounds of 'Navaarn Mantra'. Do this 5/8/11 times. When you keep the new coconut and black salt, keep the old one under the Peepal tree. And rub the lemon and rock salt in your hand and wash it with water. Relationships will improve.

Wearing nutmeg and white sandalwood around the neck or applying them as tilak daily gradually stops the **stubbornness of the child.**

By applying tilak of turmeric and saffron on the navel, neck and forehead daily, the weak 'marriage yoga' of the girl's horoscope becomes stronger.

In case of childlessness, if the person was very naughty in childhood, then a silver earring should be worn, if he was fat and very quiet, then a gold earring should be worn and if he was a gossiper/loquacious/talkative, a liar or a tall talker, then a copper earring should be worn in his right ear.

Chanting one rosary of Gayatri Mantra daily in front of someone's photograph and meditating on the photograph while offering 11 oblations with this mantra gradually attracts him towards the seeker in a positive manner.

The boys who are rejected by girls, they should donate 5 utensils made of bronze. For talking about marriage, rice should be kept in a silver pocket and red-white flowers should be taken along.

If the child lies a lot, then apply tilak on his forehead and neck daily by mixing raw milk and white sandalwood, apply saffron on his tongue. And wear pomegranate root in an orange thread. **If he cries a lot**, then wear a whole betel nut in a blue/yellow thread around his neck.

Marriage & Child Mantra (Simple Use)

For Getting a Son -

'ॐ ह्रां ह्रीं हूं पुत्र कुरु स्वाहा।'
'Om Hreem Hreem Hreem Putra Kuru Swaha.'

Sit under a mango tree and chant this mantra 21 times daily with concentration. Start chanting from an auspicious time for one year and feed 100 dogs in a year.

To Get a Wife -

'पत्नीं मनोरमां देहि मनोवृत्तानुसारिणीम्। तारिणीं दुर्गसंसारसागरस्य कुलोद्भवाम् ।।'
'Patnim Manoramaam Dehi Manovrittaanusarini. Taarini Durgasansarasagarasya Kulodbhavam.'

Start chanting this mantra 10 times daily from an auspicious time. The total number of chants is one and a quarter lakh. But it has been observed in experience that before reaching one and a quarter lakh, usually the obstacles in marriage are removed. By doing this, a compatible and supportive wife from a good family is definitely obtained.

Note: Those who are not able to get married due to 'mangaldosha' etc., due to debts of previous birth or due to very weak chances of marriage, they should chant the above mantra and recite 100 times Durga (Shatchandi). Marriage will happen.

For Early Marriage -

'स देवि नित्यं परिपूज्यमान स्त्वामेव सीतेत्यभिभाषमाण:। दृढव्रतो राजसुतो महात्मा तवैव लाभाय कृतप्रयत्न:।।'
'Sa Devi Nityam Paripujyaman Stvamev Seetetyabhibhasmaanah. Dharavrato Rajsuto Mahatma Tavaiva Labhaya Kritaprayatnah.'

(Valmiki Ramayana) By reciting at least one recitation of Valmiki's Sunderkand encapsulated with this mantra, marriage takes place quickly. Start from an auspicious time.

To Get a Husband -

'कात्यायनि महामाये महायोगिन्यधीश्वरि। नन्दगोपसुतं देवि पतिं मे कुरुते नम: ॥'
'Katyayani Mahamaye Mahayoginyadhishwari. Nandagopsutam Devi Patim Me Kurute Namah.'

Chant 5 rounds of this mantra daily in front of the picture/statue of Katyayani at an auspicious time. This helps in getting a beautiful husband soon.

Getting a Desirable Husband -

From Friday or Monday, worship Goddess Parvati and chant 5 garlands daily in front of her statue/picture

'हे गौरि! शंकरार्धाङ्गि यथा त्वं शंकर प्रिया। तथा मां कुरु कल्याणि! कांत कांतां सुदुर्लभाम् ।।'
'Gauri! Shankararardhangi Yatha Tvam Shankar Priya. Tath Maa Kuru Kalyani! Kant Kant Sudurlabham.'

Chant this mantra. Usually within 6 months, otherwise it takes a whole year to get a loving, best and agreeable husband.

For Early Marriage -

While observing sixteen fasts on Mondays and worshipping the banana tree on Thursdays, worship Goddess Parvati daily and in front of Goddess Parvati and whenever you get time, while getting up, sitting, eating, drinking, lying down or doing any work, keep on reciting/reciting with devotion or singing the lines

'जय जय गिरिराज किशोरी......मंजुल मंगल मूल वाम अंग फरकन लगे।'
'Jai Jai Giriraj Kishori....Manjul Mangal Mool Vaam Ang Farkan Lage.'

(Sunderkand, Ramcharitmanas couplets 234, 235 and 236) as much as possible, then the girl gets married very soon.

Husband Subjugation -

'ॐ नमो महायक्षिणिं पतिं मे वश्यं कुरु कुरु स्वाहा।'
'Om Namo Mahayakshini Patim Me Vashya Kuru Kuru Swaha.'

Chant 11/21 rosaries of this mantra on Diwali/eclipse. Then keep chanting one rosary daily for 31 days. Keep your husband's picture tied with a sacred thread and coconut in front of you during the chanting time and keep your gaze on your husband's picture. After chanting, apply Ashtagandha Tilak on your husband's picture. (If possible, apply it on your husband's forehead too). This method makes your husband favorable.

Note: Don't do the work that your husband doesn't like. Don't create unnecessary quarrels or speak harshly. Stop interfering and finding faults. Otherwise, it will take more time.

For a Comfortable Delivery:

Recite this mantra
"ॐ मुक्तापाशा विपाशाश्च मुक्ता: सूर्येण रश्मय:। मुक्तसर्वभयाद् गर्भ त्राहिहिं मारुत स्वाहा।"
"Om Muktapasha Vipashasch Mukta: Suryaen Rashmay:. Muktsarvabhayad Garbha Trahihi Marut Swaha"

8 times in holy water or Ganga water. Then giving this water to a pregnant woman will ensure a comfortable delivery.

Note: On the day of eclipse or Diwali, this mantra should be chanted 1008 times and made Siddha, so that its effect is infallible.

"Repeating the turmeric rake, fill the place where there is less turmeric or leave more turmeric there. Next day, put turmeric in the root of the banana tree. During the chanting, keep your face towards north. Place Ganesh ji's picture in the north. Invoke him before the sadhana. Bid him farewell after the sadhana is over. Keep the time and place of sadhana the same.

Other benefits - If this prayog is not done with the desire of marriage, but if it is done for the removal of poverty/obstacles and misfortunes, then use a red seat and a garland of red sandalwood. And instead of laddus, offer coriander and jaggery as naivedya."

For Multi-faceted Benefits -

'ॐ श्रीं ह्रीं क्लीं ऐं वृन्दावन्यै स्वाहा।'
'Om Shreem Hreem Kleem Aim Vrindavanye Swaha.'

On an auspicious day and auspicious time, install Shaligram in Tulsi. Then worship it with incense, lamp and offerings. After that, chant 5/10 rounds of the above mantra on Tulsi beads. Then read the names of Tulsi 11/21 times -

'ॐ वृन्दा वृन्दावनी विश्वपूजिता विश्वपावनी। पुण्यसारा नन्दिनी च तुलसी कृष्णजीवनी।।'
'Om Vrinda Vrindavani Vishwapoojita Vishwapaavani. Punyasara Nandini Cha Tulsi Krishnajeevani.'

Water Tulsi and circumambulate it. For one year, keep chanting at least one rosary and 11 times, keep circumambulating, watering and lighting lamps. (Must light a ghee lamp near Tulsi in the evening too.) By doing this, a suitable groom/bride is soon found. A child is born. Diseases and grief are removed and wealth and prosperity increase. After the Puja, applying tilak daily with wet mud from near the root of Tulsi increases the brilliance/influence and power of attraction.

Woman's Good Luck Mantra -

'ॐ ॐ ह्रीं ॐ क्लीं ह्रीं ॐ स्वाहा।'
'Om Om Hreem Om Kleem Hreem Om Swaha'.

Start on an auspicious day and auspicious time. Chanting 10 rosaries every day at sunrise ensures that a woman always has domestic happiness, husband's happiness and good luck. After chanting this mantra during Navratri, offer 108 oblations from the wood of the banyan tree and worship a girl and give her donations. Women who have 'Vaidhavya Yog' in their horoscope or whose husbands often stay abroad or away from home for some reason and they are not able to get much proximity to their husbands should do this. (Reciting 'Ahilya Stotra' is also beneficial).

To get the Desired Husband -

Girls who want to marry their lover, but it is not possible. Or those who want to marry a particular man. They should chant this mantra to marry the man of their choice. Chant at least one rosary after incense-lamp-worship in front of the idol of Gauri/Parvati. (5 rosary chanting shows quick results). Start from an auspicious time or from Friday Monday.

'ॐ श्री दुर्गायै सर्वविघ्नविनाशिन्यै नमः स्वाहा। सर्वमंगल मांगल्ये सर्वकामप्रदेशिवे। देहि मे वांछितं नित्यं, नमस्ते शंकरप्रिये दुर्गे शिवे'भये माये, नारायणी! सनातनी। जपे मे मंगले देहि, नमस्ते सर्वमंगले॥'
'Om Shri Durgaye Sarvavighnavinashinye Namah Swaha. Sarvamangal Mangalye Sarvakaampradeshive. Dehi Me Aanchitham Nityam, Namaste Shankarpriye Durga Shivaye Bhaye Maaye, Narayani! Sanatani. Jape Me Mangale Dehi, Namaste Sarvamangale.'
The more you do it with devotion, the quicker the effect will be. Sitaji got Ram due to the effect of this mantra.

Indrani Mantra for getting a Good Husband -

Start from an auspicious time. First of all, worship Tulsi in the morning facing east. Then chant the following mantra 5 times (at least one time) with Tulsi beads in front of Tulsi.
'ॐ देवेन्द्राणि नमस्तुभ्यं देवेन्द्र प्रिय भामिनि। विवाहं भाग्यमारोग्यं शीघ्र लाभं च देहिमे।'
'Om Devendrani Namastubhyam Devendra Priya Bhamini. Vivaham Bhagyamarogyam Sheegar Labham Cha Dehime.'

After this, do 12 rounds of Tulsi. Offer Arghya to the Sun together by holding a pot of water in the left hand and milk (raw) in the right hand (even if it is a small pot). While offering Arghya, chant the same mantra 12 times again. By doing this prayog regularly, you get a good husband in a few weeks. (The girl has to do this sadhana herself).

Infertility Destroying Mantra -

The woman who does not have a child should chant or remember the mantra

'एहिविधिगर्भ सहित सब नारी भई हृदय हर्षित सुख भारी। जा दिन से हरिगर्भहि आए। सकल लोक सुख संपति छाए।'
'Ehi Vidhi Garbha Sahit Sab Naari Bhi Hridya Harshit Sukh Bhaari. Ja Din Se Hari Garbhahi Aaye. Sakal Lok Sukh Sampati Chaaye.'

as much as possible while getting up, sitting, walking or lying down. And should drink Tulsi juice or Rudraksha water consecrated with this mantra every day on an empty stomach.

Lok Vashikaran:

'ह्रीं श्रीं क्लीं गं गणपतये वरवरद । सर्वजनं मे वशमानय स्वाहा।।'
'Hreem Shreem Kleem Gam Ganpataye Varavarad. Sarvajanam Me Vashmaanay Swaaha.'

By chanting 1008 times daily for 41 days while offering cow ghee, honey and sweet kheer in front of Ganesha idol made from bamboo soil, the whole world gets subdued.

Note: If 1008 oblations are offered with wood apple wood with the above mantra for 31 days, then the king/official gets subdued/beneficial. Afterwards offer laddus.

Getting a son and other benefits -

One who has only daughters, does not have a son or is suffering from debt/poverty/sorrow/fear of enemies, gets benefited by chanting 5 rosaries of this mantra daily.

'पुत्रान् देहि धनं देहि त्वमस्मि शरणंगता। ऋण दारिद्र्य दु:खेन शत्रूणां च भंयात्तत: ।।'
'Putran dehi dhanam dehi tvamsmi sharanangata. debt poverty dukhen shastrunam ca bhayattatah.'

(Start from an auspicious time. At least for one year).

Marriage Obstacle Removal -

When the moon of a girl who is not getting married is strong in transit, then in the amrityog or amritlabh choghadiya, wear yellow clothes on a yellow seat, make Ganesh Ji sit on a yellow seat, light a lamp of pure ghee with turmeric, worship with whole rice/kanku rice, turmeric and laccha. Remember the Guru and recite the 'Ganesh Mantra' and take a pledge. Pray to Ganesh Ji for getting a groom and offer 1/3/5 laddus and make a swastika with turmeric on a new plate and chant 'ॐ वक्रतुण्डाय हुं' **'Om Vakratundaya Hum'** 21 times on a turmeric rosary. Do this daily for at least 6 months (except 7 days of menstruation). After that distribute the laddus among children. This is a very effective prayog. It is experienced. Marriages have been seen happening with this prayog even at the age of 35 to 45 years. If this is done with investment then it gives faster results. For your benefit, the appropriation method is being given.

Appropriation : Say with water in hand 'ॐ अस्य श्री गणेश मंत्रस्य, भार्गव ऋषि: अनुष्टुप् छन्द: विघ्नेशो देवता, वं बीजं, यं शक्ति:, सर्वेष्ट सिद्धये (या 'मम विवाहार्थे') जपे विनियोग:।'
'Om Asya Shri Ganesh Mantrasya, Bhargava Rishi: Anushtup Chhand: Vighnesho Devata, Vam Bijan, Yam Shakti:, Sarveshta Siddhaye (or 'Mam Vivaharthe') Jape Viniyoga.'.Leave the water in your hand on the ground).

Rishyadinyas: ॐ भार्गव ऋषये नम: **Om Bhargav Rishaye Namah: Touch the head.** ॐ अनुष्टुप्छन्दसे नम: **Om Anushtuphandse Namah: Touch the mouth.** ॐ विघ्नेशदेवताये नम: **Om Vighneshdevataye Namah: Touch the heart.** ॐ वं बीजाय नम: **Om Vam Bijay Namah: Touch the sense organs.** ॐ यं शक्त्ये नम: **Om Yam Shaktye Namah: Touch the knees.** ॐ हुं कीलकाय नम: **Om Hum Keelakay Namah: Rotate hands around the body/head.**

Karanyas: ॐ वं अंगुष्ठाभ्यां नम: **Om and Angusthabhyam Namah.** ॐ क्रं तर्जनीभ्यां नम: **Om Kram Tarjanibhyam Namah.** ॐ टं मध्यमाभ्यां नम: **Om Tam Madhyamabhya Namah.** ॐ टां अनामिकाभ्यां नम: **Om Taan Anamikabhyan Namah.** ॐ यं कनिष्ठकाभ्यां नम: **Om Yam Kanishtha Kaabhya Namah.** ॐ हुं करतलकर पृष्ठाभ्यां नम: **Om Hum Kartalkar Prushabhya**

Namah. Touch all the thumbs, fingers, palm and back of the hand in the above manner.

Anganyas: ॐ वं हृदयाय नम: oṃ vaṃ hṛdayāya namaḥ. ॐ क्रं नम: मस्तक स्वाहा oṃ kraṃ namaḥ mastaka svāhā. ॐ टुं नम: शिखा स्थान वषट् oṃ tuṃ namaḥ śikhā sthāna vaṣaṭ. ॐ टां नम: कवचाय हुं oṃ tāṃ namaḥ kavacāya huṃ. ॐ यं नम: नेत्रत्रयाय वौषट् oṃ yaṃ namaḥ netratrayāya vaṣaṭ. ॐ हुं नम: अस्त्राय फट् oṃ huṃ namaḥ astrāya phaṭ.
After each mantra, touch the heart, forehead, crest, navel and eyes respectively and finally clap.

Varnanyas: ॐ वं नम: भुवैर्मध्ये ॐ क्रं नम: कण्ठे Om Vam Namah Bhuvairmadhe Om Kram Namah Kanthe. ॐ टुं नम: हृदये Om Tun Namah Hridaye. ॐ ॐ नम: नाभौ Om Om Namah Nabhau. ॐ यं नम: लिंगे Om Yam Namah Linge. ॐ हं नम: पादयो: Om Han Namah Padayo. Meditate or touch these body parts or wash hands. ॐ वक्रतुण्डाय हूं नम: Om Vakratundaya Hoon Namah. Saying this, splash water on yourself.

Benefits of Nyasaadi: In this way, the mantra gets connected to the body/parts of the sadhak. The body becomes full of mantras. Due to which there are no disturbances and the flow of concentration and energy improves. Then meditate on the form of Ganesha with the following mantra.

Meditation Mantra: "ॐ उद्दण्डनेत्वर रुचि निजहस्त पद्मे पाशांकुशाभयवरान् दधतंगास्यम्। रक्ताबरं सकल दु:ख हरं गणेशं ध्यायेत्प्रसन्न अखिल लाभं भरणाभिराममम्।।"
"Om Uddandanetvar Ruchi Nijahasta Padme Pashankushabhayavaran Dadhatangasyam. Raktabaran Sakal Dukh Haram Ganesam Dhayetprasanna Akhil Labham Bharanabhiramam."

Basic Mantra: ॐ वक्रतुण्डाय हुं। Om Vakratundaya Hum. Then chant this mantra 21 times.

Caution: While making the swastika with dry turmeric on a brass plate, do not touch it with the index finger. Make the swastika from right to left and from bottom to top. Do not stop where the pinch of turmeric falls short, complete the sequence.

By adding turmeric and repeating the sequence, fill the place where there is less turmeric or leave more turmeric there. Next day put that turmeric in the root of a banana tree. During chanting, keep your face towards the north. Also place the picture of Ganesh Ji in the north. Invoke him before Sadhana. Bid him farewell after the completion of Sadhana. Keep the time and place of Sadhana the same.

Other benefits: If this experiment is not done with the intention of marriage but is done to eradicate poverty/obstacles and misfortunes then use a red seat and a garland of red sandalwood. And instead of laddus, offer coriander and jaggery as naivedya.

For Multi-faceted Benefits -

'ॐ श्रीं ह्रीं क्लीं ऐं वृन्दावन्यै स्वाहा।'
'Om Shreem Hreem Kleem Aim Vrindavanye Swaha.'

On an auspicious day and auspicious time, place a Shaligram in the Tulsi plant and worship it with incense, lamp and offerings. Then chant 5/10 rounds of the above mantra on a Tulsi rosary. After this, read the names of Tulsi 11/21 times - 'ॐ वृन्दा वृन्दावनी विश्वपूजिता विश्वपावनी। पुण्यसारा नन्दिनी च तुलसी कृष्णजीवनी।।' **'Om Vrinda Vrindavani Vishwapoojita Vishwapaavani Punyasara Nandini Cha Tulsi Krishnajeevani.'** Offer water to Tulsi and circumambulate it. For one year, keep chanting at least one rosary and 11 times the names, keep circumambulating, watering and lighting lamps. Must light a ghee lamp near Tulsi in the evening too. By doing this, one gets a suitable groom/bride very soon. One gets a child. Diseases and grief are removed and wealth and prosperity increase. After the Puja, applying tilak daily with wet mud from near the root of Tulsi increases the brilliance/influence and power of attraction.

Marriage Obstacle Prevention -
The girls who are not liked, or for some reason marriage talks are not progressing, they should chant 21 rosaries in a stable Lagna on a white seat in front of 'Shri Yantra' on Diwali/Navratri, wearing white clothes, facing north, on a rosary of white sandalwood/crystal, with the mantra

'ॐ धं ह्रीं श्रीं रतिप्रियै स्वाहा।'
'Om Dham Hreem Shreem Ratipriyai Swaha.'

If the total chanting is more than one and a quarter lakh, then one should perform Havan of one tenth, Tarpan of one tenth, Marjan and feed one tenth of the Brahmins. Usually marriage happens before the experiment is complete.

Support of wife -
Men who do not get support from their wives should chant at least one rosary (sphatik rosary) of the mantra 'ॐ द्रां द्रीं द्रौं सः शुक्राय नमः।'
'Om Draam Driim Draum Sah Shukray Namah'
on a white seat and wearing white clothes. They should remain well-groomed and well-dressed

Specific Shiva Mantras- Some mantras for Shiva worshippers are as follows:

To have a child - Chant 'ॐ निधये नमः।' **'Om Nidhaye Namah'** and offer marigold flowers, milk and white sandalwood on the Shiva lingam.

To get a good body - Chant 'ॐ स्वर्ण रेतसे नमः।' **'Om Swarn Retse Namah'** and offer rose flowers and water on Shiva Linga.

For healthy child - Chant 'ॐ सुबीजाय नमः।' **'Om Subijaya Namah'** and offer honey, milk and white flowers on Shiva Linga. Men with weak semen/sperm should do this.

For family happiness - Chant 'ॐ महाबीजाय नमः।' **'Om Mahabijaya Namah'** and offer Imarti/Gulab Jamun, black sesame seeds, Dhatura and Aak flowers on the Shiva lingam.

To get the desired groom - Chant 'ॐ नीलकंठाय नमः।' **'Om Neelkanthaay Namah'.** Offer marigold and rose flowers and aak or bael leaves on the Shivling and offer ghee. Or offer Nagkesar. Note - All chanting should be done daily at least 10 times on Rudraksha rosary.

Widowhood Protector Mantra - '॰ ह्रीं क्लीं श्रीं सावित्र्यै नमः।'
'Om Hreem Kleem Shreem Savitryai Namah.' According to 'Devi Bhagwat Puran', this mantra provides and increases husband's happiness, household happiness and child happiness. Therefore, women with widowhood yoga should worship Banyan tree or banana tree every day and chant this mantra at least 11 times near Banyan tree or banana tree. And should wear marital symbols respectfully.

Removal of obstacle in child birth -

This mantra belongs to Varun (and Gayatri) who is the patron of the genital centre. Hence, due to the effect of chanting this mantra, necessary changes take place in the body of the person chanting it and obstacles in fertility are removed. It is especially useful for those who are unable to have children due to **'Nadi Dosha'.**

'॰ यं यं यं भूः भुवः स्वः ॰ तत्सवितुर्वरेण्यं भर्गो देवस्य धीमहि धियो यो नः प्रचोदयात्।'
'Om Yam Yam Yam Bhuh Bhuvah Swah Om Tatsaviturvarenya Bhargo Devasya Dhimahi Dhiyo Yo Nah Prachodayat.'

Both the husband and wife should observe fast on Sunday. Inhale and hold the breath, then chant the above mantra 3 times, keeping the wish of having a son/daughter in mind. Chant on a sandalwood rosary. Keep Gayatri's picture in front or imagine her as a child wearing white clothes holding a lotus. Exhale. Inhale again and chant 3 times. Chant 3 times in each repetition. (Total 108 times/one rosary; this way 108 will be completed in 36 pranayamas. Gradually increase the practice. After a little rest do 3/4 sets of 36 pranayamas daily. Then worship Gayatri Devi with kheer and honey and consume the prasad; rice has the power of Gayatri.

Therefore, offering of Kheer is very essential. This ritual corrects the Nadi Dosh/genital obstruction of the husband and wife in a year and makes them capable of having children. It has been tested in many cases of Nadi Dosh. Special - If there is 'Pitru Dosh' along with 'Nadi Dosh', then getting a child is almost impossible/extremely difficult. Such people should also do the remedy for 'Pitru Dosh' removal for at least 1 to 5 years.

Santan Gopal Mantra - This is the surefire and final remedy for getting a child. Both the husband and wife should do this in front of 'Santan Gopal Yantra' or in front of the picture of Laddu Gopal. Before chanting the mantra, 'Ganesh Atharvashirsha' should be recited and after chanting, 'Santan Gopal Stotra' should be recited. Once a day, some portion of 'Harivansh Purana' should also be read or heard. This not only opens the way to getting a child but also gives a healthy, intelligent and talented child (mostly a son is born). If done for a long time with faith and devotion, even an infertile woman can get a child. It has great glory among the remedies for getting a child. It is well-tested. One and a quarter lakh chants of its mantra/stotra should be done). It is better to do it in the last quarter of the day in a stable ascendant. (Santan Gopal Yantra is also consecrated and worn. Buy it readymade from the market and consecrate it with 'Santan Gopal Stotra/Mantra'.

'देवकीसुतं गोविन्द वासुदेव जगत्पते। देहि मे तनयं कृष्ण त्वामहं शरणं गतः॥'
"devakīsutaṃ govinda vāsudeva jagatpate | dehi me tanayaṃ kṛṣṇa tvāmahaṃ śaraṇaṃ gataḥ ||"

While chanting the mantra, imagine Lord Vishnu coming from the sea on Garuda and giving himself a son. It is also beneficial in abortion/pregnancy etc.

Infertility Removal Mantra -

'ॐ हं गं ग्लौं हरिद्रागणपतये वरवरद सर्वजनहृदयं स्तम्भय स्तम्भय स्वाहा।' **'Om Hoon Gan Glaun Haridraganpataye Varvarad Sarvjanahridayam Stambhay Stambhay Swaha.'**

This mantra is chanted systematically in works like Stambhan etc. But if a barren woman, after taking seasonal bath, worships Ganesha, filters 4 tola cow urine, grinds durva and turmeric in it and blesses her with 1008 chants of this mantra and after feeding laddus to the girl and children, then she will get a virtuous son. This has been said in 'Mantra Mahodadhi'.

Vastu Remedies - Totke/Solutions

As per popular belief it is said that your life is influenced by three key factors: **planets** (33%), **Vastu** (33%) and **Karma** (deeds) (34%). Together, they shape your life's experiences. If two of these factors are favorable, your life will generally go well. However, if two are unfavorable, you may face difficulties. If all three are aligned positively, you will experience great fortune. But if all three are problematic, it can lead to serious challenges.

Key Highlights:

Influence of Planets, Vastu and Karma:

Planets (33%): Beyond our control, planetary positions can significantly influence our life, but remedying their effects requires substantial effort.

Vastu (33%): The arrangement of your living space can influence your life. Fixing Vastu issues often brings quick and noticeable benefits. There are rare cases where some defects cannot be resolved.

Karma (34%): The most controllable factor. By improving your mindset and actions, you can dramatically improve your life.

Understanding and Action:

People often focus only on one aspect of their life, like planets, Vastu, or Karma. If one is in a bad state, they may overlook the others or become overly anxious. This lack of understanding leads to confusion and frustration.

Key Insight: You cannot change the planets, but you can influence Vastu and Karma.

Vastu problems can be easily fixed with simple remedies and when done, they offer quick relief.

Karma can be controlled through self-awareness, managing your mind and performing righteous deeds.

The 67% Solution:

If your **Vastu is improved** and **Karma is corrected**, you can benefit **67%** without needing to exert much effort on planetary remedies. This is the most effective and sustainable approach to improving your life.

Important Note: If your Vastu is in a bad state, fixing your Karma or doing planetary remedies will not bring lasting benefits. The bad effects of a poor Vastu will cancel out any good planetary influences, similar to how a hot object cools quickly when placed in a cold environment.

The Importance of Vastu:

Vastu defects create an imbalance between the five elements - **earth, water, fire, air and space** - which affects health, wealth, peace and prosperity.

Examples of **Vastu defects**:

Misplacement of elements: For instance, placing water in the space of fire, or fire in the space of water, causes imbalance.

Improper placement of items: Placing heavy items in the space of sky, or placing impure objects in pure areas, creates harm.

Structural issues: Defects in the roof, basement, stairs and the main door disrupt the harmony of energies, leading to negative outcomes like fear, insecurity and stress.

Planetary Placement in Vastu:

Each planet governs a particular direction in the Vastu of your home. If planets are not properly aligned, their negative influence may worsen over time, affecting both your Vastu and your personal horoscope.

Correcting Vastu: Fixing Vastu imbalances helps in improving not only the surrounding environment but also the planetary influences in your horoscope.

Vastu Tips to Bring Wealth and Prosperity

1. North Direction:

- The North direction is considered the best place to keep **money**, **pure water**, or a **money plant**.
- If this is not possible, place a picture of water here to symbolize wealth.
- Ensure that this area is **lower and lighter** than the South direction to maintain harmony.
- Keep the North direction **clean**, avoiding dirt or clutter.

2. North-East Direction:

- The **North-East** is an important area in Vastu. It is ideal to place a **Sphatik Pyramid** or a **Shriyantra** here.
- Avoid keeping **dustbins, toilets, storage, brooms, or stairs** in this area.
- This direction should be kept **pure** and **clean** and it is ideal for a **place of worship**.

3. East Direction:

- The East is the source of **light and positive energy**. Ensure that light and air can freely enter this direction.
- The **East direction** should be **clean, lower and lighter** than the West direction.
- **Planting a Tulsi plant** in the East brings prosperity.
- **Avoid keeping shoes** or other personal items in the East.

4. South-West Direction:

- Ideally, the **South-West** should be the **highest** or **heaviest** part of the house.
- If it is not possible to make it heavy, you can place a **flag** or **bamboo** on the roof.
- If the roof is not in your possession, place **heavy items** in this area.

- As an alternative, you can place a **picture of high mountains** (without water) in this direction.

5. Main Door:

- The main entrance should be **free of any obstacles** such as **dampness, dirt, garbage, or any obstructions** like a pit, pillar, drain, or tree directly in front.
- A **thick lock** on the door or **any obstruction** blocks wealth from entering.
- If an obstacle cannot be removed, place a **mirror** in front of the door to reflect the obstruction and reduce its negative impact.

6. Main Door with Two Doors:

- A **door with two doors** is said to divide happiness and wealth. It is best to have a door with a single entrance.
- If two doors are unavoidable, **open both doors** while entering and exiting the house.

7. Direction of the Door:

- The **main door** should open **outwards**, while **windows** should open **inwards**. This setup facilitates the free flow of wealth and positive energy into the home.
- Avoid having a **slope in front of the door**, as it can create imbalances in energy flow.

8. Puja Place:

- Place a picture of **Lakshmi sitting** rather than standing, as it invites more blessings.
- It is also auspicious to keep a **Lakshmi-Vishnu** picture together.
- Along with the image, **keep a conch** and a **lamp** to enhance positive energy.

9. Cleanliness of the House:

- **Cleanliness** is essential for prosperity. If there is **laziness, unrest, quarrels, intoxication, junk, dirt,** or **disorder** in the house, **Lakshmi** (goddess of wealth) will not reside.
- The house should be **clean, well-organized** and free from negative influences.
- **Daytime sleeping** or **cooking without bathing** is considered inauspicious for the housewife. She should cook with care and devotion.

10. Grihalakshmi (Housewife):

- The housewife is known as **Grihalakshmi** and her happiness is crucial for the well-being of the household.
- Respect the **elders and guests** in the house, as neglecting them can cause financial setbacks.
- If the housewife is unhappy or elders are mistreated, **Lakshmi** will not stay in the house.

Vastu tips to keep money at Home

1. Single Entrance:

- **One main entrance** is essential for the free flow of energy. If there are more than two entrances in the house, wealth does not stay in the house.
- **Solution**: Close the extra doors to ensure wealth remains in the house.

2. Direction Balance:

- **East and North** directions are considered favorable for doors and windows. These directions attract positive energy and wealth.
- **South and West** directions should ideally have smaller windows/doors compared to the East and North.
- **Solution**: If doors/windows exist in the south and west, ensure they are smaller than the ones in the east and north, or keep them closed.

3. Brahmasthan (Center of the House):

- The **center** of the house is very important in Vastu. If there are obstacles like **stairs, pillars, pits**, or any water source in the center (Brahmasthan), it blocks wealth and prosperity. It can also affect health and longevity.
- **Solution**: Keep the center of the house clear and free from obstacles.

4. Water-Related Vastu Defects:

- Issues like **waste of water, dampness, leaking taps**, leaking roofs, **water flowing from neighbors' houses**, or any construction that disturbs the natural flow of water can prevent wealth from staying in the house.
- **Solution**: Ensure proper drainage, repair leaks and maintain the purity of water sources, especially in the **north-east** direction.

5. Toilet, Kitchen and Prayer Room:

- The **toilet** should not be in the **north-east, east, or north** direction, as it disrupts prosperity and brings about diseases and quarrels.
- **Kitchen** should not be in the **north-west, north, or north-east** direction, as this negatively impacts wealth and happiness.
- The **prayer room** should not be in the **south-west**.
- **Solution**: Relocate the toilet, kitchen and prayer room to more favorable directions.

6. Stairs:

- **Stairs should descend** inside the house, not outside.
- Too many stairs, **Saudia (staircases that ascend in the northeast or east), kitchen under stairs**, or an **even number of steps** are considered bad.
- **Solution**: Keep the number of steps **odd** and make sure the total number when divided by 3 leaves a remainder of 2 (e.g., 5, 11, 17).

7. Windows:

- If the **number of stairs** is odd, then the **number of windows** should be even, but not ending in 0 (10, 20).
- **Solution**: Maintain this balance to prevent disturbances in the energy flow.

8. Tulsi Plant:

- **Tulsi (Holy Basil)** should be planted in the **east** or **north-east** direction of the house.
- **Solution**: Light a **ghee lamp** in the morning and evening and perform a **parikrama** (circumambulation) around it for prosperity.

9. Kitchen Vastu:

- The **kitchen** should not have a **bathroom** or toilet nearby, as this disrupts the balance between the **water and fire elements**, which affects both health and wealth.
- **Solution**: Keep the bathroom away from the kitchen. If this is not possible, place a **sink** on the kitchen side of the bathroom and **gas/stove** on the opposite side to balance the elements.

10. South-East Direction for Kitchen:

- The **south-east** direction is the best for the kitchen, as it is the **fire element's** direction.
- **Forbidden directions** for the kitchen include the **north-west, north, south-west, north-east and west**.
- **Solution**: If the kitchen is in a forbidden direction, remove the door or keep it open and light a lamp in the **south-east corner**.

Vastu Tips for Peace, Happiness, Love and Good Relationships at Home

Single Entrance:

- **Main Entrance**: It is essential to have a **single main entrance** to ensure the free flow of energy into the house. Multiple entrances can disrupt the flow and prevent wealth from staying in the home.

- **Solution**: Close any extra doors to retain the energy flow and wealth within the house.

Direction Balance:

- **East and North Directions**: These directions are the most favorable for doors and windows, as they attract positive energy, good health and prosperity.
- **South and West Directions**: These directions should ideally have smaller doors or windows than the east and north directions. Larger windows or doors in these directions can cause imbalance in energy.
- **Solution**: If there are doors or windows in the south and west, make them smaller, or keep them closed to maintain balance.

Brahmasthan (Center of the House):

- The **center (Brahmasthan)** of the house is a key area in Vastu. If this area contains obstacles such as stairs, pillars, pits, or water sources, it can block the flow of prosperity and harm health and longevity.
- **Solution**: Keep the center of the house clear of obstacles to allow the smooth flow of positive energy.

Water-Related Vastu Defects:

- Issues like **leaking roofs, damaged taps, waste water**, or **flooding from neighboring homes** can cause financial and health problems in the house.
- **Solution**: Ensure that water flows properly in your house. Repair leaks and prevent water-related problems, particularly in the **north-east direction**.

Toilet, Kitchen and Prayer Room Placement:

- **Toilets** should not be in the **north-east**, **east**, or **north** direction, as they disrupt prosperity and health.
- **Kitchens** should not be placed in the **north-west**, **north**, or **north-east**, as this impacts wealth and happiness.

- **Prayer Room** should not be located in the **south-west** direction.
- **Solution**: Relocate the toilet, kitchen and prayer room to more suitable directions for better energy flow and prosperity.

Stairs:

- Stairs should always **descend inside the house**, not outside. Avoid **Saudia** (staircases that ascend in the northeast or east) or a **kitchen under stairs**.
- **Solution**: Keep stairs with an **odd number** of steps and ensure that the number of steps, when divided by 3, leaves a remainder of 2 (e.g., 5, 11, 17).

Windows:

- **Windows** should be balanced in terms of the number of stairs. If the number of stairs is odd, the number of windows should be **even**, but not ending in 0 (e.g., 10, 20).
- **Solution**: Maintain balance between the number of stairs and windows for smooth energy flow.

Tulsi Plant:

- The **Tulsi plant (Holy Basil)** should be planted in the **east** or **north-east** direction to bring prosperity and positive energy.
- **Solution**: Light a **ghee lamp** in the morning and evening and perform **parikrama (circumambulation)** around the plant for added benefits.

Kitchen Vastu:

- A **bathroom or toilet** near the kitchen disrupts the balance of water and fire elements, leading to health and wealth issues.
- **Solution**: Keep the bathroom away from the kitchen. If relocation is not possible, place a **sink** on the kitchen side of the bathroom and the **gas/stove** on the opposite side to balance the elements.

South-East Direction for Kitchen:

- The **south-east** direction is considered ideal for the kitchen because it represents the **fire element**, which is crucial for cooking.
- **Forbidden Directions for Kitchen**: Avoid placing the kitchen in the **north-west**, **north**, **south-west**, **north-east** and **west** directions.
- **Solution**: If your kitchen is in an unfavorable direction, remove the door or keep it open and light a lamp in the **south-east corner** to improve energy flow.

Vastu Tips for Livelihood, Growth and Success

If you are not getting a job or are facing problems in your job, or you are facing losses in business, or you are trapped in debt, then follow these Vastu tips:

If you are not getting a job or are facing problems in a government job, then plant 5 Tulsi or sunflower plants in the east direction of the house and offer water to the rising sun every day. Recite 'Adityahridaya Stotra'. On any Sunday, tie the root of Bel Patthar tree in a white thread and wear it around your neck and give 5 almonds and milk to your father or grandfather every day. By doing this, job and money problems in your life can be removed.

If you are facing losses in your business or trade, then put a picture of Krishna Ji or a small statue of Ganesh Ji in the north direction. (Silver or crystal statue is the best). Keep a conch and crystal Sriyantra in front of them. Offer mung to Ganesh Ji every Wednesday or Chaturthi and distribute it among the poor. By doing this, losses in your business can be stopped.

If you are often in a position to take loans or have trouble repaying them (even if you are a good person and have good habits), then hammer copper nails at the head of your bed. While sleeping, keep your feet towards the west. Plant a potato or gooseberry plant in the north direction. Recite 'Rinmochak Mangal' or 'Rinmochak Ganesh' stotra daily.

If you often do not get your money back from others, then do not lend money to anyone on Tuesdays during Rahukaal, Jwalamukhi Yoga, Rikta or Kshaya Tithi. Put a green flag in the north direction of your house. Always keep the mirror and wall clock in the north or east direction. On Wednesday, sometimes fill 5 empty pitchers with water and put them in flowing water.

If despite your qualifications and despite the job being vacant, you are not able to get a transfer, then float 4 spotless lemons in a river in Pushya Nakshatra. Apart from this, sleep or sit in the north-west direction for a few days.

If you want to get progress, position and respect, then plant a white water lily in Ravi Pushya Yoga in the east direction of the house. Put a picture of copper sun on the eastern wall of the house. Chant 'Gayatri Mantra' under the vine tree every day. Gift a cane to your father. Do not make an open courtyard in the west direction of the house (if there is one, cover it) or if there is a courtyard in the east direction, keep it small. Feed a bull or sheep or feed jaggery and gram to a monkey.

If you are losing your job repeatedly or are afraid of starting a new job, then go for a few days with dhatura seeds in your pocket. Keep a brass Gangajali airtight in the puja room of your house or plant a pomegranate plant in the east of the house. Before going to work, bow to the mango tree.

Sit in the south direction in your office or work place, face north. There should be a wall behind your back. This will increase your influence on the people in front and will give you stability. Do not put any picture or photograph behind your back. This can distract the attention of the person in front. If you have to put a picture, then put a picture of a mountain or a big building so that your words carry weight and you get courage.

If any item is not selling in your shop, then keep it in the north-west corner of the shop. This increases the chances of it selling quickly. Because in this direction there is an effect of things ending quickly. This direction does not allow anything to remain there for a long time.

If your shop is not doing well or the number of customers is less, then try these Vastu tips:

- **Hang a ding:** Hang a ding tied with a white thread in the shop and replace it when it gets damaged.
- **Peepal leaf:** Keep a fresh peepal leaf in the cash box every day and remove it in the evening.
- **Swastik symbol**: Make a swastik symbol with turmeric on both sides of the shop entrance.
- **Picture of deities**: Keep the picture or temple of deities in the east or north direction of the shop. Do not put the picture of a dead person. If you have to put it, then keep it in the south direction.
- **Worship**: Offer incense and lamp to God every day, light rose or sandalwood incense sticks, worship Ganesha and Lakshmi, then start work.
- **Bisa Yantra:** Place 'Bisa Yantra' in the eastern direction of the shop and worship it daily.
- **Sphatik Pyramid:** Keep a pyramid of sphatik on the counter.
- **Shape of the counter:** Get the corners of the counter rounded or keep a semi-circular (D-shaped) counter.
- **Intoxication and Eating:** Do not consume intoxicants at the shop and do not eat on the seat.

By following these tips, you can bring success and prosperity to your shop.

Labour problem: If your factory does not have labour or you face problems with labor, then on Saturday while going from home to factory, pick up any nail lying on the way - small, big, new, old, bent or rusted, any nail. Wash that nail with buffalo urine and clean it with Gangajal and hammer it so deep into the door frame or wall of the factory gate that nothing can be hung on it. This will solve your problem. But remember, pay attention to your behavior and giving proper remuneration to the labor.

By keeping in mind these Vastu tips, you can get success and progress in your work.

To Remove some more Vastu Defects, follow these Simple Remedies

1. High Houses Around Your House:

- **Problem**: If there are taller houses around yours, the good energy coming from the sky gets blocked, leading to stress, scarcity and obstacles in progress.
- **Solution**: If you cannot make your house taller, place a **white flag**, a **five-colored flag**, or **bamboo** on your roof to increase its height and balance the surrounding energy. If the taller house is only on one side, place an **arrow-shaped figure** on that side of your roof to redirect the energy.

2. Temple or High House in Front of Your House:

- **Problem**: A temple or a tall house directly in front of your home or on the opposite side of the street can have a negative effect on your house.
- **Solution**: Hang a **toran** (decorative band) made of **auspicious cowries** on your main door to block the negative impact and attract positive energy.

3. Peepal/Banyan Tree or Temple Near Your House:

- **Problem**: Having a **Peepal tree**, **Banyan tree**, or a **temple** nearby can create negative effects such as hindering peace and happiness in your home.
- **Solution**: Ensure that their shadow does not fall on your house. If it does, raise the height of your roof. If you have a **Peepal tree** in your home, do not cut it. Instead, **worship it daily**, as neglecting it can lead to financial losses and family issues.

4. Protection from Evil Eye:

- **Solution**: **Plant coriander** in your home to protect against the evil eye. Additionally, **plant henna** or **mahua plants** outside your house, or keep the root of **henna** inside to safeguard against negative energy and harmful forces.

5. Stairs in the Wrong Direction:

- **Problem**: Stairs in an unfavorable direction can cause energy imbalances in your house.

- **Solution**: If the stairs cannot be moved, **wipe them daily** with water mixed with **Gangajal** and burn **frankincense** and **gugal** incense in the evening to cleanse the energy.

6. Main Door Enhancements:

- **Solution**:
    - **Garland of fresh mango leaves**: Hang a garland of fresh **mango leaves** on the main door to invite positive energy.
    - **Swastika symbol**: Make a **swastika** on both sides of the main door with **turmeric or roli** to enhance good luck.
    - **Peacock feather plant**: Place a **peacock feather plant** near the main door to bring prosperity and reduce bad luck.

7. Height of the House:

- **Problem**: If your house is lower than the road or has an uneven floor, it can cause energy imbalance.
- **Solution**: The house should be **3 feet higher** than the road and the **floor should be flat** to allow proper energy flow and prosperity.

8. Conch for Vastu Defects:

- **Solution**: **Fill a conch** with water and sprinkle it in all the rooms of your house daily to help neutralize any Vastu defects. This simple remedy helps in balancing energy and improving harmony.

Infallible Tricks of Lal Kitab

Lal Kitab mentions some such tricks and remedies which provide instant relief in many kinds of problems. These tricks work like injections or painkillers and show quick results. However, astrological remedies should also be done for permanent solutions. Lal Kitab also says to follow some special rules, which you must follow. Here, the major rules, abstinence, tricks and remedies are mentioned in 12 houses according to the position of various planets.

Understand the effects of Sun: According to Lal Kitab

Lal Kitab describes the different effects of Sun in different Bhaavs (houses). Here are some remedies to understand these effects and overcome them:

Remedies for Sun:

Sun in House-1:
- Honesty, charity and service will make you progress.
- If House-7 is vacant then get a hand pump installed in your ancestral house. This will improve your fortunes after 10 years.
- If Mars is in House-5 or Saturn is in House-8 then get a hand pump installed. Otherwise it can have a bad effect on the health of your child or wife.

Sun in House-2:
- Service will bring you progress.
- If Sun is weak then donate coconut oil and almonds in the temple.
- Avoid disputes related to land, wife and money. Otherwise the Sun will become weaker.
- If Moon is in House-8 then do not take anything for free, it may cause loss.

Sun in House-3:
- Keep your conduct good until Surya gives bad results.
- If House-1 is bad then Surya in House-3 can harm your neighbors.

Sun in House 4:
- Avoid theft, bad habits and greed.
- If the Sun is weak and other malefic planets are also bad then your child may suffer.
- If Sun and Moon are together then you will benefit from new discoveries or inventions.
- If Sun and Mercury are together then you will benefit from travels, you will become a good businessman.
- If Sun is alone then you will benefit from charity.
- Being in the company of another woman is not good for your child.

Sun in House-5:
- With increasing age and experience, your wealth will also increase.
- A kitchen built in the east direction will be very good.

Sun in House-6:
- Do not interfere in other's work.
- Follow the traditions of the house.
- Keep or donate three dogs, support brother-in-law and son-in-law.
- Keep silver and Gangajal in the house.
- Surfing the fire of the stove with milk at night will prevent Sun from giving bad results.
- If there is a health problem, donate wheat.

Sun in House-7:
- If the health of the wife is bad, make the child sleep between them at night or sleep separately.
- If the condition of the house is bad, bury a square piece of copper in the ground on Sunday.
- If Saturn is with you, extinguish the fire of the stove with milk at night.
- If Saturn is in House-1, go to work after eating sweets and drinking water.
- Serve a hornless or black cow.
- Lighting up the fire before building a house will improve the condition of the house.

Sun in House-8:
- Always be charitable, never beg.

- Serve elder brother and cow.
- Avoid bad habits and wrong relationships.

Sun in House-9:
- Medical profession will be good.
- Give medicines to patients occasionally.
- Do not accept silver in donation, do not take anything for free.
- If Mercury is with you then keep brass utensils in the house.

Sun in House-10:
- Wear white or light coloured turban or cap. Avoid wearing black or blue cap.
- If Saturn is weak then get a hand pump installed.
- If House-4 is empty then float a copper coin in the river for 43 days. This will increase respect in your work.

Sun in house 11:
- The more you do good to others, the more you will progress.
- Avoid non-vegetarian food and alcohol.
- If Moon is in house 5, then sleep with vegetables, radish, carrot, turnip near your pillow and donate them in the temple in the morning.
- If Mercury is weak, then donate a goat.

Sun in House-12:
- Avoid criticizing religion.
- Serve sadhus, cows and wife.
- If Venus and Mercury are together then keep a flour mill in the house.
- If sinful planets are in House-1 then forgive enemies.
- If Sun is alone then there can be loss due to working with machines.

Some additional tips:
- The more open the courtyard of the house, the more luck will shine.
- If the Sun is in the later houses and Saturn in the first houses, then bury a vessel filled with water in the south of the house.

- If the Sun is getting help from any other planet, then eat less salt.
- If the Sun is alone or weak, then stay calm and do charity.
- It is considered good to offer water to the rising Sun when the Sun is high, low and equal.
- Reciting 'Adityahridaya Strotram', donating gold and copper, not telling lies, good conduct, donating wheat/jaggery/copper, flowing a copper coin in the river, living in an east-facing house, staying away from dishonesty, wearing ruby, serving father and officers, not sleeping during the day, staying away from intoxication, etc. are measures beneficial for the Sun.
- By doing these measures, you can bring the auspicious effects of the Sun in your life and avoid troubles.

Remedies for Moon

Lal Kitab tells about the different effects of the Moon in different houses. Here are some remedies to understand the effects of Moon and improve them:

Moon in House-1:
- Always keep the silver or rice given to you by your mother. It will always bring you wealth and prosperity.
- Respect your mother and if her health is bad, bury the object of Mars (like a red cloth) in the ground.
- If Venus is in House-7, keep a dog after marriage. This will save the child from harm.
- Never sell milk, silver and rice, it can lead to a shortage in the family.
- If House-7 is empty, keep rain water, silver and rice in the house.
- Serve your mother and mother-like women and take their blessings.
- Keep a cow or do Gau Seva. Otherwise, there can be bad effects at the age of 25.

Moon in House-2:
- Building a temple in the house or ringing a bell can make you childless.
- If Mercury is in House-3 and Jupiter is in House-9, then donate a green cloth to a girl every day for 43 days.

Moon in house-3:
- If there is a bad effect then worship girls.
- Feed fodder to goat and mung or grains to birds.
- If you have a daughter then donate rice, silver and milk.
- If you have a son then donate wheat, jaggery, wood apple and copper.
- If Ketu is having an effect then donate copper, wood apple and wheat.
- If Rahu is having an effect then do Surya Kanyadan.

Moon in House-4:
- Serving your mother will benefit you.

- Work related to milk, farming, water and medicine will benefit you.
- Establish a milk urn before starting any auspicious work.
- Donate milk.
- Selling, burning or spilling milk is harmful.
- If Jupiter is in House-6, you will benefit from ancestral work.
- If Jupiter is in House-2, go to a religious place with your father and grandson/grandson and perform Yagya.

Moon in house-5:
- Avoid bad manners, abusive language and Mercury things (like goat meat, pigeon meat, greed).
- If house-9 is empty then eat something sweet before going for any work.

Moon in House-6:
- If Jupiter is in House-2 then in case of any trouble donate milk in the temple and feed milk to your father yourself.
- If Moon House-6 is affected by Ketu then one should avoid donating water.
- Do not drink milk at night.
- Curdled milk or cheese at night is auspicious.
- Bow head in the temple.
- Sometimes donate things related to Sun, Jupiter and Mars.

Moon in House-7:
- Never quarrel with your mother, especially an old mother.
- Do not sell milk, water, silver and rice.
- Keep milk, silver or Gangajal equal to your weight in the house.
- If Mercury or Venus is in House-1 and is influenced by Saturn then on the day of marriage of a man, the woman should bring milk, silver or Gangajal equal to her weight.
- At the time of marriage of a woman, her in-laws should keep milk, silver or Gangajal equal to her weight in the house before she comes to their house.

Moon in house-8:

- Having a well or pond in an ancestral house can cause loss.
- If Mercury is in house-4 or 12, Saturn or Rahu in house-12 and Sun, Mercury are weak then get your nose pierced.
- If Mars, Mercury, or the malefic planets are weak then keep your conduct good.
- Keep water from a well or hand pump near the crematorium in the house.
- Donate milk or perform Shraddh in the name of ancestors.
- If Jupiter and Venus are in house-4 then touch the feet of elders or wash them with water.
- Build a house on the roof of a well or keep a hand pump, well, milk, or horse in the house.
- A person having Moon in house-8 should not work as a jeweler.

Moon in house 9:

- Follow religion, go on pilgrimages, bathe in Ganga, take parents/elders on pilgrimages.

Moon in house 10:

- Visiting religious places increases luck, but flirting can cause harm.
- If there are malefic planets or Mercury, Venus in house 2, 3, or malefic planets or Mercury-Venus in house 5, 6, or Saturn in house 3, or Moon itself is weak, then liquid medicines, treatment at night, drinking milk at night, building/buying house with brothers, buying machines, rearing animals, or doing work related to Moon will give inauspicious results.
- Keep water (rain, hail, Ganga, underground) in the house continuously for 10 years, you will get benefit in 15 years.

Moon in 11th house:

- If Saturn is good then donating milk will bring a son and wealth.
- If 3rd house is weak then take/give donation in the morning or give/listen to sermon in the evening.
- Buying, building or demolishing a house on Saturday, buying or working on things related to Saturn, doing

things or work related to Mercury on Wednesday and getting married on Friday is harmful.
- If Ketu is in the 3rd house then digging a well, getting a hand pump installed or boring done will be beneficial.
- Send your grandmother (mother-in-law) out somewhere for 43 days after the birth of the child, otherwise grandmother or grandson may suffer loss.
- If Moon is in 11th house and Ketu is in 3rd house then digging a well, getting a hand pump installed or boring done will be beneficial.
- Your mother or child or both may die.
- Donate milk for the diet of 11 people or distribute 121 pedas made from milk among children or throw them in a river.

Moon in House-12:
- If Mercury, Venus, or malefic planets are in House-2, 12, then do not keep property in your name.
- Do not get a hand pump or boring done under the roof of the house.
- Keep rain water stored on the roof of the house.

By following these measures, you can avoid the bad effects of the Moon and bring prosperity in your life.

Remedies for Mars

Lal Kitab tells about the different effects of Mars in different houses. Here are some remedies to understand the effects of Mars and improve them:

Mars in House-1:
- If Mars is weak then avoid bad deeds. Do not take anything for free, otherwise you may face problems or problems of not having children.
- If Mercury is in House-3 and 7, 9, 11 houses are empty then keep and read Gangajal, gold, saffron, turmeric, religious texts in the house. Apply saffron-turmeric tilak. For House-7 (householder/life partner) keep silver, cow, or do cow service.
- Avoid the company of a fakir or sadhu. Keeping brother-in-law at home can have a bad effect on your brother's health.
- If Sun and Moon are in House-2, 12 then avoid taking donations, taking anything for free, or earning money without hard work (bribe, brokerage, interest, rent, loan, etc.). Stay away from things like shares, gambling, or speculation.

Mars in House-2:
- If Mars is good then keep helping your younger brothers, this will give you money. Otherwise your savings will always be less.

Mars in House-3:
- If Mars is weak then keep ivory or things made of ivory in the house.
- If Mars is good then you will progress due to your soft nature.

Mars in House-4:
- If Mars is weak then do these remedies: Keep teeth clean. Pour sweet milk at the root of banyan tree and do Tilak with wet soil. Keep empty bags of sugar candy on the roof of the house. Feed desi ghee to the horse. For problems related to children, bury a vessel filled with honey in the cremation ground.

- Keep a square piece of silver with you. Nail the south door of the house.
- Stay away from one-eyed, childless, black person and Dhaak tree.
- Keep copper, jaggery, silver, well, hand pump, gold, saffron, or elderly in the house. Feed sweets to birds. Keep elephant tusks with you or in the house.
- If Mars or Venus is in House-4 or 8 then take blessings from widow aunt, aunt, widower uncle, uncle.

Mars in House-5:
- If Moon is in House-8 then perform Shradh and donate milk in the name of elders and ancestors.
- If Mars is weak then staying away from your ancestral home can cause the problem of not having children. Girlfriend or boyfriend can also harm you.
- If Mercury and Ketu are in House-9, 10 then sleep with water near your head.

Mars in House 6:
- For happiness in the house, do Kanya Pujan. Helping brothers will protect you from enemies and Ketu.
- If Mars is weak, then your brothers should give you something or if they cannot give, then throw their share in the river.
- If Ketu is weak, then do not celebrate the birth of a child. On his birthday, distribute salty snacks instead of sweets.

Mars in 7th house:
- If you don't have a child, then take care of your brother's child.
- If Mars is bad or Mercury is weak in any house, then avoid dry well, business of Mercury's things (toys, books, moong), or people related to Mercury.
- Stay away from widow sister, aunt, sister-in-law, niece, sister-in-law, granddaughter, granddaughter.
- Don't take Mercury's things for free.
- Avoid bat, broad leaf milk, seal, parrot, myna, pigeon, goat, dholak, tabla, empty bamboo, dry grass, dry flowers, whitewash, tinned goods, savanna, guava tree.
- Build a small wall every day and demolish it.

- If your sister comes home, give her sweets and send her away.
- If your widow sister lives with you, then eat sweets in the morning and start work.
- Keep solid silver in the house.
- If Mars is in 7th house and Mercury and Saturn are in 6th and 7th house, then behave well with your nephews.

Mars in House-8:
- If Mars is weak then do not take abuse from widows. Serve them and take their blessings.
- If there is illness in the house or the condition of the house is bad then sprinkle water on a hot pan and then cook roti on it.
- If Mercury and Mars are in House-8 then keep a dark room at the end of the ancestral house.
- If Mars in House-8 is bad or House-2 is empty then always wear silver around the neck.
- Do not live in a house facing south.
- Do not make a furnace or tandoor in the house.
- Give sweet roti made in tandoor to a dog for 43 days.

Mars in House-9:
- If Mars is alone and good then serving your sister in law will bring good luck.

Mars in House-10:
- If Mars is good then you will get wealth and respect as long as your elder brother is alive.
- If Mars is weak or is with enemy planets then do not sell gold. Do not let milk burn or spill.
- If Venus, Moon, or malefic planets are in House-2 then keep a deer or serve a black-eyed person, childless. Keep a deerskin in the house.
- If Sun is in House-4 or Moon is in House-6 then do not keep your child with your mother.
- If Saturn is in House-4 then avoid bad company, otherwise you may get punished without any crime.

Mars in House-11:

- Keep three dogs, serve fish and serve fakirs. Maintain good relations with brother-in-law, son-in-law, or nephew.
- If House-3 is empty or weak, you will have a lack of money until the father's property is completely sold.
- If Mars is bad, then also keep three dogs. Help brother-in-law, son-in-law, or nephew and distribute namkeen on son's birthday.

Mars in House-12:
- If Mars is weak then offer water to the Sun by adding jaggery to it. Eat sweet roti yourself and give some part of it to a Darvesh, Fakir, or a dog. Visit a temple or religious place.
- Give honey or sugar mixed in milk to people or friends, this will help you and give you good results.

By doing these remedies, you can avoid the bad effects of Mars and bring success and happiness in your life.

Remedies for Mercury

Lal Kitab tells about the different effects of Mercury in different Bhavas (houses). Here are some remedies to understand these effects and overcome them:

Mercury in House-1:
- If Mercury is weak then do not eat eggs.
- If Moon is in House-1 then avoid intoxication and talking too much.
- If House-7 is empty and Mercury is alone then keeping or playing Tabla in the house can have bad effects.

Mercury in House-2:
- If Mercury is weak then avoid trading in counterfeit goods, gambling, speculation, shares, or lottery. This may cause loss.
- Your father's money may be wasted.
- All the things related to Mercury may harm you. In this situation, getting your nose pierced may help.
- If Venus is in House-12 then both your sister-in-law and wife may suffer loss.
- If Venus is in House 3, 8, 9 then also both your sister-in-law and wife may suffer loss.
- Do not keep parrot or sheep.
- If Moon and Saturn are in House-12 then donate milk, rice and silver in the temple.

Mercury in House-3:
- If Mars is in House-1 then business of things related to Venus (cow, art, music, makeup) will be good for you and your brother.
- If you stutter or stammer then Mercury in House-3 generally does not give bad effects.
- If still there is bad effect then keep 3 dogs. Help son-in-law, nephew, brother-in-law. Do not eat things related to Mercury (moong, Bhadra, guava etc.). Serve birds and donate goat. Do not live in a south facing house. Brush your teeth with alum daily. Wash the stone kept in the house with milk daily. Burn 51 yellow cowries in ghee and flow them in the river.

Mercury in House-4:
- If Mercury is weak then do not keep goat, parrot, or mynah. This may have a bad effect on your mother and moon.
- Money situation may worsen.
- Offering water to the Sun and applying turmeric-saffron tilak will be beneficial in terms of money.

Mercury in House-5:
- If Mercury is weak then things related to the Moon will help you. Wear a copper coin around your neck.

Mercury in House-6:
- If Mercury is good then patience, contentment and honesty will bring you happiness.
- It is good to use Mercury items (flowers, girl, ball, bangle, green gram) in auspicious works.
- If Mercury is alone and not affected by any planet then work related to paper, publishing, or printing press will bring you benefits.
- If Mercury is weak then do not make any new path or door in the north of the house. Do not marry your daughter in the north of the house.
- If Mercury is weak and Venus is also bad then bury a milk pot in the forest.
- If Moon is good then bury a bottle of Gangajal in the field instead of milk.
- If Venus is in House-4 and Ketu is weak then put a silver ring on your wife's hand. This will help in having children.

Mercury in House-7:
- If the Moon is in House-1 then there will be benefits from water or sea travel.

Mercury in House-8:
- If Mercury is weak, demolishing the stairs of the house and then rebuilding them can be harmful.
- The stairs falling down on their own can also be a sign of bad times.
- Never change the place of worship.
- Make a mole on your buttock with black Surma.

- Keep milk or rain water on the roof.
- Make a girl wear a silver nose ring.
- If there is a planet in House-2, give milk, rice or silver to the animal associated with that planet.

Mercury in House-9:
- If Mercury is giving bad effects then wear new yellow or saffron coloured clothes after washing them in Gangajal.
- Get your wife to wear a round iron object coloured red on her head.
- Get her nose pierced.
- Bury silver in the ground of the house.
- Feed a cow wearing silver.
- For success in work, fill mushrooms in an earthen pot and donate them in a temple.
- If Mercury goes from House-9 to House-11 then do not wear amulets, especially not from any sadhu or fakir.

Mercury in house-10:
- Avoid alcohol and meat, else Saturn will give bad effects.
- Avoid talking too much.

Mercury in house 11:
- If Mercury is weak then wear a copper coin around your neck. This will save you from losses due to foolish acts.

Mercury in House-12:
- Avoid alcohol, lies, hypocrisy and greed.
- Do not marry before the age of 25.
- Serve dogs and dervishes.
- Help son-in-law, nephew, or brother-in-law.
- Get your nose pierced.
- Follow brothers' advice.
- Wear gold and yellow clothes as advised by Guru.
- Apply saffron tilak on your forehead.
- Wear an iron ring (without joints).
- Sometimes throw an empty pot in water.
- Do not apply ash or bhasma tilak.
- If House-2 is empty then go to the temple.

- If Rahu is in House-8, 12 then do not go to temple.
- If Moon is in House-2 then keeping water without a vessel will benefit you in wealth, work and employment.
- If Mercury and Rahu both are in House-12 then control your speech, do not get angry and do not break promises.

Some additional suggestions:
- If Mercury and Rahu are together, or are weak separately (especially Mercury in houses 3, 8, 9, 12 and Rahu in houses 5, 7, 8, 11), then there may be a fear of going to jail, mental asylum, hospital, cemetery, or a desolate place. In this situation, wearing an iron ring (jointed) is helpful.
- If Mercury and Rahu are weak, demolishing the stairs of the house and rebuilding them or changing the stairs without changing the boundary wall and roof will have a bad effect.
- Brushing teeth with alum, performing Kanya Pujan and getting the nose pierced are good remedies to reduce the weak effects of Mercury.
- If many members of the family have a bad Mercury, then serve or donate a goat.
- If someone in the house is constantly ill, then donate a yellow pumpkin to the temple.
- If Mercury and Saturn are together, then making a courtyard under the roof in the house can have a bad effect.
- Do not eat eggs when Mercury is weak.

By following these measures, you can avoid the bad effects of Mercury and bring prosperity in your life.

Remedies for Jupiter

Lal Kitab describes the different effects of Jupiter in different Bhavas (houses). Here are some remedies to understand these effects and correct them:

Jupiter in House-1:
- If house-7 is empty then marriage, rearing a cow, or doing work related to Venus will increase the influence of Jupiter.
- Marriage before 28 years, marriage of relatives, or having a son can have a bad effect on your father's age.
- If house-11 is good then you will get wealth from a beautiful woman, wife, rearing a cow, or cow service.
- If Jupiter is weak, Sun is also weak, or Mercury, Venus, Saturn, Rahu are in house-2, 5, 9, 12, then there can be Pitra Dosha.
- Be content, patient, do not ask for donations from anyone.
- If Saturn is in house-9 then your health can deteriorate. Apply turmeric-saffron tilak, feed a cow, crow or dog.

Jupiter in House-2:
- If Jupiter is good then wealth will increase by giving charity. Serve travelers. Avoid work related to gold. Work related to soil (like kutcha house, farming, road construction) and work related to women will be beneficial.
- If Jupiter is weak then there can be loss due to things related to Ketu (like son, dog).

Jupiter in House-3:
- If Jupiter is weak or sleeping, or Moon is in House-12, or Jupiter is with enemy planets, then do not be happy on hearing your praise, it may cause harm.

Jupiter in House-4:
- If House-10 is empty then you may become poor by showing a naked body.

- Keeping your character good will increase your lifespan.
- If Jupiter is weak then falling in love before 34 years may harm you and your family.
- Control your desires. Obey elders.
- Avoid jealousy, killing snakes, demolishing houses, alcohol, meat, gambling and adultery.

Jupiter in House-5:

- If Jupiter is good then you will get luck from your children.
- Business will grow due to honesty and good behavior.
- Appreciating your children will give you happiness in old age.
- If Saturn is in House-9 then you will benefit from a child born on Saturday.
- If Jupiter is weak and Ketu is in House-11 then asking for donations in the name of religion can harm your child. Maternal uncle or maternal uncle's child can also be harmed.

Jupiter in House-6:

- If Jupiter is good then nephews, maternal uncles and nieces will bring you luck.
- Donating in the name of elders will increase luck.
- If Jupiter is weak and Mercury, Ketu are also weak then feed dogs or keep a dog.
- Maintain good relations with brother-in-law, nephews and son-in-law.

Jupiter in House-7:

- If Jupiter is good then you will get luck from your wife and muscular power.
- Building a temple in the house, converting the house into a temple, or selling children in the name of religion is harmful.
- If Jupiter is weak then avoid preaching religion or roaming with sadhus.
- Avoid living with a widowed sister or aunt and bad habits.
- Keep red rattis in a yellow cloth or with gold and do remedies related to the moon.

Jupiter in house-8:
- If Jupiter is good then religion, spiritual power and wearing gold on the body will increase luck.
- If Jupiter is weak then donate things related to Jupiter or Venus in the temple.

Jupiter in House-9:
- If Jupiter is good then you will get luck from religion and elders.
- If Jupiter is weak then avoid irreligion, atheism, selfishness and pride.

Jupiter in House-10:
- If Jupiter is good then people doing manual work will get luck.
- Donating too much can make you poor, being clever will give you happiness.
- Avoid immorality and alcohol.
- If Jupiter is weak then apply yellow tilak on forehead or turban and keep nose clean.
- If your father's health is not good then flow a copper coin in river for 43 days.
- If Jupiter is in House-10 and Saturn is good, along with Venus or Mars in House-4 then do not hide your love.
- If Sun is in House-4 then the effect of Jupiter will be even better.
- If Sun is in House-3 or 5 and Saturn is in House-9 then there will be profit from gold and silver work, but Saturn's work (like iron, cement, liquor, junk etc.) can cause loss or accidents.
- If Saturn is in House-4, 10, or 1 or Moon is in House-4 then keep gold, saffron, musk and dog in the house.
- If Mercury is in house 4, 9, 10 then get your nose pierced and keep it clean.

Jupiter in House-11:
- If Jupiter is good then be kind to the poor, follow religion and preach.
- Living in a joint family will benefit you.
- You may face troubles after the death of your father. Fulfilling your promises will give you relief.
- Avoid immorality.
- Donate shroud on the death of others.

- If Mercury is in House-6 and Moon is in House-2 then avoid jealousy, envy, competition and love.
- Do not show your naked body to anyone.
- Avoid meat, alcohol, flirtation, demolition of house, etc.

Jupiter in house-12:
- If Jupiter is good then you will get luck by worshiping.
- You will get wealth by speaking less.
- You will get wealth and happiness by doing noble work and wearing religious bracelet.
- Avoid false testimony, cheating and dishonesty.
- If Saturn is also with or in house-9 then you will benefit from machine, motor, lorry, etc.
- Do auspicious work while breathing right.
- Do not take tobacco.
- Avoid bribery, brokerage, interest, shares, speculation, lottery.
- Do not spoil relations with brother-in-law or in-laws.
- Serve dog, fakir, or dervish.
- If Jupiter is weak and Mercury is also weak then avoid bad deeds.
- Wear rosary all the time.
- Do not insult Jupiter, sadhu, temple, deity, scholar, Brahmin, or tree like Peepal.
- Apply tilak of turmeric or saffron, wear gold or yellow clothes and keep the nose clean.

Some additional suggestions:
- The bad effects of Jupiter are indicated by things related to Saturn.
- The good effects of Jupiter are indicated by things related to Jupiter or ancestral place.
- Before Rahu or Ketu causes evil, Jupiter tells through its factors.
- If Jupiter is weak from house 6 to 11, then float coconut or almond in the river.
- If Saturn is looking at Jupiter of house 9 or 12 or Saturn is in house 2 or 5, then do not lock the house.
- If it is mandatory for everyone to go, then do not put an iron lock and do not hang the lock on the door.

By following these measures, you can avoid the bad effects of Jupiter and bring success and happiness in your life.

Remedies for Venus

Lal Kitab describes the different effects of Venus in different Bhaavs (houses). Here are some remedies to understand these effects and correct them:

Venus in House-1:
- If you have a Venus-Chakra (crescent-shaped line) below your ring finger, it will be good for you to take advice from others before doing any work.
- If Venus is weak, then flirting in youth and the desire to be the head of the house can harm you and your relatives.
- If House-7 and 10 are empty, then do not marry at the age of 25, otherwise both your wealth and wife can be ruined.
- If Saturn is in House-7 or 10, then also Venus is considered empty in House-1.
- If Venus is with Ketu or Rahu is in House-7, then at the time of marriage, take pure silver from in-laws and keep it in the house.
- If Sun, Moon, or Rahu are in House-1 or Venus is in House-1 and these are in House-7 and Mercury is not in House-3, then you may suffer from asthma, tuberculosis, or venereal diseases.
- Consume cow urine and barley. Donate Sanije or mustard seeds. Men should do Kanyadan and women should do Cow donation..

Venus in House-2:
- If Saturn is with Venus or in House-9 then you will get wealth and children from work related to animals, soil and art.
- If Jupiter is in House-8, 9, or 10 then keep your conduct good.
- If Rahu or Ketu is in House-2, 5, 9, 12 then avoid wayward love.
- If Venus is weak then you may suffer from lack of blood and semen, no child or sick child. Take medicines to increase blood and semen.

Venus in House-3:
- Respect your wife and fulfill her needs.

Venus in House-4:

- If Venus is weak and Saturn is related to Jupiter then do remedies related to Moon or put turmeric and saffron in the well.
- Avoid love and bad habits.
- Do not build a house by putting a roof on the well.
- If Venus is alone and House-2 and 7 are empty then do not pay attention to the bad things of people, focus only on good qualities.

Venus in House-5:

- If Venus is good then your wealth will never end if you keep raw soil, cow, silver, or fresh flowers in the house.
- Keep your conduct good.
- Serve cow and mother and keep the heart clean.
- Wash the private parts with raw milk and curd.

Venus in House-6:

- Never let your wife walk barefoot.
- Keep things related to moon (silver, rice, cow, mother).
- Do not marry an only child, sister, or brother.
- If Venus is not alone in House-6 or House-7 is not empty then keep solid silver in the house.
- If Mercury is in House-5 then take good care of your wife.
- If Saturn is weak or you do the work of alcohol, meat, gambling, or snake catching etc. then your wealth will decrease.
- If Ketu is with Venus or is weak then avoid other women.
- Wash the private parts with curd.
- Give two gold pieces to the son-in-law or daughter-in-law at the time of marriage.

Venus in House-7:

- If Venus is good then marriage and work related to Venus will benefit you.
- If Venus is weak then you may lose money due to lovemaking.

- If Saturn is in House-9 or 11 then the business of mattresses, beds, or such comfort items will give you money.
- If Sun is in House-8 then keep repairing the roof of the house.
- If Rahu is in House-8 then do not always wear blue clothes.
- If there is no planet in House-1 then anger and passion of a woman may harm you.
- If Saturn is in House-6 and Venus is in House-7 then seek medical advice in case of genital or heart diseases.

Venus in House-8:
- If wife's health is bad then donate millet or bury it in the ground.
- Do not scold wife.
- Do not accept donation and bow head in temples.
- Take blessings of mother, brother, sister, or aunt.
- Keep silver, jaggery, copper, or goat in the house.
- Bow head in temples.
- Take blessings from eunuch.
- Flow flowers or copper coin in a dirty drain.
- Donate cow or do cow service.

Venus in House-9:
- Bury a piece of silver in a neem tree.
- Avoid working too hard.
- If Moon or Mars are also with Venus, then keep silver, mare, well/handpump (Moon) and honey, jaggery or copper (Mars) in the house.
- If Venus is weak, then do not marry before 25 years.
- Do not buy things related to Venus (cow, bull, art items etc.).
- Do not do work related to Venus (farming, music, art, cosmetics etc.).
- If Venus is related to a sinful planet or Mercury, then make your wife wear a silver bangle with red color on it.

Venus in House-10:
- If Saturn is in House-1 or with Venus then avoid bad deeds.

- If Saturn is in House-9 or 11 or is good then as long as the western wall is raw then wealth will be there and your old age will be peaceful.
- If Saturn is in House-5 then rearing a goat will be good for the cow of the house or for the wife.
- If there is a problem related to children then wash your private parts with curd.
- If your health is bad then donate a Kapila cow.

Venus in House-11:

- If Venus is weak then do not let the wife keep money.
- Give up the habit of changing your nature and donate a Kapila cow.

Venus in House-12:

- Respect wife and serve cow.
- If wife's health is bad then donate cow, curd, or silver from your own self.
- Be a theist.
- If there is a lot of trouble then woman should bury blue flower in forest.
- If Rahu is also with Venus or in House-2, 6, or 7 then keep white cow.
- Avoid things related to Rahu (tobacco, radish, umbrella, chhaj/sieve, winnowing basket, chimney, blue clothes) and work (electrical work, crime, cheating, making fake goods, shares, gambling, lottery, mechanic work) and relations (brother-in-law, in-laws).

By doing these remedies you can avoid the bad effects of Venus and bring happiness in your life.

Remedies for Saturn

Lal Kitab describes the different effects of Saturn in different Bhavas (houses). Here are some remedies to understand these effects and correct them:

To avoid the negative effects of Saturn:
- Avoid dishonesty, killing snakes, gambling, cutting Peepal tree, drinking alcohol, worrying, bad habits, lying, injustice and sleeping or waking up at odd hours. These things make the negative Saturn even worse. Even if Saturn is good, these things make it weak gradually.

Saturn in House-1:
- Do not live in a west facing house.
- Avoid alcohol and romance.
- Bury antimony in the ground and apply sweet milk on the root of a banyan tree and apply tilak with it.
- If there is a shortage of money then offer water to the rising sun.

Saturn in House-2:
- Apply tilak with milk or curd (especially if Jupiter is also in House-2).
- Keep a brown buffalo or serve it.
- If Rahu is in House-8 or House-12 then feed milk to a snake or go to a temple and apologize for your mistakes.
- Do not keep things related to Saturn in the house.
- Avoid lying or abusing.
- Do not drink alcohol.

Saturn in House-3:
- Avoid talking too much and drinking alcohol.
- Do not eat meat.
- Distribute eye medicine for free.
- If Ketu is in House-3 or 10, keep a dog. Serve son-in-law, nephew, or brother-in-law.
- If Surya is in House-5 or 1 or Saturn is in House-3 itself, do not install stone along the south door of the house.

- Make a dark room behind the house.
- If Chandra is in House-10, well or hand pump in the house can cause death or loss of wealth.

Saturn in House-4:
- Avoid flirting, drinking alcohol, killing a snake, selling oil and laying the foundation of a house at night.
- Do not drink milk at night.
- If you are ill, take oil, poison, or alcohol (as advised by a doctor), myrobalan, jamun, walnuts, etc., but do not take milk, rice, ash gourd, litchi, or medicines.
- Feed milk to a snake or feed a fish, crow, or buffalo.
- Help a laborer.
- Pour milk in a well.

Saturn in House-5:
- If Saturn is good then keep copper, honey, jaggery, saffron, turmeric, or gold in the ancestral house.
- A house built or bought by your child will be good for you, but a house built or bought by you may be harmful for your child.
- If Ketu is in House-4 then keep 3 dogs, help son-in-law, nephew and brother-in-law.
- If Saturn is weak then keep copper, honey, gold, saffron, turmeric, sugar, fennel, milk, or rice in the west of the ancestral house.
- If Rahu or Ketu is in House-10 then burn things of Mars (jaggery, neem, honey, red coral etc.) in the ancestral house.
- If House-10 is vacant then do not build or buy a house before 48 years.

Saturn in House-6:
- Do not get married before 28 years, especially if Rahu is in House-8 and Ketu in House-2.
- If Saturn is weak then losing shoes is the first sign of bad times.
- Do not buy new leather shoes, machines, or alcohol.
- Do not drink milk at night.
- Avoid building a house.
- Flow coconut or almond in the river.
- Serve a snake.
- Do not build a house before 48 years.
- Keep a black dog.

- Bury an earthen pot filled with mustard oil in a pond or river.
- If House-2 is empty then Saturn is considered blind.
- Do or take things or work related to Saturn at night.

Saturn in House-7:
- Stay away from other women.
- Do not drink alcohol.
- Maintain the threshold of ancestral house.
- If House-1 is vacant then keep a pot of honey in the house.
- If House-1 is not vacant then fill sugar candy in a flute and bury it in the forest.

Saturn in House-8:
- Don't drink alcohol until Saturn gives Manda results.
- Keep a pure piece of silver with you.
- Sit on a stone and take a bath with milk.
- Don't let the feet touch the ground or floor.

Saturn in House-9:
- If Saturn is good, you will die before you have three houses.
- Do charity.
- If a stone is buried in the house at the time of birth, it is auspicious.
- If you are facing problems after the death of your parents, then do measures that strengthen Jupiter.
- If Venus is in House-7 or Mercury is in House-6, then mattress, bed, or sofa work will benefit you.
- If Sun, Mars, or Moon is in House-3, then keep the room behind the house dark.
- If the wall of that room is demolished or a window is made, then Saturn-9 will ruin you within three years.
- Avoid arguing too much.
- If your house was built before your birth, then your father may die at the age of 36.
- Do not keep fuel, wood, or door frame on the roof.
- In bad times, do measures related to Jupiter.
- If Rahu or Ketu is with Saturn or aspecting Saturn, then there will be benefits from gold, air, saffron, turmeric, silver, milk, rice, horse, Bajaji etc.
- Things related to Saturn (alcohol, oil, cement, coal, iron, gambling, house etc.) can harm you.

- Avoid the feeling of revenge.

Saturn in House-10:
- If Saturn is good, you will benefit from sitting work.
- Respect others.
- Be cautious and disciplined.
- Your fortune will be good as long as you don't drink alcohol.
- Being too religious can harm you.
- You will gain wealth as long as you don't build a house.
- If Saturn is weak, avoid violence, crime, gambling and alcohol.
- Apply turmeric-saffron tilak.
- If House-4 is weak, or Sun, Moon, or Mars are in House-4 or 10, feed 10 blind people.

Saturn in house 11:
- If Saturn is weak then generally do the remedies of Jupiter.
- If Saturn itself is weak then do the remedies related to Saturn.
- If Rahu or Ketu are weak or are with Sun or Moon, then do the remedies related to Mars and remain celibate for one year.
- If Saturn is alone and not affected by any planet then keep an earthen pot filled with water during any auspicious work.
- Avoid drinking alcohol and doing injustice.
- Do not build a house before 54 years.
- Spill some alcohol on the ground.
- Avoid a house facing south.
- Avoid deceit, dishonesty, Mercury things and working girls.
- Do not change the direction of houses and doors built before birth.
- If your health is bad then stay away from a woman for one year.
- If Jupiter is also weak or weak or you do not have a father, then do the remedies related to Jupiter.
- Keep water (Kumbha) in the house.
- In the morning at the time of rising sun, drop oil, wine, or spirit on the ground for Saturn.

Saturn in House-12:

- Do not stop building your house.
- Your house will be ready within 6 to 12 years.
- If Ketu is in House-9 or 12 or Rahu is in House-3 or 6 then maintain a dark room behind the house.
- Keep almonds in the eastern or southern corner of the room.
- Avoid talking too much, lying, abusing, badmouthing, arguing and flirting.
- If Surya is in House-6 then your wife may get hurt due to the fall of the back wall of the house.
- If Mercury is weak then the work, things and relatives related to Mercury may harm you.
- If Surya and Saturn are in House-12 then there will be quarrel or discord with the government, officer, king, master, or father.

Some additional tips:

- Saturn gives good results to those who are hardworking, just, tolerant, patient, mother-loving and those who serve animals, patients, or birds.
- By following these remedies, you can avoid the bad effects of Saturn and bring success and happiness in your life.

Remedies for Rahu

Lal Kitab describes the different effects of Rahu in different Bhaavs (houses). Here are some remedies to understand these effects and correct them:

Rahu in House-1:
- If Rahu is weak then the electrical goods, motor, cupboard, machine, box etc. taken from in-laws after marriage can harm you.
- If Rahu is with the Sun or is influenced by it then keep a cat's placenta in a pink, khaki or golden coloured cloth in the house.
- Donating things related to the Sun can benefit you.
- If Rahu is in House-1 and the Sun is weak then you may have the disease of talking to yourself. In this situation, take measures related to the Moon.

Rahu in House-2:
- Making roti or doing chimney/smoke work facing east on the southwest corner or roof of the house can harm you and your in-laws.
- Rahu can also cause theft in House-2.
- Wearing a solid silver ball will protect you from theft and in-laws' problems.
- If Rahu is weak, apply saffron tilak, wear gold or yellow clothes, wear a solid silver ball and keep silver, water, milk, or rice in the northwest corner of the house.
- Avoid eating meat, abusing, alcohol, lying and insulting the mother.

Rahu in house-3:
- If Rahu is weak then do remedies related to Moon.
- If Sun and Mercury are together then do not keep ivory or things made of ivory in the house.
- Do not quarrel unnecessarily.
- Do not sign papers without reading them, you may get cheated.

Rahu in House-4:

- Do not unnecessarily accumulate toilet, loft, attic, roof, stairs, coal storage, dustbin etc.
- If the roof has to be changed then change the walls too.
- If it is not possible to change the entire walls then make a new roof by combining some part of the old roof.

Rahu in House 5:
- If Rahu is weak, then marry your wife twice.
- Keep a cow.
- Keep a silver elephant with you.
- Do not do bad deeds related to Saturn.
- Press a silver plate under the entrance of the ancestral house and cross that part to enter the house.

Rahu in house-6:
- Keep a black dog.
- Keep a coin bullet with you or put black mirrors in the house.
- If Rahu is weak then do not start work if someone sneezes in front of you.
- If Mars is in house-12 then do not quarrel with elder brother or sister.

Rahu in House-7:
- If Rahu is weak then do not marry before 22 years.
- Things, work, or relatives related to Mercury and Venus can also harm you.
- Avoid work related to electricity, jail, police, gambling, crime, mental asylum.
- At the time of marriage, after Kanyadan, donate a silver brick to the girl.
- Flow a coconut in a river.
- Avoid dogs.

Rahu in House-8:
- If Rahu is weak, then money earned through dishonest means can harm you.
- Just changing the roof of the house, lowering the south door, or having a furnace attached to the house can harm you.

- If the eldest member of the house is black, one-eyed, fat, or childless, then you can get some protection.
- If Rahu is in House-8, then take almonds to the temple every day for 8 months before your next birthday and bring back half of them.

Rahu in House-9:
- If Rahu is weak then the roof, furnace, toilet, dirty water passing under the threshold, black dog going missing, crying of a cat, death of a black relative, or falling of nails can harm you.
- Keep 3 dogs or help son-in-law, brother-in-law, or brother-in-law.
- Live in a joint family.
- Don't take your own decisions.
- Don't break ties with in-laws.
- Don't seek advice from people close to Mars.
- Keep things related to Jupiter (gold, air, saffron, turmeric) with you.
- Avoid court disputes with relatives.
- If a dog dies or gets lost, immediately keep another dog.

Rahu in house 10:
- If Moon is in house 4 then take measures related to Mars.
- Avoid being narrow minded and miserly.
- Wearing a black cap or being bare headed can cause you financial loss.

Rahu in House-11:
- If Saturn is not in House-3 or 5 then keep gold or things related to Jupiter in the house.
- Father, son and grandson will not be able to live together.
- Religion, temple and charity are beneficial for Rahu in House-11.
- Wear gold.
- Avoid blue clothes, freebies, things related to Rahu, or work related to Rahu (electricity, smoke, weapons, magic, crime, gambling, lottery, speculation, shares, or mechanic work).
- If Jupiter is with Rahu or in House-3 then wear iron.
- Give money to a scavenger occasionally.

- Drink beverages in silver glasses.
- If you smoke cigarettes, use a silver pipe or cigarette case.

Rahu in house 12:
- Sleep with sugar candy or fennel near your pillow at night.
- Eat food in the kitchen only.
- If someone sneezes before starting work, do not start the work.
- Avoid criminal cases, theft, embezzlement, litigation, restlessness, false accusations and unnecessary expenditure.
- If Saturn is also weak, then avoid stubbornness.

Some additional suggestions:
- If Rahu is weak, do not live in a house facing south.
- The bad effects of Rahu do not end before 42 years.
- Wear or keep silver with you.
- Donate red lentils to a sweeper.
- During illness, donate barley equal to the patient's weight or throw it in the river.
- If there are disputes in business or livelihood, throw raw coal equal to your weight in the river.
- Avoid tobacco, too much haste, self-governance, interest, bribery, brokerage, shares, horse racing, speculation, gambling, lottery, theft, cheating, etc.

By following these measures, you can avoid the bad effects of Rahu and bring success and prosperity in your life.

Remedies for Ketu

Lal Kitab describes the different effects of Ketu in different Bhaavs (houses). Here are some remedies to understand these effects and correct them:

Ketu in House-1:
- Serve dervishes, sadhus, Guru and treat them like God.
- Wash the feet of father and Guru.
- If Mars is in House-12 then Ketu will not give bad results in House-1.
- Ketu never gives bad results in House-1.
- If Sun is in House-6 or 7 then do not give things related to Sun (like copper coins) to children in the evening.
- If Ketu is weak then do remedies related to Saturn.
- If Ketu is weak then things related to Mercury and later things related to Venus and Mars will start getting bad and then things related to Jupiter will also get affected.
- If House-2 and 7 are empty then Mercury and Venus may get weak from Ketu House-1.
- If Sun is in House-7 then your health may get bad after the birth of your grandson or granddaughter.

Ketu in House 2:
- If Ketu is good then you will progress through land travel.
- If Ketu is weak then avoid using your tongue wrongly and avoid quarrels in the family.

Ketu in House-3:
- If Ketu is weak then children may face problems if you live in a house facing south.
- You may face financial loss in court cases.
- The distance between wife and sister-in-law may increase.
- Keeping brother-in-law with you may cause problems to your brother.
- Having brother-in-law or in-laws' dog may also cause loss in the house.
- Neighbor's house may also become vacant.

- A fight with brother will cause loss.
- Children may become lazy.
- Apply saffron tilak or float Jupiter's things in the river.
- Wear gold.

Ketu in House-4:
- If Ketu is weak then your mother and children may face problems.
- There may also be a risk of diabetes.
- Take measures related to Jupiter and give gold or yellow things to the family priest.

Ketu in house-5:
- Son's health may remain bad for 45 years.
- If Jupiter is also weak then the cry of a dog can be heard in the house.
- If there are malefic planets in house-2, 5, 9, 12 then there can be ancestral debt, illness of children or illness of pets.
- Strengthen religion and faith.

Ketu in house-6:
- If there is a long straight line on your soles, you will get a car.
- The results of Ketu will be as per the Jupiter.
- Keep Jupiter strong.
- Avoid ego.
- If Jupiter or Mars is not in house-6 or 12 and Mercury is not in house-12, then Ketu will not let Jupiter weaken.
- Avoid selfishness, ego and the feeling of not forgiving.
- If Ketu is having a bad effect on house-6 from house-2, then wear a gold ring in the left hand.

Ketu in 7th house:
- If Ketu is good then avoid breaking promises.
- If Ketu is weak then avoid ego, selfishness, pride and unforgiveness.
- If Mercury is also in the 7th house then you may face problems from enemies for 34 years.
- Apply saffron tilak on your forehead and speak less.

Ketu in house-8:

- If Ketu is weak then you cannot have a child before 34 years.
- Serve a dog.
- If Moon is also weak then worship Moon.
- If Mars is good or Jupiter is in house-1 or 2 or Moon is in house-2 then there is no need to do any remedy.
- If Ketu is weak then worship Ketu for the health of the wife.
- A dog crying on the roof or in the courtyard is a sign of Ketu's bad times.
- Donate a two coloured blanket in the temple.
- If there is a planet with Ketu then tie the object of that planet in a piece of two coloured blanket and bury it in the forest.
- Wear gold or saffron.
- Get your ears pierced.

Ketu in house-9:
- Keep 3 dogs or serve son-in-law, brother-in-law and brother-in-law.
- Keep gold and saffron in the house and wear gold.
- Birth of a child is auspicious.
- If Ketu is weak or Chandra or Mars is in house-3, you may have trouble with luck, children and maternal uncle.
- Serve dogs and lepers, worship elders and saints.
- Respect gurus, brahmans and learned men.
- Perform cow service and perform satsangs or religious rituals.
- Learn to ask for forgiveness and forgive.
- Do not harm dogs, sadhus, or elders.

Ketu in house 10:
- If Ketu is good then the more harm your brother will do to you, the more progress you will make.
- Avoid immorality.
- If Ketu is weak then bury a pot full of honey in the forest before the age of 48.
- After the age of 48, keep a dog.
- If Mars is also in house 10 then Mars will control Ketu to some extent.
- If Ketu is weak and Saturn is in weak houses then bury milk and honey under the house.

Ketu in house 11:
- If Ketu is weak then you may suffer loss due to noise from behind or interruption while doing some work.
- If Saturn is also weak then your son may suffer loss.
- Keep Saturn related things or white radish at wife's bedside at night and donate it in the temple in the morning.

Ketu in house-12:
- If Ketu is weak then you cannot have children.
- If Mars is in house-6 then you cannot have children for 28 years, Moon is in house-6 then you cannot have children for 32 years and Sun is in house-6 then you cannot have children for 42 years.
- If you have bad habits, then you can have children.
- Avoid taking money from a widow and getting injuries in the feet.
- The curse of a widow can harm you.
- Do not take a house from a childless person.
- Avoid killing or torturing dogs.
- If you cannot have children or the children do not survive, then keep a dog.
- If you have children but there is a lack of money, then put your thumb in milk and suck it.

Some additional suggestions:
- If Ketu is weak, do not tell anyone about your weakness.
- Take measures related to Jupiter.
- If your health is bad, take measures related to Moon.
- If the child's body is dry, then rub the mud of a river or stream on him.
- If Mercury is very good, then Ketu is usually bad.
- If Jupiter or Sun is bad, then Ketu is also bad.
- The remedies or remedies for Ketu are known from the planet in house 10.
- In Lal Kitab, the ears of a dog (Ketu) are considered to be in house 8, mouth in house 2 and tail in house 6.
- Ketu is a black and white dog, not red and white.
- If Ketu is weak and Venus and Moon are together in any house, then the child's body may become dry. In this situation, rub mud on his body.

- By taking these measures, you can avoid the bad effects of Ketu and bring success and happiness in your life.

General Use Mantras

Easy mantras are given which you can use to overcome many kinds of problems.

For business/job:

Mantra: "ॐ वक्रतुण्डाय हुं।" "Om Vakratundaya Hum."

Chanting: Chant this mantra 21 or 11 times every morning while sitting near a white ark tree.

Method: Chant using a red sandalwood rosary on a red seat. Worship Ganesha with kumku rice and offer coriander and jaggery.

Effect: This mantra shows results in 45 days to 3 months. This mantra will help you get success in job or business. This mantra is associated with Ganesha, who is considered to be the destroyer of obstacles. Chanting while sitting near a white ark tree helps in getting the blessings of Ganesha.

For success in interview:

Mantra: "ॐ नमो भगवती पद्मावती ऋद्धि-सिद्धिदायिनी दुःखदारिद्र्यहारिणी श्रीं श्रीं नमः कामाक्षाय ह्रीं ह्रीं फट् स्वाहा।"

"Om Namo Bhagwati Padmavati Riddhi-Siddhidayini Dukhdaridryaharini Shreem Shreem Namah Kamakshaya Hreem Hreem Phat Swaaha."

Jaap: Chant this mantra 11 times.

Method: Feed jaggery to a cow before going for the interview.

Effect: This mantra will help you get employment. This is a Jain Sadhana mantra and has been used many times. This mantra is associated with Goddess Padmavati, who is believed to bestow wealth, splendor and prosperity.

For getting a higher position:

Mantra: "ॐ नमो भगवती त्रिलोचनं त्रिपुटं देवि। अंजलीम्भू में कल्याणं कुरु कुरु स्वाहा।"

"Om Namo Bhagwati Trilochanam Triputam Devi. Anjalimbhu Me Kalyanam Kuru Kuru Swaha."

Jaap: Chant this mantra 108 times daily while sitting on a blanket, kusha, or deerskin facing east during any auspicious time.

Effect: This mantra can get you a higher position or promotion within 3 months to a year. This mantra is associated with Goddess Parvati, who is believed to bestow advancement, power and success.

To remove obstacles to success:

Mantra: "ॐ नमः शांते प्रशांते ॐ ही हा सर्व क्रोध प्रशमनी स्वाहा।"

"Om Namah Shante Prashante Om Hi Ha Sarva Krodh Prashmani Swaha."

Jaap: Chant 1 or 5 rosaries of this mantra daily.

Effect: This mantra shows effect in 2 to 6 weeks. Sometimes it may take three to four months. This mantra is related to peace and destruction of enemies.

For material progress:

Mantra: "ॐ नमो नारायणाय।" **"Om Namo Narayanaya."**

Recite: Chant this mantra 5 or 10 times daily.

Method: Chant using Tulsi, sandalwood, or Vaijayanti beads. Face east-northeast. Say "Narayan-Narayan" before starting any work.

Effect: This mantra can help you gain wealth, prosperity and wealth. This mantra is associated with Lord Vishnu, who is considered the god of prosperity, happiness and peace.

For destruction of obstacles:

Mantra: "सकल विघ्न व्यापहि नहि तेही राम सुकृपां बिलोकहि जेहि।"

 "Sakala Vighna Vyapahi Nahi Tehi Ram Sukripa Bilokhi Jehi."

Jaap: Keep chanting this mantra every day everywhere.

Effect: This mantra will protect you from minor troubles. This mantra is associated with Lord Rama, who is considered to be the remover of all obstacles.

To gain prestige and please the authorities:

Mantra:"ॐ भूर्भुवः स्वः तत्सवितुर्वरेण्यं भर्गो देवस्य धीमहि धियो यो नः प्रचोदयात्।"
 "Om Bhurbhuvah Swah Tatsaviturvarenyam Bhargo Devasya Dhimahi Dhiyo Yo Nah Prachodayat." (Gayatri Mantra)

Chant: Chant one rosary of this mantra every morning at sunrise under a Bael tree.

Effect: This mantra will start showing effect in 1 week to 1 month. This mantra is associated with the Sun God, who is believed to bestow knowledge, power and prestige.

For victory in a lawsuit:

Method: Recite "Gajendra Moksha" in the morning and "Shaniwajrapanjar Kavach" or "Shanidasharath Stotra" in the evening.

Jaap: "राजिव नयन धरे धनुसायक। भगतविपति भंजन सुखदायक।"
"Rajiv Nayan Dhaare Dhanusayak. Bhagatvipati Bhanjan Sukhadayak."
 Chant or remember this mantra several times a day.

Mantra: Recite this mantra 51 times in the afternoon:

"जो प्रभु दीनदयाल कहावा। आरति हरन बेद जसु गावा॥ जपहिं नाम जन आरत भारी। मिटहिं कुसंकट होहिं सुखारी॥ दीनदयाल बिरदु संभारी। हरहु नाथ मम संकट भारी॥"

"Jo Prabhu Deendayal Kahaawa. Aarti Haran Veda Jasu Gaava. Japahin Naam Jan Aarat Bhaari. Mitahi Kusankat Hohin Sukhari. Deendayal Birdu Sambhari. Harahu Nath Mam Sankat Bhaari.".

Effect: This mantra can help in winning a lawsuit.

By chanting these mantras regularly, you can get rid of many types of problems. It is important to remember that while chanting mantras, one should chant with concentration and sincerity.

Shiva's special mantras - for Shiva worshippers:

By using these mantras, you can get rid of many kinds of problems.
These mantras should be chanted 5 or 11 times daily and Rudrakshamala should be used. While chanting, keep your face in the north-east or north direction.

To get things done:

Mantra: "ॐ शिवकर्मणे नमः।" **"Om Shivkarmane Namah."**
Effect: This mantra can help you get success in work and progress in your field.

For victory in dispute/litigation:

Mantra: "ॐ आद्याय नमः।" **"Om Aadyaay Namah."**
Effect: This mantra can help you win litigation and settle disputes.

For stability in business:

Mantra: "ॐ नियमाय नमः।" **"Om Niyamaya Namah."**
Effect: This mantra can help you in bringing stability and success in business.

To gain strength:

Mantra: "ॐ महाबलाय नमः।" "Om Mahabalaya Namah."
Effect: This mantra can provide you with power, strength and courage.

For destruction of troubles:

Mantra: "ॐ सर्वज्ञाय नमः।" "Om Sarvagya Namah."
Effect: This mantra can help you in getting rid of all troubles.

By using these mantras, you can get the blessings of Lord Shiva and get happiness, prosperity and success in your life.

Destroyer of Obstacles, Ganapati Mantra - When all Work is stopping:

When none of your work is getting done, there are obstacles in every work, then chant this powerful mantra of Ganesh ji.

Mantra:
"वक्रतुण्डं महाकायं सूर्यकोटि समप्रभम्। निर्विघ्नं कुरु मे देव सर्वकार्येषु सर्वदा।।"
"Vakratundam Mahakayam Suryakoti Samaprabham. Nirvighnam Kuru Me Deva Sarvakaryeshu Sarvada."

Jaap: Chant this mantra 108 times (one rosary) daily.

Method: Use turmeric or sandalwood rosary. Offer modak (modak is Ganesh ji's favorite bhog) and durva (doob grass) to Ganesh ji.

Effect: This mantra will free you from all kinds of obstacles and help you get success in all your work.

Ganesh ji is the remover of obstacles. This mantra will help you get his blessings and remove all the obstacles coming in your life.

Specific Mantras of Goddess Durga:

Some special mantras have been given for the worship of Goddess Durga. By chanting these mantras or performing havan, you can fulfill many wishes.

For wealth, good luck and political success:

Mantra: "ॐ श्रीं ह्रीं क्लीं ऐं कमलवासिन्यै स्वाहा।" "Om Shreem Hreem Kleem Aim Kamalavasinye Swaaha."

Effect: This mantra can help you get wealth, good luck and political success.

For wish fulfillment and success in work:

Mantra: "ॐ श्रीं ह्रीं वह्निजायायै नमः।"
 "Om Shreem Hreem Vahnijayaye Namah."

Effect: This mantra can help you fulfill your wishes and get success in your work.

For the fulfillment of grains and food:
Mantra: "ॐ सुरभ्यै नमः।" "Om Surabhyai Namah."

Effect: This mantra can help in removing the shortage of food and money in your house.

For victory:

Mantra: "ॐ ह्रीं भुवनेश्वर्यै नमः।" "Om Hreem Bhuvaneshwaryai Namah."

Effect: This mantra can help you overcome all kinds of obstacles and enemies.

For protection and destruction of troubles/ calamities:

Mantra:"ॐ ऐं ह्रीं क्लीं चामुण्डायै विच्चै।" "Om Aim Hreem Kleem Chamundaye Viccha"

Method: Perform Havan with at least 21 mantras.

Effect: This mantra can help protect you from all kinds of troubles and calamities.

For success in work, reputation, health and fearlessness:

Mantra: "ॐ भूर्भुवः स्वः तत्सवितुर्वरेण्यं भर्गो देवस्य धीमहि धियो यो नः प्रचोदयात्।" **"Om Bhurbhuvah Swaha Tatsaviturvarenyam Bhargo Devasya Dheemahi Dhiyo Yo Nah Prachodayat."** **(Gayatri Mantra)**

Method: Chant Gayatri Mantra and recite "Gayatri Kavach" every morning.

Effect: This mantra can give you success in your work, reputation, good health and fearlessness.

For special crisis/calamity:

Method: Recite or get "Shatchandi" recited.
Effect: This recitation can help you get rid of big crisis or difficult situations.

For progress against fate:

Method: On an auspicious day, keep 21 white Ratti grains in a silver or copper vessel for worship. Apply vermilion on them daily. Spread a white cloth on a blanket and consume only milk and fruits for 9 days. Chant 11 rounds of the mantra "ॐ दुं दुर्गाय नमः।" **"Om Dum Durgay Namah"** every morning and evening.

Tie three copper coins in a red, yellow, or white thread and place them at the feet of Durga. Chant 5 rounds of the eighth verse of "Argala Stotra" in "Durga Saptashati" in the morning and evening.

Shloka: "अचिन्त्य रूपचरिते सर्वशत्रु विनाशिनि। रूपं देहि जयं देहि यशो देहि द्विषो जहि।"
"Achintya Roopcharite Sarvashatru Vinashini. Roopam Dehi Jayam Dehi Yasho Dehi Dwisho Jahi."

Effect: This prayog shows the best effect if done during Navratri. This prayog will give amazing results in 9 days.

Addition: Keep chanting 1 round of both the mantras every day.

Ninth day: Wear copper coins around your neck and apply vermillion on white Ratti beads daily.

By using these mantras you can get the blessings of Goddess Durga and get happiness, prosperity and success in your life.
To achieve the goal - If you want to achieve a particular goal and despite your ability and efforts you are not getting success, then go to a pilgrimage place for 11 days.

Stay there with restraint and purity and stand on the banks of the river Ganga or in the Ganga water and face east in the morning and face north in the evening and chant 5-5 rounds of the mantra "ॐ खगोल्काय नमः स्वाहा।" **"Om Akashghoshkaay Namah Swaha"** daily. This will create reasons for success in achieving your goal.

If for some reason it is not possible to go to a pilgrimage place or to the banks of the river Ganga, then you can offer water to the rising Sun and chant near Tulsi or hang a copper Sun on the eastern wall and chant near it. By doing this you will have to chant for 41 days.

Freedom from trouble from officer:

If the relationship between you and the officer is not good, even if you are working honestly, but you are facing trouble due to your speech defect, the officer's malice or wickedness or someone else's whispering, then write the name of your officer on a betel nut and place it in front of Ganesh ji on a betel leaf.

It is best to place it on Wednesday or Chaturthi Tithi and chant 10 rosaries of "ॐ गं गणपतये नमः।" **"Om Gan Ganpataye Namah"** daily for 11 days.

After chanting, get the betel nut mounted in silver and wear it around your neck. This will improve the relationship between you and the officer and will also reduce your speech defect. But then keep chanting the above mantra one rosary daily.

Freedom from instability or stress in job:

Consecrate the root of Ashwagandha with ten recitations of 'Ganesh Sahasranama' and tie it in a grey thread on Wednesday or Chaturthi Tithi and wear it around your neck. This will make your thoughts good, your personality will improve and become positive. You will be free from stress and there will be stability in work/job.

Freedom from obstacles in promotion:

If you are facing obstacles in promotion despite being eligible or Sun/Saturn is an obstacle in marriage, then offer madaar/ak flowers/leaves to Lord Ganesha in the evening and light a ghee lamp and recite 'Ganesh Chalisa'/'Ganesh Atharva Shirsha' daily. Or chant "ॐ गं गणपतये नमः।" **"Om Gan Ganpataye Namah"** mantra 10 times (take a garland of turmeric/sandalwood). This will give benefits in 45 days to 6 months.

Freedom from Job/Business Problems:

When you are facing a lot of problems in your job/business/trade and are not getting help/relief from anyone, then on Trayodashi, make a small Shivling yourself from cow dung, cow urine and Ganga water. Place it in the North/Ishan. Offer 5 black sesame seeds and 2 drops of water on it daily and chant the mantra

"ॐ नमः शिवाय मृत्युंजय महादेवाय नमोऽस्तुते।"
"Om Namah Shivaya Mrityunjaya Mahadevaya Namostute" 108 times on a Rudraksha rosary in front of it; at least one rosary daily. Changes will start coming within a week or two.

Protection from misfortune and crisis:

Daily recitation of 'Durga Ashtottarashat Naam Stotra' or

"ॐ जयन्ती मंगला काली भद्रकाली कपालिनी। दुर्गा क्षमा शिवा धात्री स्वाहा स्वधा नमोऽस्तुते।।"

"**Om Jayanti Mangala Kali Bhadrakali Kapalini. Durga Ksama, Shiva Dhatri Swaha Swadha Namostute.**" Chanting a rosary of the mantra will protect you from all troubles and adversities and provide success, good fortune and peace.

Freedom from lawsuits:

Mix sulphur and dhatura in cow urine and dry it. Later grind it and mix it in the havan material, or use this as havan material and offer 540 oblations in the fire during Navratri with the mantra

"ॐ जयन्ती मंगला काली भद्रकाली कपालिनी। दुर्गा क्षमा शिवा धात्री स्वाहा स्वधा नमोऽस्तुते।।"

"**Om Jayanti Mangala Kali Bhadrakali Kapalini. Durga Ksama, Shiva Dhatri Swaha Swadha Namostute.**" and pray to Mother Kali to solve your problem.

By this you will be honorably acquitted and will not get trapped in such cases again.

For Victory Honor:

Offer water to the rising sun and chant 11 rosaries of **'Om Hreem Hansah'** mantra and wear a bael root around your neck on Sunday. Or keep a bael leaf in your right hand and recite **'Adityahridaya Stotra'** three times in front of the rising sun. Or stand under a bael tree at the time of rising sun and chant a rosary of **'Gayatri Mantra'**. Do any of these things continuously for a year (at least). Although its effect starts showing in 3-4 months.

Success/Victory and Wealth:

By reading 'Durga Saptashati' with 'Keelak' every day with Amrit Siddhi Yoga, you soon start getting good luck, wealth, success and victory. If you want, you can also chant "ॐ ह्रीं" **"Om Hreem"** mantra 5 times on a rosary of red sandalwood to increase your strength (self-confidence) and influence.

Getting Caught in a Scandal:

One who is caught in a scandal despite being innocent should chant "ॐ धूं रां राहवे नमः।" **"Om Dhoom Raam Rahve Namah"** in the evening, in the twilight, facing south-west and without a rosary (do it for 15 to 30 minutes). If you are uncomfortable chanting without a rosary, chant 11 rosaries (at least) on a black hakik rosary.

To avoid getting caught in a scandal again without any reason, chant the Surya Mantra every morning by holding 5 betel nuts and 2 cloves in your right fist and keep them at the place of worship.

Enemy Affliction/Oppression by Officers:

In spite of being righteous and honest, if due to being weak, you are afflicted by enemies/evil people/officers (unnecessarily oppressed or harassed), then sitting in front of Durga idol/picture or Bagalamukhi Devi's picture/yantra facing east, on a yellow or red seat, recite one rosary of the mantra

"ॐ ज्वल-ज्वल शूलिनी दुष्ट ग्रहान् हुं फट् स्वाहा।"

"Om Jwal-Jwal Shoolini Dushta Grahan Hum Phat Swaaha" every morning and evening. Start from Ashtami. Do it continuously for 31/41/51 days. Then keep doing it only on Ashtami. It is very beneficial.

Protection from loss of money and robbers:

Those whose money is stolen or there is loss of money, or those who often have to travel with money and are afraid of attack by thieves and robbers, should keep the 'Ram Raksha Yantra' in front of them in an auspicious time and make it consecrated by chanting 1008 (ten rosaries) of the 'Ram Gayatri'

("ॐ दाशरथाय विद्महे सीतावल्लभाय धीमहि तन्नो रामः प्रचोदयात्"

"Om Dasharathaay Vidmahe Sitavallabhya Dheemahi Tanno Ram: Prachodayat") mantra and keep it with them.

When going on a journey, it should be carried with you in a clean manner. This prevents loss of money and also protects from thieves and robbers.

For promotion:

If you are not getting promotion despite being eligible, then on the day of Dhanteras, facing north in front of the idol of Ganesh ji, chant the mantra "ॐ गं गणपतये नमः।" **"Om Gan Ganpataye**

Namah" 10 times on a turmeric rosary. After this, chant one rosary every day for 31, 41 or 51 days.

This removes the obstacles in promotion, removes the defects of Mercury and if you are not getting success according to your ability and efforts, then this problem also goes away.

To avoid falling prey to politics in the job:

If you are facing trouble in the job despite being truthful or there is politics against you, then chant a rosary of "ॐ सत्यं सत्यं सत्यं विजेयते ॐ"

"Om Satyam Satyam Satyam Vijayate Om" mantra by keeping a cardamom in the left hand. Go to work every day keeping that cardamom in your mouth. Gradually the situation will improve.

To get the desired results:

Ganesh's Agartinsh Mantra is very effective and infallible for the accomplishment of any kind of work. It has to be chanted with celibacy and purity in the number of 15000 (usually 9 rosaries daily) in 6 months. The mantra is

"रायस्पोषस्य दिदितानिधि रत्नधातु मान्नक्षोहणोबल गहनो वक्रतुण्डाय हुम्।"

"Raisposhasya   Diditanidhi   Ratnadhatu Mannakshohanobal Gahano Vakratundaya Hum." (Start this from Chaturthi. If it is recited 10,000 times (usually 4 malas daily) till the next Chaturthi, it removes poverty. Those who find this difficult should chant 31 malas of Uchchhisht Ganapati's mantra "हस्ति पिशाचिलिखे स्वाहा" "Hasti Pishachilikhe Swaha", potter's clay One should make a Ganesha idol from it and do it in front of it. It helps one to attain a kingdom in 6 months and removes poverty in three months. Or chant 10 rounds of the mantra "मेधोल्काय स्वाहा" "Medholkay Swaha" in front of Ganesha made from bamboo soil and chant one round of the mantra Make an offering. This experiment bears fruit in one year.

To get wealth and victory:

"ऐं ह्रीं श्रीं आद्यलक्ष्मी स्वयंभुवे ह्रीं ज्येष्ठायै नमः।"
"Aim Hreem Shreem Aadyalakshmi Swayambhuve Hreem Jyeshthayai Namah."

Chant this mantra 21 times every day under a mango, amla or parijat tree. This mantra provides wealth and victory in 6 months to 1 year. It has been experienced. Jyeshtha Lakshmi has special significance in relation to wealth and prosperity, but this practice demands sattvikta (purity), restraint and purity.

Narasimha Mantra to increase influence:

Chanting "ॐ क्ष्मौं ॐ" **"Om Kshom Om"** or "ह्रीं क्ष्मौं ह्रीं" **"Hreem Kshom Hreem"** mantra 1000 times with vine flowers, fruits and wood for 11 days or chanting 21 rosaries of this mantra for 10 days removes all troubles and fears, influence and glory increase and success starts coming. After this, chant one rosary every day.

Mrityunjaya Mantra for many benefits:

This is one mantra, but gives success to the practitioner in different fields depending on the way it is used.
"ॐ हौं ॐ जूं सः भूर्भुवः स्वः त्र्यम्बकं यजामहे सुगन्धिं पुष्टिवर्धनम्। उर्वारुकमिव बन्धनान्मृत्योर्मुक्षीय माऽमृतात् भूर्भुवः स्वः र्यों जूं सः हौं ॐ।"
"Om Hom Om Joon Sah Bhurbhuvah Swah Tryambakam Yajamahe Sugandhim Pushtivardhanam. Urvarukamiv Bandhanan Mrityormukshiya Ma'mritat Bhurbhuvah Swah Ryon Joon Sah Hom Om."

This mantra is proved by chanting it 1.25 lakh times. Chant at least 10 rounds or 5 rounds every day on a Rudraksha rosary. By performing havan with 11 finger long sticks of Giloy in the 20th or 21st nakshatra from one's birthday, a person conquers his diseases and enemies and lives for 100 years, the life crisis goes away.

Acquisition of wealth:
Wealth is obtained by performing havan using vine wood.

Celibate groom:
By performing havan with the wood of Palash (Dhak), semen, strength, sharpness increase and celibacy increases.

Wealth, good fortune:

Performing havan with wood of Banyan tree increases good fortune.

Influence, attraction:
Performing havan with the wood of Khadir (Khair) increases the luster, attraction and influence.

Destruction of enemies:
Performing havan with mustard seeds destroys enemies. Destruction of sins: Performing havan with sesame seeds destroys sins/adharma.

Fame and glory:
Performing havan with kheer increases radiance, wealth, Lakshmi, fame and glory as well as happiness.

Victory, fearlessness:
The fire of curd leads to victory in a dispute/lawsuit and the fear of untimely death also goes away.

Fulfillment of wishes:
By performing havan with Amrita soaked in milk, all types of wishes are fulfilled.

Note: Number of offerings in all homas is 10000.

Mantras of the Nine Planets

Vedic mantras for the nine planets in Kaliyug. Kaliyug mantras (including chanting number)

- **Sun**
  'ॐ ह्रां ह्रीं सूर्यादित्य ॐ ।'
  'Om Hreem Hreem Suryaditya Om.'
  (1,24,000) - Chant this mantra for Sun God and repeat it 1 lakh 24 thousand times.

- **Moon**
  'ॐ घौं स्रौं सः चन्द्रदेवाय ॐ ।'
  'Om Ghoum Sroum Sah Chandradevaya Om.'
  (1,40,000) - Chant this mantra for Moon God and repeat it 1 lakh 40 thousand times.

- **Mars**
  'ॐ ह्रां ह्रीं सः भौमाय भूमिपुत्राय ॐ ।'
  'Om Hreem Hreem Sah Bhaumay Bhoomiputray Om.'
  (1,28,000) - Chant this mantra for Lord Mars and repeat it 1 lakh 28 thousand times.

- **Mercury**
  'ॐ ह्रौं ह्रौं सः बुधाय ह्रौं ह्रौं ॐ ।'
  'Om Hroum Hroum Sah Budhaya Hroum Hroum Om.'
  (1,68,000) - Chant this mantra for Lord Mercury and repeat it 1 lakh 68 thousand times.

- **Jupiter**
  'ॐ ह्रीं ह्रीं श्रीं क्लीं अंगिरापुत्राय ह्रीं ॐ ।'
  'Om Hreem Hreem Shreem Kleem Angiraputraya Hreem Om.'
  (1,64,000) - Chant this mantra for Guru Dev and repeat it 1 lakh 64 thousand times.

- **Venus**
  'ॐ ह्रौं ह्रीं सः शुक्राय भृगुनंदनाय ह्रौं ह्रीं ॐ ।'
  'Om Hroum Hreem Sah Shukraya Bhrigunandanay Hroum Hreem Om.'

(1,80,000) - Chant this mantra for Venus and repeat it
1 lakh 80 thousand times.

- **Saturn**
  'ॐ शौं शौं सः रविछायापुत्राय शं सौं ॐ ।'
  'Om Shaum Shaum Sah Ravichhayaputraya Sham
  Soum Om.'
  (1,76,000) - Chant this mantra for Shani Dev and
  repeat it 1 lakh 76 thousand times.

- **Rahu**
  'ॐ छौं छां छौं सः राहवे छौं छां ॐ ।'
  'Om Chhaum Chhaum Chhaum Sah Rahve Chhaum
  Chhaum Om.'
  (1,72,000) - Chant this mantra for Rahu Dev and
  repeat it 1 lakh 72 thousand times.

- **Ketu**
  'ॐ फौं फां फौं सः केतवे फौं फां फौं ॐ ।'
  'Om Faum Faum Faum Sa: Ketave Faum Faum Faum
  Faum Om.'
  (1,28,000) - Chant this mantra for Ketu Dev and
  repeat it 1 lakh 28 thousand times.

Gems, Metals, Colors, Herbs, Substances etc. of the Planets

Sun

- Gemstone: Ruby
- Sub-gemstone: Lalri, Garnet
- Metal: Copper
- Substitute: Gold
- Direction: East
- Deity: Narayan/Shiva/Gayatri
- Color: Bright pink, golden, khaki
- Factors: Father, King, Heart, Right Eye, Bone and Bile, Light, Soul, Bull, Sheep, Garuda etc.
- Substance: Wheat, Jaggery, Salt, Rajmaah, Bael, Pomegranate, Aak, Mango, Royal Court, Throne, Turban, Ajwain, Saunth, Ginger etc.

Moon

- Gemstone: Pearl
- Sub-gemstone: Moonstone, Quartz
- Metal: Silver
- Direction: Northwest
- Deity: Shiva/Gauri
- Color: White, Milky
- Factors: Mother, Queen, Mind, Left Eye, Juice, Water, Phlegm, Cow, Horse, Rabbit, Duck etc.
- Substance: Milk, Rice, Mishri, Sandalwood, Refined Flour, Sharbat, Litchi, Ashgourd, Muskmelon, Coconut Water, Wood Apple, Creepers, Water Chestnut, Butter etc.

Mars

- Gemstone: Coral
- Sub-gemstone: Kaharwa, Red Hakik
- Metal: Copper
- Direction: South
- Deity: Hanuman/Kartikeya/Kali
- Color: Red, Bloody Red, Orange
- Factor: Brother, soldier, warrior, courage, valour, arm, back, fire, weapon, land, bile, pancreas, meat, electricity, labourer, blood, wound, ram, monkey, lion, eagle, energy, power etc.

- Substance: Jaggery, Giloy, chilli, honey, vermilion, plum, cactus, kikar, gum etc.

Mercury

- Gemstone: Emerald
- Sub-gemstone: Onyx, Ghritmani
- Metal: Brass
- Substitute: Copper
- Direction: North
- Deity: Durga/Ganesh/Vishnu
- Color: Green
- Factors: Speech, intestine, skin, kidney, child, daughter, sister, aunt, eunuch, bark, education, business, cleverness, goat, laughter, cat, pigeon, parrot etc.
- Material: Moong, spinach, green vegetables, mulberry, guava, Ashoka, alum, belt, bangle, ball etc.

Jupiter

- Gemstone: Topaz
- Sub-gemstone: Sunela, Amber
- Metal: Gold
- Substitute: Brass
- Direction: Ishan
- God: Narayan/Brahma/Dattatreya
- Color: Yellow
- Factors: Acharya, priest, Pujari, husband, son, wisdom, religion, dignity, tradition, patience, forgiveness, tolerance, rituals, knowledge, learning, Shikha-sthan, stomach, cow, swan, elephant, liver, fat etc.
- Material: Turmeric, Banyan, Saffron, Gram flour, Gram, Banana, Papaya, Dushaala/Cover, Japa-mala, Kamandalu, Temple etc.

Venus

- Gemstone: Diamond
- Sub-gemstone: Fire Opal, Zircon
- Metal: Platinum
- Substitute: Silver
- Direction: South-East
- Deity: Durga/Lakshmi/Kamadeva
- Color: White, Shiny, Silver

- Factor: Semen, genitals, pelvis, joy, citizenship, tenderness, art, music, decoration, makeup, tantrums, woman, love, marriage, wife, breast, uterus, celebration etc.
- Substance: Amla, lotus seeds, sugarcane, basmati rice, bamboo, fragrant flowers, perfume, cow, white pigeon, sago, jalebi, curd, cream, ghee, lotus seeds etc.

Saturn

- Gemstone: Blue Sapphire
- Sub-gemstone: Blue, Jamunia Kataila, Black Hakik
- Metal: Iron
- Direction: West
- Deity: Rudra/Bhairav/Kali
- Color: Black/Blue
- Factors: Sorrow, sadness, grief, disease, wind, obstruction, laxity, slave, feet, nerves, nervous system, hair, nails, camel, jackal, buffalo, crow, vulture, snake, etc.
- Substance: Urad, sesame, oil, berries, peepal, poison, alcohol, cement, woolen clothes, etc.
- Other factors: Research, science, justice, renunciation, renunciation

Rahu

- Gemstone: Onyx
- Sub-gemstone: Black Onyx, Lapis Lazuli
- Metal: Zinc, Lead, Tin
- Direction: South-West
- Deity: Saraswati/Durga/Rudra
- Color: Black/Brown/Purple/Blue
- Factors: Separation, separation, accident, breakup, fainting, shock, poison, infection, confusion, dilemma, illusion, hypocrisy, cheating, fraud, coal, stone, sunlight, shade, clouds, photography, spying, idea, snake smell, snake, scorpion, spider, ant, elephant, cat, pig, bat, owl, electricity, radio, magic, ghost, staircase, roof, etc.
- Substance: Chhaj, tobacco, opium, oleander, dhatura, radish, evening, garbage, rotting/foul smell etc.

Ketu

- Gemstone: Lahsuniya/Vaidurya
- Sub-gemstone: Turquoise, Agate, Ruby Metal: Ashtadhatu/Panchdhatu
- Direction: Upward
- Deity: Durga/Ganesha/Shiva
- Color: Grey/Two-Colored/Pied Bar
- Factors: Foot, Ear, Travel, Espionage, Contingency, Eccentricity, Destruction, illusion, inspiration, belief, faith, spirituality, public service, salvation, widow etc.
- Substances: Musk, flag, gloves, saber, dogrose, ashwagandha, pheasant/quail, lion etc.

Short Mantras of the Gods of the Constellations (Nakshatras)

Ashwini:
ॐ अश्विनी कुमाराभ्यां नमः ॥
Om Ashvinee Kumarabhyam Namaha ||

Bharani:
ॐ यमाय नमः ॥
Om Yamaya Namaha ||

Krittika:
ॐ अग्नये नमः ॥
Om Agnaye Namaha ||

Rohini:
ॐ ब्रह्मणे नमः ॥
Om Brahmane Namaha ||

Mrigashira:
ॐ चन्द्रमसे नमः ॥
Om Chandramase Namaha ||

Ardra:
ॐ रुद्राय नमः ॥
Om Rudraya Namaha ||

Punarvasu:
ॐ अदिते नमः ॥
Om Adite Namaha ||

Pushya:
ॐ बृहस्पतये नमः ॥
Om Brihaspataye Namaha ||

Ashlesha:
ॐ सर्पेभ्यो नमः ॥
Om Sarpebhyo Namaha ||

Magha:

ॐ पितराय नमः ॥
Om Pitaraya Namaha ||

Purva Phalguni:
ॐ भगाय नमः ॥
Om Bhagaya Namaha ||

Uttara Phalguni:
ॐ अर्यम्णे नमः ॥
Om Aryamne Namaha ||

Hasta:
ॐ सवित्रे नमः ॥
Om Savitre Namaha ||

Chitra:
ॐ विश्वकर्मणे नमः ॥
Om Vishvakarmane Namaha ||

Swati:
ॐ वायवे नमः ॥
Om Vayave Namaha ||

Vishakha:
ॐ इन्द्राग्निभ्यां नमः ॥
Om Indragnibhyam Namaha ||

Anuradha:
ॐ मित्राय नमः ॥
Om Mitraya Namaha ||

Jyeshtha:
ॐ शक्राय नमः ॥
Om Shakraya Namaha ||

Mula:
ॐ निरृत्ये नमः ॥
Om Nirritye Namaha ||

Purva Ashadha:

ॐ अद्भ्यो नमः ॥
Om Adbhya Namaha ||

Uttara Ashadha:
ॐ विश्वेभ्यो देवेभ्यो नमः ॥
Om Vishvebhyo Devebhyo Namaha ||

Shravana:
ॐ विष्णवे नमः ॥
Om Vishnave Namaha ||

Dhanishta:
ॐ वसुभ्यो नमः ॥
Om Vasubhyo Namaha ||

Shatabhisha:
ॐ वरुणाय नमः ॥
Om Varunaya Namaha ||

Purva Bhadrapada:
ॐ अजैकपदे नमः ॥
Om Ajekapade Namaha ||

Uttara Bhadrapada:
ॐ अहिर्बुध्न्याय नमः ॥
Om Ahirbudhnyaya Namaha ||

Revati:
ॐ पूष्णे नमः ॥
Om Pushne Namaha ||

Strengthening a Weak Planet

Remedies
- Wear the gemstone/metal/herb of the planet on the day of the planet
- Chant the mantra of the planet daily (more on the day of the planet)
- Wear or worship the yantra of the planet
- Consume the substances/foods/fruits/colors etc. of the planet
- Serve the factors/persons/relatives/animals-birds/plants of the planet and stay in contact with them more
- Bathe with the roots of the planet and worship with its substances

Example
To offer sacrifice to the Sun
- Worship of the rising Sun
- Respect for father
- Respect for authority/obeying orders
- Wearing ruby in gold/copper
- Worshipping/watering/planting trees like bael, mango, guava, aak, tulsi etc.
- Consuming jaggery, wheat, salt, pomegranate, bael etc.
- Feeding bull/monkey/sheep
- Wearing bael root etc. or taking bath by adding bael leaves, tulsi leaves or their roots in water etc.

Weakening a Strong Planet

If a planet is inauspicious, harmful, unprofitable or ineffective, but is strong in the horoscope or transit, then its strength should be reduced. This will minimize the suffering/loss to oneself.

Remedy
- Donate/remove the objects and factors of the planet
- Chant the Shanti Mantras/Podahar Mantras of the planet (more on the day of the planet) daily
- Do not consume/use the objects/grains/fruits/colors etc. of the planet
- Do not annoy the person related to the planet
    - Behave sweetly with them
    - Do not anger them
- Strengthen the objects, gems, factors, plants, fruits, grains, colors etc. of the enemy but auspicious planets of the planet by consuming them

Pacify the Agitated Planets

If any planet is aggravated due to malefic afflictions or inauspicious situations, then it is necessary to pacify it so that it can come to a balanced/happy state.

Remedies
- Chanting planet stotras and peace mantras

Chant planet stotras and peace mantras in their days specially or in more rosaries. Recite planet mother stotra.

- Tantra and Totka

Combine the factors or substances of those planets with the factors or substances of those planets by tantra and totka which can pacify them.

- Serving planet factors

Serve the factors, persons, relatives, animals, birds and plants of those planets. Offer them food etc.

- Wearing planet gems and metals

Wear the gems, metals and roots of those planets in different fingers, combinations of metals, gems and roots. So that they can get free from the infection by taking the influence of other planets in themselves.

- Planet peace rituals

Use planet peace rituals, fasts and worships.

Do not do activities that increase the wrath of the planets.

Method and fingers of wearing Gemstone

Select the following days for wearing gemstones:

- Sunday for gems/metals/herbs etc. of Sun
- Monday for pearls etc. of Moon
- Tuesday for coral etc. of Mars
- Wednesday for emerald etc. of Mercury
- Thursday for topaz etc. of Jupiter
- Friday for diamond etc. of Venus
- Saturday for sapphire etc. of Saturn
- Wednesday (or Saturday) for Onyx etc. of Rahu and Thursday (or Tuesday) for Cat's Eye etc. of Ketu are appropriate to accept.

Wear gems in the Shukla Paksha and in the Hora of the planet to which the gem belongs. Before wearing gems, they should be purified. For this, soak them in raw milk and Ganga water or Panchagavya for 12 hours. In the morning, when you want to wear them, clean them and burn incense, then keep them in front respectfully or in the left fist and with the right hand chant the first rosary of Ganesh mantra, with the second rosary of the planet's deity and five rosaries of the planet's mantra (11 rosaries / 10 rosaries are best, five are medium and one is normal. But in the absence of time, do chant one rosary of the planet). In the end, chant the rosary of the planet's mother as well and it is good, otherwise bow to her and touch the gem to the feet of the deity and then wear it.

Generally, Jupiter's gems/metals are worn in the index finger, Saturn/Rahu/Ketu in the middle finger, Sun/Mars in the ring finger, Mercury/Moon in the little finger. Venus' gems are worn in the ring finger, metals are also worn in the thumb. Moon's gem pearl can also be worn in the index finger (fingers can be changed in special problems). Metals are also worn in the neck or arm. Generally, opposing gems are not worn together (except for prevention).

Gemstones and Rudraksha in Disease Prevention

It is also possible to cure diseases by wearing/consuming gems, Rudrakshas, metals, herbs, substances etc., because diseases are also the result of the ill-effects of planets. Here we will briefly discuss remedies for some major diseases.

Heart disease
To get rid of heart disease, wear 5 1/4 Ratti ruby in gold in the ring finger. Also wear Arjuna root or bark in orange thread around the neck on Sunday. Also consume Arjunarishta, Manik Pishti/Bhasm, Bael/Bel Murabba, Carrot Murabba, Pomegranate juice, Walnut, Almond, Sunflower oil, Bottle gourd juice, Tulsi juice etc.

Low morale, nervousness
To get rid of the problem of low morale and nervousness, wear a 4 1/4 ratti pearl in silver on the little finger. Apart from this, wear a solid silver ball around the neck, take bath by adding Ashoka leaves in water, consume pearl ash, take Pravalpishti. Also consume Ashgourd, gourd, litchi, grapes, coconut water etc. Drink conch water, wear two-faced Rudraksha or rub it and lick it, or put it in water and drink that water.

Arthritis
To get rid of arthritis, wear 9 ratti red coral in silver in the ring finger and 5 ratti blue sapphire in gold in the little finger. Also consume dry ginger, carom seeds, black pepper, bay leaf, ginger, myrobalan etc. Eat food cooked in sesame oil or massage with sesame oil. Boil garlic/black pepper/cloves in oil and massage the affected area with it for pain.

Appendicitis
To get rid of appendicitis, avoid consuming cold things. Protect the joints from cold.

Anemia
To get rid of anemia, wear 7 ratti topaz in gold in the ring finger and 5 ratti coral in copper in the other ring finger. Mix pomegranate juice with radish juice. Mix raisins soaked overnight with lemon juice. Drink juice of papaya root/leaves. Eat Prabalpishti. Drink carrot and spinach juice. Drink beetroot,

tomato, carrot juice. Eat raw papaya or radish by adding it in vinegar. Eat dates.

Asthma, epilepsy, mental problems

To get rid of asthma, epilepsy, mental problems, wear 6.25 Ratti Emerald in gold with 7.25 Ratti Topaz in the ring finger (or you can wear Topaz in the ring finger of the other hand as well). And wear 6.25 Ratti Chandrakant Mani in silver in the little finger. Wear Punarnava root around the neck. Avoid sour and cold things. Take Mulhathi, honey, Tulsi. Massage red oil on the head and raw milk on the soles with light hands. Take dates/jaggery with milk or suck old jaggery with black pepper. Wear a garland of garlic.

Piles, Asthma, Hernia, Kidney Diseases, Urine Problems

To get rid of piles, asthma, hernia, kidney diseases, urine problems, wear 7 and a half ratti coral in copper in the ring finger. Wear 5 and a quarter ratti topaz in gold in the second ring finger (in case of kidney wear 6 ratti Danafirang in silver or emerald in gold in the little finger). Wear a garland of garlic cloves, drink goat milk. Eat old jaggery with dry ginger. Eat guava after roasting it on ash. Drink the water of four faced Rudraksha or wear it around the neck, or wear the root of Vidhara.

Mania/Madness

To get rid of mania/madness, wear 7 ratti emerald in gold in the ring finger and 7 ratti topaz in gold in the other ring finger, or wear both together in one ring finger if the problem is mental. If the problem is mental, wear 7 ratti emerald and 7 ratti pearl in silver together in the little finger or wear them separately in both the little fingers. Take pearl ash. Take Brahmi. Smell the smoke of spikenard and guggul, camphor. Wear spikenard in the neck. Take carrot and amla murabba. Eat uprooted white onion immediately at sunrise in the morning.

Wear it together on the little finger or separately on both the little fingers. To get rid of insanity/madness, do the following remedies:

- Take pearl ash.
- Take brahmi.
- Smell the smoke of spikenard, guggul and camphor.

- Wear spikenard on the neck.
- Take carrot and amla jam.
- Eat uprooted white onion immediately after sunrise in the morning.

Jaundice, Liver Disease

To get rid of jaundice, liver disease, wear 5 ratti topaz and 7 ratti emerald in gold in the ring finger and wear 3 ratti lapis lazuli or chitti (tiger eye) in gold in the little finger. Take Makoy juice/extract/sugarcane juice or suck Gaderi. Drink radish leaf juice. Eat radish. Raw papaya or radish put in vinegar and eat 4-5 pieces of it with food. Take curd and buttermilk. Drink pomegranate juice. Wear the root of papaya/punarnava. Consume Punarnavarishta. Wear three faced Rudraksha.

Eczema, Ringworm

To get rid of eczema, ringworm, wear 7.5 ratti white coral in gold in the middle finger and 7 ratti topaz in gold in the ring finger. Take juice of neem leaves in basil juice and honey. Take Safi/blood purifier medicine. Apply Vanshlochan/sandalwood-turmeric by rubbing or apply sulphur oil or neem oil. Dry cow dung and rub its powder. Wear three copper coins in a green thread around the neck.

Brain Tumor and Migraine

To get rid of brain tumor and migraine, wear 7.25 Ratti Emerald in gold in the ring finger. Wear 6 Ratti Pearl in silver in the little finger. Wear 5 Ratti Blue Sapphire in gold in the middle finger. In case of migraine, wear 7.25 Ratti Black Hakik in silver in the middle finger, consume sunflower oil. Cut half an apple and eat it in the morning on an empty stomach. Keep a proper routine of eating, sleeping and waking up.

Lung Cancer, Breast Cancer

To get rid of lung cancer, breast cancer, wear 9 ratti coral in copper in the ring finger. Wear 7 ratti emerald in gold in the middle finger. Wear 5 ratti sapphire in panchdhatu in the little finger. Consume basil juice, tomato, ginger, honey, turmeric. Drink giloy.

Tongue/Throat/Mouth Cancer

To get rid of tongue/throat/mouth cancer, wear 11 ratti topaz in gold in the ring finger. Wear 5 ratti red coral in copper in the second ring finger and wear 3 ratti cat's eye (lahsuniya) in the middle finger on Thursday. Drink turmeric in milk. Lick ginger juice mixed with honey. Drink ½ to 2 teaspoons of fresh cow urine in the morning. Drink Tulsi juice and Giloy juice. Eat cinnamon.

Blood Cancer

To get rid of blood cancer, wear 9 ratti coral in copper in the ring finger. Wear 13 ratti topaz in gold in the second ring finger. Wear 5 ratti Cats Eye in gold on Thursday in the middle finger. Consume urine of Kapila cow or calf in the morning and after lunch. Take juice of Giloy, Neem, Tulsi. Take powder of nutmeg in honey. Take ginger and honey. Consume turmeric, Indian gooseberry, aloe vera.

Diabetes

To get rid of diabetes, wear white coral of 7.5 Ratti in gold in the ring finger, wear silver rings in the toes or tie white silk thread. Wear the root of Sharpokha in a white thread around the neck. Walk. Eat neem, bitter gourd, jamun, gurmar, sadasuhagan, fenugreek etc. Eat soybean and gram. Drink basil juice. If sugar is present in urine, then definitely drink water of paneer flowers/doda paneer. If it is present in blood, then put a handful of cow husk in water at night, strain it in the morning and drink it on an empty stomach.

High/Low Blood Pressure

To get rid of high blood pressure, wear pearl, Rudraksha beads in silver wire, burn acacia. Drink banana root juice. Take basil juice and cow urine, take less salt. To get rid of low blood pressure, wear coral, Rudraksha beads in copper/gold wire. Eat honey and cinnamon mixed together. Eat jaggery and sesame.

Lack of memory

To overcome lack of memory, wear four-faced Rudraksha or rub it in milk and drink it for twenty days. Consume Brahmi, Amla. Eat almonds or massage almond oil on the head. Wear 6 ratti emerald and 6 ratti pearl in gold and silver in both little fingers. Do Shirshasana.

Impotence, low semen, premature ejaculation
To get rid of impotence, low semen, premature ejaculation, wear a 2½ ratti diamond in gold in the ring finger. Or consume gold ash and diamond ash. Rub raw milk on the thumbs of both hands. Eat milk-jalebi. Eat makhana or urad kheer. Eat white musli, shatavar, ashwagandha, salam mishri. Eat basil seeds or basil root by putting it in betel leaf. Roast a clove of garlic in cow ghee and take it daily or eat banyan milk by adding it to batasha. Take amla-mishri.

Deafness and muteness/ speaking-hearing problems
To get rid of deafness and muteness/ speaking-hearing problems, if the child is suffering from deafness, rub Jahar Mohra at night and apply it behind the ear. Rub milk (raw) on the soles/massage red oil on the head. In case of speaking problems, feed green chillies (especially seeds) daily. Make the child eat food. Make the aunt talk to him. Make him wear 4 Mukhi Rudraksha.

Vision and Eye Problems
To get rid of vision and eye problems, wear a 5.25 Ratti ruby in gold in the ring finger and a 4.25 Ratti pearl in silver in the little finger. Consume Triphala. Wash the eyes with Triphala and rose water. Watch the rising sun. Drink carrot juice.

Thyroid, Hormonal Disorders
To get rid of thyroid, hormonal disorders, wear the root of Sarpounkha in a white thread, a knot of turmeric in a yellow thread and the root of pomegranate in an orange thread around the neck. Wear a six-faced Rudraksha. Do Ujjayi Pranayam. Wear a silver ring on the thumb of the hand.

Pain in Heels and Ankles
To get relief from pain in heels and ankles, wear a copper ring on the middle finger (wear it on the finger of the opposite hand). Boil dry ginger in water and sit with your feet dipped in it. Grind Amarbel and apply it on the heels. Do not wear slippers with hard soles.

In Depression, Sadness etc.
To get rid of depression, sadness etc., wear 11 ratti Kataila in silver in the middle finger or 8 ratti Rose Quartz in silver in the ring finger. Wear a solid copper ball around the neck or wear a

locket of red Hakik in silver. (If the heart is nervous or sinking, wear Hauldil). Pour raw milk at the root of the banyan tree and apply a Tilak of wet mud.
Herbs for Low / Enemy Zodiac Planets:

Sun: If the Sun is weak, wear the root of the vine around your neck. If it is in the enemy sign, wear the root of the white water lily around your neck. If it is in a low sign, wear the root of the red oleander around your neck. If it is in a friendly sign, wear the root of the pomegranate. The best remedy for low Sun is to pour jaggery in flowing water on Sunday Amavasya.

Moon: If the Moon is weak, wear the root of Khirni. If it is in enemy sign or under evil influence, wear the root of Banyan tree. If it is in low sign, wear the root of Gular or Anantmool. If it is in friendly sign, wear a solid copper ball. Flowing litchi/petha in the river on Somvati Amavasya is also an excellent remedy for low Moon.

Mars: If Mars is weak, wear the root of Anantmool. If it is in enemy sign, wear the root of Shami. If it is in low sign, wear the root of banana tree. If it is in friendly sign, wear the root of fig tree. Floating jaggery rolls in the river on Bhaumvati Amavasya is the best remedy for low Mars.

Mercury: If Mercury is weak, wear the root of Vidhara. If it is in enemy sign, wear a copper coin around the neck. If it is in a low sign, wear the root of Punarnava or the root of Palash. If it is in a friendly sign, wear the root of Amla. The remedy for low Mercury is to flow mung beans in flowing water on Budhvasari Amavasya.

Jupiter: If the Jupiter is weak, wear the root of Punarnava around your neck. If it is an enemy sign, wear the root of Papaya. If it is a low sign, wear the root of fig or banyan. If it is a friendly sign, wear a knot of turmeric or the root of banana. Flowing turmeric or gram lentils in the river on Guruvasari Amavasya is also a good remedy for a low Jupiter.

Venus: If Venus is weak, wear the root of Sharapokha around your neck. If it is in enemy sign, wear the root of Palash/Sandalwood pendant. If it is in low sign, wear the root of Amla.

Remedies and Control of Planets

Venus: If Venus is weak or in enemy sign, wear white sandalwood root. If it is in a friendly sign, wear a rosary of crystal or Rudraksha. Flowing rice/curd in the river on Friday's Amavasya is the remedy for low Venus.

Saturn: If Saturn is weak, wear the root of scorpion grass. If it is in enemy sign, wear the root of Peepal. If it is in low sign, wear the root of Apamarg. If it is in friendly sign, wear the bark of Jamun/Peepal in a black thread. On Saturday Amavasya, pouring oil in the root of Aak or pouring liquor in the drain is the remedy for low Saturn.

Rahu: If Rahu is weak or in enemy sign, wear the root of Sarpagandh. If it is in low sign, wear a locket of white sandalwood and keep a square piece of silver with you. If it is in friendly sign, wear the root of Dhatura, or keep Dhatura seeds or white leaves with you. The remedy for low Rahu is to throw a coin or tobacco in the drain on Saturday or burn Peepal wood and throw its coal in the drain.

Ketu: If Ketu is weak or in enemy sign, wear the root of Ashwagandha. If it is in low sign, wear papaya seeds in a cloth amulet or wear the root of Nirgundi/Palash. If it is in friendly sign, wear the root of yellow/red oleander. The remedy for low sign of Ketu is to flow black and white sesame seeds in flowing water in equal quantity or feed Satanja tablets to fish.

Control of Planets:

Wearing a silver ring on the index finger controls Jupiter.

Wearing a gold ring on the ring finger controls Venus.

Applying turmeric on the thumbs of both hands before sleeping at night controls both Jupiter and Venus.

Wearing a copper ring on the middle finger controls Saturn.

Wearing a gold ring on the little finger controls Mercury.

Wearing a iron ring on the ring finger controls the Sun.

An iron ring on the little finger controls the Moon.

Licking honey from the index finger controls Mars. The root of a banana also controls Mars.

Pitra Dosh

What is Pitra Dosh? Pitra Dosh is a significant and long-lasting issue among the debts, faults and curses of past lives. It is one of the most serious types of doshas (flaws) that can affect a person and their family. This dosh is passed down through generations and can trouble up to three to seven generations if left unresolved. In many cases, it is inherited either from the paternal or maternal side of the family and can affect not just one individual but the entire family line.

How Does Pitra Dosh Form?

Inherited or Acquired: Pitra Dosh can be inherited due to the actions or sins of one's ancestors, either from the paternal or maternal side. It can also be acquired by an individual due to their own misdeeds or wrongdoings in their past life. Such actions could include violating religious principles, causing harm to elders, or neglecting ancestral rituals and duties.

Continued Impact: If not rectified, Pitra Dosh can persist for several generations and the effects may be seen in every member of the family. The curses and debts of the ancestors affect the living descendants, causing problems in their personal and professional lives.

Impact on Family: Often, the family may suffer collectively from this dosh, or individual members may face repeated misfortunes, such as health issues, financial difficulties, relationship problems, or blocked career progress.

Astrological Indicators of Pitra Dosh In astrology, Pitra Dosh is indicated by certain placements of planets in a person's birth chart:

Afflicted Sun and Jupiter: These planets, when they are placed in an angry or negative state, point to the presence of Pitra Dosh. The Sun represents the father and ancestors, while Jupiter signifies wisdom and blessings, often linked to family prosperity.

Weak Moon and Mercury: The Moon, representing the mother and family's emotional stability and Mercury, which governs communication, when in afflicted or weak positions, can contribute to Pitra Dosh.

Influence of Rahu, Ketu and Saturn: These planets have an adverse effect when they influence the aforementioned benefic planets (Sun, Moon and Jupiter). When placed in houses 2, 4, 5, or 9, they intensify the dosh.

Afflicted Lagna (Ascendant) and Lagnesh (Ascendant Lord): If the Ascendant or its lord is afflicted or weak, it may indicate a serious form of Pitra Dosh. Similarly, an uncomfortable position of planets like Mars or Venus can also contribute to the issue.

Severity and Diagnosis: It is important to note that the severity of Pitra Dosh and its origin (whether from the mother's side, father's side, or one's own past life) cannot be determined easily without a deep understanding of astrology. Consulting a skilled astrologer can help in identifying the specific planetary afflictions and their impacts on an individual's life.

Symptoms of Pitra Dosh:

It is not necessary that all the symptoms given below are found in a single person. But most of them are found. If most of them are found, then it is considered a serious Pitra Dosh. If only one or two are found, then it is considered a mere shadow of Pitra Dosh.

- Mysterious death of any elder in the last 4-5 generations of the family.
- All the members of the family face problems in studies/livelihood/marriage/children.
- All the members of the family remain worried for each other when they are away from each other, but when they stay together/sit together, there is commotion/debate/quarrel/quarrel among them.
- Almost all/most of the members of the family are atheist/anti-religion/alcoholic and egoistic and do not believe in things that are beneficial or make fun of religion/saints/scriptures etc./get angry when religious activities are performed.

- Gradual loss of hair on the head or eyebrows of almost all the members of the family (especially men).
- Excessive expenditure of money on diseases/lawsuits/gambling-alcohol etc./no prosperity in the house.
- Disorder/dirt/junk/old or useless things in the house, lizards/spider/ants/termites, dampness/slippery/moss/mud, water dripping, walls/roofs/floors getting damaged/peepal or wild bushes growing in or around the house/any part of the house (especially the back) getting broken or damaged.
- The toilet/lavatory in the north-east/east direction of the house or stairs/junk/garbage etc. in this direction/Brahmasthan or main door getting defective/boring/tap getting in the wrong direction/the house facing south or west/the house getting near a dirty drain/crematorium/graveyard/garbage/vastu defects.
- At least one member of the family getting strange/weird/scary dreams or repeatedly seeing dead people/ancestors/snakes in dreams or seeing dreams of death. This can be a sign of Pitra Dosha.
- Guests coming to the house very rarely or not coming at all. If they come, they do not leave satisfied due to lack of proper hospitality. Or as soon as they leave, people in the house start criticizing them.
- No auspicious event or festival or religious work takes place in the house for a long time. If it does, it is interrupted/the mood is spoiled or some sad news is received after that.
- The pet does not stay in the house, it tries to go out again and again. Or it gets stolen/got lost or dies. Or it keeps falling sick again and again.
- Almost always there is unrest, quarrel, chaos in the house or silence and ominousness in the house even when the members are present, as if there are no people living in the house.
- Diseases enter the house. Almost everyone suffers from some mental disease or such incidents happen again and again. At least one member is suffering from an incurable/complex disease or there is a series of deaths in the house.
- Litigation/quarrels with brothers/relatives or fights, lawsuits/oppositions between husband-wife/father-son

and everyone is troubled, stressed and dissatisfied but the one among them who starts living separately becomes relatively happy.

- The Shraddha of ancestors is not performed in the house/ is not performed properly/ nothing is done for them during the Shraddha period/ it is done irreverently or in an evasive manner. Or the living elders are not given due respect and are neglected.
- Quarrels while eating or insects/hairs etc. are often found in the food or food is thrown away (in the garbage etc.). Disrespect for food or milk/salt/ghee/oil etc. being spilled repeatedly or utensils being empty/unwashed or defective or broken.
- Shoes and socks of the members being dirty/ getting dirty quickly/ getting spoilt. Vests, undergarments etc. and socks being damaged, torn, loose, yellow etc. with holes. Even if new ones are bought, they will get spoilt relatively quickly/ sweat will smell bad.
- There is no puja room/pictures of deities etc. in the house, if there is, then they are damaged/ broken/ torn or they are not given respect and honour daily. They are neglected/hanging/kept unattended. They are not even cleaned or are neglected. This can be the effect of Pitra Dosha.
- Almost all the family members are independent or do as they please. It is very difficult to touch the feet (charansparsh), ask for forgiveness and forgive. Having an erratic daily routine (staying awake till late at night, sleeping till late in the morning/sleeping during the day).

Causes of Pitra Dosh:

There are many reasons for Pitra Dosh. It is not possible to tell all the reasons here. Here we will tell the main reasons which create Pitra Dosh. If it is already present, it increases it. If it is increased, it makes it complicated and incurable. Hence, this is also a forbidden/prohibited act. At least those with Pitra Dosh should strictly avoid them. The rest of the people should also avoid them as much as possible because if these doshas are done repeatedly for a long time or if they increase in quantity, they create Pitra Dosh. Apart from this, they also gradually spoil the good planets of the horoscope.

- **Insulting respectable people:**
  Insulting or misbehaving with Guru, elders, Brahmins, scholars, sages, religious persons, gentlemen, parents etc.
  Insulting or harming guests, deities, religion, religious places, religious scriptures, religious materials, religious activities, revered trees like Peepal-Banyan, Tulsi etc. and revered rivers like Ganga etc.

- **Killing and torturing living creatures:**
  Killing or torturing cows, dogs, calves, birds, orphans, the downtrodden, the helpless, the handicapped and refugee creatures.

- **Injustice and Exploitation:**
  Injustice, exploitation, adulteration, corruption, fraud, tyranny, wickedness, oppression and suppression of the weak/ decent/ honest/ helpless person or taking advantage of his helplessness.

- **Violation of decorum:**
  Abandoning or violating the path of decorum, justice, traditions, hard work and honesty and adopting wrong methods, adopting politics/conspiracy or unethical methods or condemning these and inciting/motivating others to violate these.

- **Abortion and killing of newborn babies:**
  Causing or causing or inciting abortion.

Torturing or starving or killing or harming a pregnant woman or pregnant female animal.

Killing or torturing/separating a newborn baby (animal/bird/human/creature) from its mother.

Breaking/damaging eggs.

Feeding orphans only on meat.

- **Damage to home and environment:**
Destroying/breaking/occupying the home of any human being/animal or bird.

Destroying nests.

Keeping birds in cages (even for rearing), killing/torturing them etc.

- **Disrespect for food and health:**
Disrespecting food, throwing it away/wasting it/destroying it (burning fields etc.).

Contaminating/infecting food, drinks and medicines or adulterating or counterfeiting them and playing with people's health and life.

Washing dirty hands in the utensils after eating or throwing away the utensils.

- **Disrespecting Sacred Directions:**
Disrespecting sacred directions/sacred places/sacred occasions/sacred times/sacred activities/sacred purposes, sacred spirits or performing unholy/prohibited/forbidden sinful acts in front of them.

- **Damage to vegetation:**
Breaking/damaging vegetation, grass, trees, plants, gardens, forests etc. without any reason.

If these are cut or uprooted for a good purpose, then arrangements should be made so that new trees can grow.

Especially if it becomes necessary to cut/take life-giving trees or medicines like Peepal etc. for a good purpose, then five times more of those medicines/Peepal should be planted and an apology should be sought.

- **Breaking the trust of your dependent:**
  Breaking the trust/cheating of someone who is dependent on you or is under your protection or believes in you or is your devotee/devotee.
  Ignoring/not protecting him/her/sacrificing him/her for your own protection or benefit or using him/her by putting emotional pressure on him/her.

- **Usurping rights and exploitation:**
  Usurping someone's rights, especially those of workers or the helpless/not paying them proper wages.
  Exploiting intellectuals and scholars/usurping their rights/stealing their ideas/themes.
  Theft of knowledge/scriptures/books (obtaining them without paying dakshina/price).
  Taking astrologer's/doctor's advice for free (taking anything for free spoils the planets).

- **Inappropriate receipt of wealth:**
  Accepting wealth for which one has not established one's right by hard work and ability (bribery, brokerage, gambling, theft, lottery, speculation, fraud, interest, shares, found/lying money etc.).
  Or depending only on asking/loan/rent etc., not working hard yourself etc., taking everything for free.

- **Atheism and inhumanity:**
  Atheism, inhumanity, being overly wealthy/selfless, not helping a distressed/destitute/needy person despite being capable of helping or despite being asked for it.
  Not imparting knowledge/learning to a deserving, inquisitive and dedicated seeker of knowledge, despite being knowledgeable, with the intention of maintaining monopoly.

- **Discrimination and Prejudice:**
  Discriminating on the basis of caste/sex/color/status etc. and behaving in a biased manner.

Hurts others by practicing untouchability or embarrasses or humiliates others by making them feel inferior.

Even discriminating on the basis of gender in the upbringing of one's own children is wrong.

Remedies to remove Pitra Dosh:

The most important thing to do in Pitra Dosh remedy is that we do not perform those forbidden/prohibited actions which create and increase Pitra Dosha. We should strictly abstain from these actions and do penance and correction. The last mentioned penance actions are mandatory to be done simultaneously.

If we do not follow these measures, then we will not be able to get complete and permanent benefit just by the measures and tricks given below. If there is a serious Pitra Dosh, then even this much will not be achieved.

- Chant at least one rosary of the mantra "ॐ ग्रां ग्रीं ग्रौं स: गुरुवे नम:" "Om Graam Greem Groum Sah Guruve Namah" daily. For this, sit on a turmeric rosary facing north/east and offer water to the rising sun. Make sure that the water does not fall on your feet nor does it splash on your feet.

- Chant the above mantra at least 5 times every Thursday. For this, sit near a banana tree/in a temple or do it at home by keeping a turmeric lump in your left hand. Later, dedicate that turmeric lump to a banana tree and burn it.

- Chant the above mantra at least 11 times on every Amavasya. For this, keep a turmeric knot and a coin/money in your hand and keep a coconut with husk in front of you. If chanting 11 times is not possible, then perform havan by offering 108 oblations with the above mantra. Mix black sesame seeds and kusha in the havan samagri. Later, keep the turmeric knot under a banana tree. Give the money/coin to a beggar and float the coconut in the river. On your return, feed or donate to a leper.

- During Navaratri and Shraadh Paksha, while observing restraint and purity, one should chant the aforementioned mantra as much as possible, study/swadhyaya of religious scriptures, attend satsang/dharma discussions, perform/get religious rituals done, visit pilgrimage or religious places and offer water to ancestors from an earthen pot in the south direction or do charity in their name. Because these occasions multiply the effect of Pitra Dosh prevention measures.

- On Mauni Amavasya, Pitru Visarjani Amavasya (Somvati Amavasya also has special importance), Amavasya with Bharani Nakshatra, one should chant 21 or 11 rosaries of the mantra 'Om Graam Greem Groum Sah Guruve Namah' and perform a havan of 108 oblations. On this occasion, all the family members should sit and offer oblations in the havan. All the members should keep a lump of turmeric and a coin in their left hand and keep their own coconut with them/in front of them. Later, everyone should offer turmeric to a banana tree. Money should be given to a beggar and each one should float his own coconut in the river. On the way back, feed as many lepers as there are members. Make donations in the name of ancestors. In the morning, mix black sesame seeds in water in an earthen pot in the south and offer it to the ancestors and ask for forgiveness from them.

- If you are suffering a lot, then every Sunday perform a havan at home using mango wood. All the family members should participate in it and offer oblations using the 'Gayatri Mantra'. Offer at least 21 oblations. If this can be done daily, it is even better.

- If the shraddha ceremony of an ancestor has not been performed or his shraddha has not been performed in Gaya etc., then it must be done with respect and soon. But do it with devotion. Go and come only for this work. Stay away from any other work/entertainment/intoxication/sexual intercourse etc. during that time, otherwise you will not get any benefit.

Note: The above remedies definitely start bringing changes/showing auspicious results within a year, yet they should be continued for 5 years. If the defect is serious then do it for life.

Totke and Supportive Measures:

It is best that the above measures should be adopted. Along with this, any one or some of these should be adopted as per the need. But if for some reason all the above measures are not possible, then definitely adopt measures no. 1, 3 and 7 and do these supporting measures and tricks from time to time.

- Serve cow, crow, dog, leper, gentleman/saint/scholar and Guru as much as possible. Adopt a Guru and remain devoted to him.
- Stay completely away from intoxication, meat, slander, criticism and injustice. Do not even have close relations or contact with such people.
- In a family with Pitra Dosh, other members should not sleep in the same room/together except husband and wife.
- Junk, old useless things, dampness, dirt and disorder should not be kept in the house. Dispose of garbage properly.
- In the morning and evening (especially in the evening), burn cow dung cakes in the house and put pure desi camphor, pure guggul, pure frankincense, pure sandalwood powder on it and smoke it. This gradually removes the negativity of the house and the people living in it.

Weekly and yearly remedies:

- Mop the house with salt once a week. All members should bathe in water mixed with salt once a week (afterwards bathe with clean water). Or bathe in Ganga or a flowing river at least once a month. It is better if done on Poornima/Amavasya.
- Planting 5 banana and 5 Peepal trees in a year and taking care of them until they grow a little big/strong gives very good and quick results. If not possible,

then plant at least one tree each every year. If you cannot do even that, then plant them once in your life and keep watering, lighting lamps and worshipping the banana and Peepal trees daily.

- Offering raw milk and black sesame seeds or offering Bel leaves or Dhatura flowers on Shivling also gives benefits. But its full benefit is only when you also do 'meditation' afterwards. Be spiritual/give priority to knowledge and satisfaction.
- Keep a portion of your food for ancestors daily. Ask for forgiveness from your ancestors every day and offer them water in the south direction. Install a drinking water facility/tap etc. in the name of your ancestors or do some charity work and keep dedicating its fruits to your ancestors.
- Once a year collect money/coins from all the family members and go to a pilgrimage site and flow it in a river. Feed the lepers and beggars there and return.
- Once a year, send an elderly person on a pilgrimage (at your own expense). Or take blessings of the elderly by serving them in an old age home. (Obviously, one should not neglect the elderly in one's own home). Serve/help the sick/orphans. Donate medicines
- Doing shramdaan at religious places or renovating temples etc. or donating to cow shelters or orphanages, giving food to hungry creatures and water to the thirsty (humans or animals or birds) also gives very good results.
- Incidentally, let us tell you that if any human/animal/bird comes to the front of a house/courtyard, on the roof/gate to rest/take shelter (even if only for a short time), the good fortune of the people of that house increases. They should not be chased away/removed/rebuked/forbade.
- Every third month/every sixth month/at least once a year, some religious event/ritual etc. (Satyanarayan ki Katha/Sundarkand Paath/Akhand Ramayan Paath/Jagran/Bhajan-Sandhya/Kirtan/Yagna etc.) should be organized in the house, in which others should also be invited.
- Efforts should be made to have more/frequent guests in the house. Until they start coming, a religious/ascetic/learned Brahmin/Guru/Sadhu should

be fed every week. It is best that at least one outsider should eat at home every day.

- Every Saturday, one should throw a coin (lead) in a dirty drain, feed a buffalo with lotus or offer water to the Peepal tree growing in the cremation ground and give food, money or clothes to a sweeper. (If the pain is more, then offer water to the Peepal tree in the cremation ground for the first 45 days continuously, then keep offering every Saturday.)
- Burying silver under the threshold of the main door of the house and entering the house by crossing that part is also a good solution - if the whole house / family is affected by Pitra Dosha. Also, keep a clean Toran of yellow cloth tied on the main door.
- Usually in families affected by Pitra Dosha or when bad luck / negativity increases, the trees and plants planted in the house, especially Tulsi and Aak, dry up / fall / get spoiled. They do not survive even after being planted again and again. But somehow they should be made to flourish by making efforts, taking full care and maintaining purity. If Tulsi or Aak grows and starts increasing in such a family, then relief, auspiciousness and protection are attained soon.
- Take blessings from a Hijra on Wednesday and offer yellow flowers/laddu/yellow cloth to Guru on Thursday. On Wednesday feed fodder to a goat or spinach to a cow or free birds. Use only good utensils. Do not use broken/torn/crooked/damaged or triangular/square/crooked shaped utensils.

Penance:

By atonement, by removing the guilt from the mind, satisfaction and peace are attained and the punishment is also reduced. Therefore, as a measure and prevention, along with staying away from the prohibited acts mentioned in the beginning, at least one of the following atonement acts must be performed. This is very important.

- Clean the shoes of devotees or mop the stairs and floor of the temple (at least once a week on Saturday).
- Do Shramdaan for charity at a religious place. As far as possible, donate food/money/clothes etc. along

with Shramdaan (once a month is a must, if possible do it every week).

- Teach an orphan/ needy/ poor/ curious person for free. Or bear the responsibility of his education/ food expenses for at least one year. Or donate educational material.
- Serve any one category of plants/ animals/ lepers/ patients/ handicapped/ orphans/ displaced/ abandoned people with body, mind, money and words throughout your life.
- Bear the expenses of arranging for the cremation of unclaimed dead bodies (human/animal).

Special:

When the Pitra Dosh is very big or the misfortune is more, then even the animal desired for the totka is not found. If it is found, then on the day it is to be fed, it will not be found easily. If it is found, it will not eat, it will sniff and leave. If there is a complex Pitra Dosha or the planet is very angry, then far from accepting food, it tries to attack/grow/bite/push even if it comes near it. Even then, by not getting disheartened and trying again and again with devotion, success is achieved.

Actually, these are a kind of previous symptoms/omens. If the problem related to the planet is not relieved soon (the planet is very angry), then the animal/creature related to it does not accept the donation, or is not found at all, or shows displeasure. But if it accepts peacefully or shows love or is found easily (comes on its own), then it is an auspicious sign. It means that the troubles related to that planet will be removed soon.

It is also not true that if your luck is not changing soon or good times are not coming, then you do not get remedies. You are not able to meet an astrologer or a doctor (if you meet him, he is not suitable). Even if you meet him and get remedies, you are not able to start it due to some reason or the other. Even if you start, you are not able to continue. Either you leave it yourself or you leave it due to some reason or the other. Or there are repeated obstacles. Many times the planet scares you by giving negative results in the beginning, due to which you get scared/believe the remedy to be bad and leave it yourself. Because if you do the remedy, then the planet will have to become good. Whereas it does not want to become good without punishing the previous sins of the doer. That is why it creates obstacles.

Keep giving 5 flour cakes with a pinch of turmeric to a cow on Thursdays and Saturdays. Give millet to birds or soaked green gram to pigeons every day.

All this information has been provided so that you do not remain in any confusion and do not have any misunderstanding or doubt about the remedies. Also, you do not get discouraged or troubled by the symptoms that occur. Also, you can understand that for improvement, it is necessary for the doer to do the remedies correctly, continuously, for the specified period with determination.

If you leave it in the middle, or do it irregularly, or do it in a hurry, half-heartedly or in a makeshift manner, then you will not get any benefit. Your hard work will go in vain. Later you will have no faith in astrology/remedies, while the mistake will be yours. Therefore, without getting discouraged, it is necessary to do any remedy continuously/regularly for the specified period with faith, devotion, concentration, emotion and patience.

Kaal Sarp Dosh and its Remedy: Basis and Definition

Does Kaal Sarp Dosh Really Exist?

The existence of **Kaal Sarp Dosh** (or **Kaal Sarp Yoga**) is often debated, but it's more important to understand its effects rather than focus on its existence. Once you understand how this yoga affects a horoscope, its significance becomes clear.

What is Kaal Sarp Dosh?

Kaal Sarp Dosh occurs when **all the planets** in a person's horoscope are located **between Rahu and Ketu**. Rahu and Ketu are considered shadow planets in astrology, meaning they don't have a physical existence but are points where the Sun and Moon intersect. Rahu and Ketu are always **180 degrees apart**, moving in opposite directions.

- **Rahu and Ketu** affect the **5th, 7th and 9th houses** in the horoscope, influencing a large part of the chart.
- If even **one planet** is outside the boundary between Rahu and Ketu, then this yoga is not formed.

Rahu and Ketu:

- **Rahu** is related to material desires, obsession and challenges.
- **Ketu** represents spirituality, detachment and unfulfilled desires.
- Together, they impact a person's psychological and karmic life journey.

Effects of Kaal Sarp Dosh:

1. **Imbalance in the Horoscope:**
   - When all planets are confined between Rahu and Ketu, the chart becomes unbalanced, affecting half of the houses in the horoscope. This causes problems in various life areas, such as career, relationships and health.
2. **Weak Planets:**

- Planets in this restricted zone are less likely to be in their **own signs**, **exalted positions**, or **mool trikona** (most powerful placements). This weakens their positive influence, making it harder for them to work at their best.

3. **Limited Positive Influence:**
   - With planets trapped between Rahu and Ketu, their potential to bring success, happiness and good results is reduced. This often leads to delays, struggles, or a sense of things not working out.

4. **Disruptive Influence:**
   - The confinement of planets causes disruption in the overall energy flow of the horoscope, making it hard for the individual to achieve harmony and success in life. People with Kaal Sarp Dosh may feel stuck, as if something is holding them back.

5. **Psychological Impact:**
   - Rahu's desire for material success conflicts with Ketu's detachment. This internal struggle can lead to emotional and mental confusion, making it difficult to align personal goals with spiritual or emotional needs.

Why Kaal Sarp Dosh is Problematic:

The **Kaal Sarp Yoga** causes a **weak** and **imbalanced horoscope**. When planets are confined to only one part of the chart, they cannot function in their natural, strong positions. This makes the individual's life challenging and creates obstacles in career, relationships and personal growth.

Why is Kaal Sarp Yog Formed?

Kaal Sarp Yog is believed to form in a person's horoscope as a result of bad deeds or negative actions performed in previous lifetimes. These actions are thought to cause karmic consequences that manifest in this life as Kaal Sarp Yog. Some of the reasons for this formation include:

1. **Killing or torturing animals**, particularly snakes and dogs.

2. **Harming children or vulnerable people**.
3. **Exploiting or taking advantage of others**.
4. **Damaging someone's property**, such as burning a house or destroying a farm.
5. **Causing or performing abortions**.
6. **Committing serious crimes**, including murder or rape.
7. **Damaging religious or sacred places**.
8. **Hunting animals** unnecessarily.
9. **Betraying or abusing someone's trust**.

These actions are believed to create negative karmic imprints that lead to the formation of Kaal Sarp Yog in the individual's chart, influencing their life in various challenging ways.

Is Shanti of Kaal Sarp Yog Necessary?

While **Kaal Sarp Yog** is an important astrological factor, sometimes people without this yoga in their horoscope may still experience its effects. This can often be seen in palmistry, where an experienced palmist may detect a **snake-like line** cutting through the **Bhagya Rekha** (Line of Destiny). In such cases, it is believed that the person may still be affected by the negative karmas from past lives.

Thus, whether or not Kaal Sarp Yog is present in the horoscope, if a person feels its negative influence, it is advisable to perform **Shanti** (a peace-giving remedy). If Kaal Sarp Yog is present, then Shanti should definitely be done.

When to Perform Shanti of Kaal Sarp Yog?

The best time to perform Shanti for **Kaal Sarp Yog** is based on the movement of **Rahu and Ketu**. These two planets complete a full revolution in **18 years**. Some important points to consider:

1. **Within 9 years of birth** is the ideal time for Kaal Sarp Shanti. This is when the influence of Rahu-Ketu is most malefic and the remedy is most effective.
2. Performing it **before 18 years** is very beneficial.
3. Performing it **until 27 years** is moderately beneficial.
4. Performing it **until 36 years** is still helpful.

5. Performing it **until 45 years** mainly offers peace of mind, but the adverse effects may already have taken root.
6. **After 45 years**, it is less effective because by this time, the individual's habits are fully formed and they may have already experienced the full impact of the adverse effects of Kaal Sarp Yog.

Dasha/Antar Dasha/Pratyantar Dasha of Rahu-Ketu are also powerful times to perform Shanti. These periods amplify the effects of Rahu and Ketu and performing remedies during these phases is particularly potent.

How to Reduce the Impact of Kaal Sarp Yog?

While performing **Shanti Puja** or **Anushthan** (rituals) is effective, there are other ways to make Rahu and Ketu less malefic:

1. **Avoid negative behaviors** like anger, immorality, injustice and indiscipline.
2. **Focus on self-improvement**, including self-study, maintaining good company and engaging in religious and pious activities.
3. **Perform your duties sincerely and responsibly**, following ethical values and honesty.
4. **Maintain a balanced lifestyle**, including a healthy diet, proper sleep and exercise.
5. **Cultivate virtues** like generosity, gentleness, kindness, forgiveness and contentment.

By practicing these behaviors, the influence of Rahu and Ketu gradually becomes more positive, regardless of the presence of Kaal Sarp Yog or adverse Dasha/Transit periods. The positive actions help to make Rahu and Ketu more harmonious, reducing the overall impact of any negative influences.

Prohibited Actions for Rahu and Ketu:

Rahu and Ketu, being powerful and deceptive planets in astrology, can cause confusion, wrong decisions and bad karma when their energy is misaligned. To avoid angering them and making Kaal Sarp Yog more harmful, it is important to refrain from certain actions that displeases them.

Negative Habits to Avoid:

1. **Bad Behavioral Traits:**
   - Intoxication, impatience, greed, stubbornness, pride, arrogance, jealousy, vengeance, over-ambition, anger, bad company, carelessness and overconfidence.
2. **Unethical and Immoral Actions:**
   - Atheism, superstition, injustice, exploitation, taking advantage of the helpless and corruption.
   - Engaging in crimes such as theft, cheating, bribery, gambling and consuming meat and alcohol.
   - Slander, criticism, finding faults and unnecessary debates.
   - Harming or abusing children, orphans, vulnerable people, or animals (especially dogs, cows, cats, snakes).
3. **Disrespecting Sacred Entities:**
   - Disrespecting saints, scholars, Brahmins, elders, gods, or religious beliefs.
   - Damaging sacred places, or mistreating others based on caste, religion, or status.
4. **Home-related Guidelines:**
   - Keep the **north-east** direction of your home clean.
   - Dispose of garbage properly and avoid making decisions in areas like **stairs**, **crossroads**, **toilets**, **dirty places**, or near **swamps**, **crematoriums**, **graveyards** and **dustbins**.
   - Avoid making important decisions when angry, greedy, or intoxicated and try to avoid decisions after sunset.
5. **Stay Away from Malpractices:**
   - Avoid politics, deceit, theft, fraud, gambling and dishonest practices like bribes, lotteries and shares.
   - Refrain from fights, lying, gossiping, taunting, or spreading falsehoods.

6. **Specific Prohibited Actions:**
    - Do not eat salt in a **girl's in-laws' house**, avoid **smoking tobacco** and maintain good relations with **in-laws**.
    - Avoid insulting a **handicapped person** or a **saint** and do not engage with a **bald** or **black** person.
    - Do not buy property from a **childless person** or live in a house facing **south** or with **Vastu defects**.
    - Avoid wearing **blue/black clothes**, or engaging in excessive **Vata-enhancing foods**.
    - Ensure your house does not have a **toilet** in the **north-east** or keep **empty utensils**.

These actions are believed to worsen the effects of **Kaal Sarp Yog** and bring misfortune in various aspects of life, such as luck, health, career and relationships.

Puja and Ritual Remedies:

A **Kaal Sarp Yog Puja** is an effective but costly way to mitigate the negative effects of this yoga. It requires **seven scholars** and takes **7 hours** to perform, so it is not something one can do alone. The puja is typically done in temples like **Mahakaleshwar** (Ujjain, Nashik, etc.) and group pujas are also held on special days such as **Nag Panchami** or **Maha Shivratri**. While group pujas are less effective, they are a more affordable option for those with limited resources.

Lal Kitab Totka:

For those who cannot afford the elaborate puja, a simpler and cheaper remedy is the **Lal Kitab Totka**, which is quick and highly effective if performed correctly and with devotion. However, it is important to note that people who are reluctant to do the puja or remedy out of stinginess often do not experience the full benefits of this totka.

Method:

1. Perform this totka on **Surya Sankranti**, the day when the Sun changes its zodiac sign. You can find the exact date and time from the **Panchang** or a **temple priest**. If the individual is in the **Rahu/Ketu Dasha**, it's even more effective.
2. **Prepare semolina halwa** in **desi ghee** and place it in a **brass plate** with high edges to cool.
3. Once the halwa solidifies, **place a big bowl upside down** in the middle and press it gently. This will create a well-like shape in the middle of the halwa.
4. **Fill the well with melted ghee** and place a **pair of silver Naag-Nagin (snake figures)** and one or more **coins** inside.
5. The person whose horoscope has **Kaal Sarp Yog** should look into the well filled with ghee and concentrate on their **reflection**. They should focus on every part of their face, deeply and with sincerity.
6. Afterward, cover the plate with a **clean newspaper** and take it along with some **clothes** and **dakshina** to a **priest** (preferably aged **50-55 years**).
7. After returning, bow to **Lord Shiva** and consume the halwa as **prasad** (sacred food offered to deities).

Effectiveness and Timing:

- **One-time performance** is usually enough, especially when done before the age of 9 years.
- If done at an older age, the benefits might be less certain, but it can still be performed again when needed.

By performing this **totka** with devotion, you can start to see positive changes in behavior and the reduction of the effects of **Kaal Sarp Yog**. This remedy is a good, affordable option for those who cannot afford the full puja.

Remedies for Kaal Sarp Yog:

To alleviate the negative effects of **Kaal Sarp Yog**, there are various remedies using **gems, herbs, mantras** and rituals. Here are some effective ways to reduce its impact:

Gems and Metals:

1. **Snake-shaped Ring:**
   - Wear a **snake-shaped ring** made of **copper**, **bronze**, or **ashtadhatu** (an alloy of several metals) on the middle finger of the **right hand**.
   - Before wearing it, purify the ring, chant "ॐ नमः शिवाय" **(Om Namah Shivaya)** 11 times and wear it on auspicious days like **Mahashivratri, Nagpanchami,** or **Sankranti**.
2. **Gomed (Hessonite) and Cat's Eye Locket:**
   - Take a locket made of **copper**, **bronze**, or **panchdhatu** (five metals), with equal weights of **Gomed** and **Cat's Eye**.
   - Tie it with a **black thread** and wear it on **Mahashivratri, Nagpanchami,** or **Navratri** after purifying it and chanting "ॐ नमः शिवाय" 11 times or "ॐ ऐं ह्रीं क्लीं चामुण्डायै विच्चै" 1008 times.
   - **Note:** After three years, dispose of the old ring/locket in water and replace it with a new one, purified and consecrated in the same way.
3. **Silver Navratna Swastika:**
   - Wear a **silver Navratna Swastika** around your neck on a **silver chain**.
   - Additionally, **Sarpagandha** or **Ashwagandha root** can be worn on the arm using a **black or red thread** (replace these every 2-3 months).

Mantras and Rituals:

1. **Daily Mantra Chanting:**
   - Chant "ॐ नमः शिवाय" (Om Namah Shivaya) mantra **5 rounds** daily on a **Rudraksha rosary**.
   - Alternatively, chant **Mrityunjaya Mantra** daily and offer water to the **Shivling**.
   - Offer **milk on Monday, honey on Tuesday, Gangajal on Wednesday, ghee on Thursday, curd on Friday, black sesame seeds on Saturday** and **Belpatra on Sunday**.

2. **Shiv Tandav Stotra and Rudrashtakshari:**
    - Recite **Shiv Tandav Stotra** (written by Ravana) and **Rudrashtakshari** (written by Tulsi) once every morning and evening.
    - Alternatively, chant **Gayatri Mantra** 108 times at sunrise and offer water to the Sun, followed by **Adityahridaya Stotra**.
3. **Nilsaraswati and Sankatnashak Ganpati Stotra:**
    - Recite **Nilsaraswati Stotra** once and **Sankatnashak Ganpati Stotra** 21 times daily.
    - If unable to recite daily, you can recite **four times in all three evenings** or **write** the stotra and give it to **8 Brahmins** or needy people every month.
4. **Peepal Tree Remedy:**
    - Take **a pair of moon snakes, 5 Tulsi leaves, 3 pairs of whole cloves** and **4 black peppers** on a **Peepal leaf** and bury them **one foot below the main door** of your house on the day of **eclipse/Sankranti**. This remedy helps with **Vastu Dosha, Pitru Dosha** and **Kaal Sarp Dosha**.

Physical Remedies:

1. **Wear Crown and Saffron Tilak:**
    - Wearing a **crown** on your head and getting **ears pierced** can enhance positive energy.
    - Apply **saffron** and **white sandalwood tilak** daily.
    - Wear a **white sandalwood locket** or a **square piece of moon** around your neck.
    - Observe **silence for two hours daily** and **one day a week** for spiritual benefits.
2. **Bath in Flowing River:**
    - Bathe in a **flowing river** (preferably the **Ganga**) on **Amavasya** or **Purnima** and recite **"Hanuman Bahuk"** daily.

Behavioral Remedies:

1. **Serve Parents and Guru:**

- o **Serving your parents and Guru** is essential to mitigate the bad effects of Rahu, Ketu and Saturn. This brings peace, happiness and stability in life.

2. **Exercise Regularly:**
   - o **Regular exercise/running** helps expel excess energy, keeping both body and mind healthy and reduces Rahu's disruptive influence.

3. **Avoid Debt:**
   - o People with Kaal Sarp Yog should avoid **lending money** and **taking loans** as it can cause financial troubles and further distress in life.

4. **Remedies for Saturday and Tuesday:**
   - o **Throw a lead coin** in the **drain** every **Saturday**.
   - o **Donate a flag** at a **Durga temple** every **Tuesday** to bring prosperity and happiness.

5. **Beans and Flour Mill:**
   - o Keep **beans** and a **small stone flour mill** in your house. This remedy helps in promoting happiness and peace.

6. **Avoid Anger:**
   - o If **Rahu** is placed in the **1st, 2nd, 4th, 6th, 7th, or 9th houses**, **anger** should be avoided as it exacerbates problems.

7. **Make Rahu Positive:**
   - o **Make Rahu positive** and strengthen **Jupiter** to bring stability, prosperity and happiness into your life.

Switchwords: A Guide to Manifesting Wealth, Health and Success

Switchwords are simple, powerful words that can influence your subconscious mind and help you manifest your desires. They work by activating specific energies in your mind and body to achieve your goals. This book provides a comprehensive list of switchwords, their meanings and how to use them effectively.

Wealth and Prosperity

Core Switchwords for Wealth

- **COUNT**: The essence of all money-making activities. Chanting "COUNT" helps you attract money and financial growth.
- **FIND**: To build a fortune and attract valuable things, including money and opportunities.
- **TOGETHER-COUNT**: A combination to harmoniously attract financial prosperity.
- **TOGETHER-FIND**: For collaborative wealth-building and ethical financial success.
- **DIVINE-COUNT**: To request financial miracles and extraordinary results.
- **TOGETHER-DIVINE-COUNT**: Ideal for groups or companies to achieve financial success.

Additional Combinations for Financial Miracles

- **TOGETHER-DIVINE-ORDER-COUNT**: Useful for cleaning up financial messes or starting a new venture.
- **FINDIVINE**: A combination for discovering unexpected financial opportunities.
- **FINDIVINEORDERCOUNT**: Brings miraculous fortune, optimal order and financial gain.
- **CANCEL**: To eliminate debts or financial worries.
- **MAGNANIMITY**: Encourages generosity, which leads to greater prosperity.
- **SCHEME**: To advertise or design successful financial strategies.
- **SPEND**: To dress better and project affluence.

- **BRING COUNT ON**: Removes blocks to payment or financial flow.

Health and Wellness

Core Switchwords for Physical Health

- **CHANGE**: Dispels aches and pains in the body.
- **CLEAR**: Removes anger, promoting emotional and physical well-being.
- **SWIVEL**: Relieves irregularities in the body, including constipation and digestive issues.
- **GUARD**: Enhances personal safety and health protection.
- **LEARN**: Promotes youthful appearance and vitality.

For Emotional and Mental Health

- **QUIET**: Soothes selfishness and promotes peace of mind.
- **BLUFF**: Dispels conscious fear and nervousness.
- **UP**: Lifts the mood and removes feelings of inferiority.
- **BE**: Maintains good health and inner peace.

Success and Achievement

Core Switchwords for Success

- **TOGETHER**: The master switchword to align energies for any activity or goal.
- **ACT**: Develops oratory skills and public speaking confidence.
- **DONE**: Helps meet deadlines and build willpower.
- **ADJUST**: Balances life and handles unpleasant experiences effectively.
- **ELATE**: Turns setbacks into uplifting outcomes.
- **FIGHT**: Increases competitiveness and ensures victory in challenges.
- **GIVE**: Enhances selling abilities and creates success in transactions.
- **NEXT**: Boosts efficiency and completes detailed work.
- **ON**: Stimulates creative ideas and ambition.

Advanced Combinations for Success

- **TOGETHER-DIVINE-GIVE-COUNT**: Drives extraordinary results in sales and teamwork.
- **TOGETHER-DIVINE-ORDER-CANCEL**: Resolves financial disputes and eliminates poverty.

Relationships and Emotional Well-Being

Switchwords for Harmony and Love

- **TOGETHER-DIVINE-LOVE**: Strengthens bonds and resolves conflicts in relationships.
- **THANKS**: Releases past regrets and cultivates gratitude.
- **SWEET**: Makes interactions soothing and pleasant.
- **CHUCKLE**: Enhances personality and spreads joy.
- **CIRCULATE**: Eliminates loneliness and attracts new relationships.
- **HOLE**: Enhances attraction and charm.
- **HOLD**: Builds character and creates emotional stability.

Practical Applications

How to Use Switchwords

1. **Chanting**: Repeat the switchwords silently or aloud in a rhythmic manner. For example, chant "TOGETHER-COUNT" 28 times daily to manifest wealth.
2. **Writing**: Write down the switchwords in your journal or on a piece of paper and keep it in a visible place.
3. **Visualization**: Imagine achieving your desired goal while chanting the corresponding switchword.
4. **Affirmations**: Use switchwords in your daily affirmations to amplify their effects.

Comprehensive Alphabetical List of Switchwords

- **ACT**: Develop public speaking skills.
- **ADD**: To calculate percentages or attract financial growth.

- **ADJUST**: Balance life and handle discomfort.
- **AROUND**: Gain perspective and clarity.
- **ATTENTION**: Avoid carelessness.
- **BE**: Maintain health and achieve inner peace.
- **BLUFF**: Dispels fear and nervousness.
- **CANCEL**: Eliminates negativity and debts.
- **COUNT**: Attracts money and financial opportunities.
- **DIVINE**: Calls forth miraculous outcomes.
- **DONE**: Completes tasks and builds determination.
- **FIND**: Builds fortunes and attracts opportunities.
- **QUIET**: Promotes inner peace.
- **REACH**: Finds lost items and solutions.
- **TOGETHER**: Aligns energies for any goal.

Switchwords for Unique Situations

For Eliminating Debt

- **TOGETHER-DIVINE-CANCEL**: Resolves financial burdens for groups and individuals.
- **CANCEL**: Clears debts and unwanted financial commitments.

For Boosting Sales

- **DIVINE-GIVE**: Ensures miraculous sales results.
- **TOGETHER-DIVINE-GIVE**: Elevates team sales performance.

For Emotional Healing

- **SHUT**: Stops complaining and fosters calmness.
- **RESTORE**: Reestablishes fairness and honesty in relationships.

Switchwords are simple yet powerful tools to transform your life. Use them consistently and intentionally to unlock their full potential. With regular practice, you can achieve financial prosperity, emotional well-being and success in all areas of your life

Vedic Switchword

What are Vedic switch words?

Vedic Switch words are also words, these are seed-Beej mantras which are related to Gods from our Vedas, Puranas, Mahabharat, Ramayan. These too when used with full faith and belief give us positive results. They are very sacred and powerful mantras. These are tested mantras.

It can be a single word, phrases or in the form of verses. These words have some vibrations so when we chant or speak them repetitively, they create a positive vibration in our subconscious mind and when done regularly it gets programmed, fixed in our mind and help us to get the desired positive results for the purpose/issue we are working for.
Vedic Switch words are also called Chhu-mantar words. These Vedic Switch words (V SW) are a unique collection of tested and powerful Sanatan Mantras.

How do they help?

Vedic switch words help you in every field of your life where you are looking for solutions Or results like
1. Health
2. Wealth/Money
3. Prosperity
4. Abundance
5. Obstacles in our work/life/relationships.
6. Relationship
7. Job/Career/Business
8. Any type of addiction
9. Diseases
10. Weight Loss / Weight Gain
11. Beauty Related
12. Hairloss or hair fall
13. Any type of Fear
14. Evil eye
15. Black Magic

16. For kids – in their Exams, Career
17. Focus, Concentration
18. Communication
19. To balance 7 Chakras
20. Wish Fulfilment
21. Manifestation

How do Vedic Switch words work?

Vedic switch words need to be installed first before using them. Installations means getting connected to these mantras or phrases. When you get connected to a particular word it enters into your energy field and works faster and gives you the desired results.

All these Vedic Switch words are very sacred and powerful. So, for these Vedic Switch words to work for you, you need to have full faith and belief before you start to use them.

Vedic Switch words can be used by anyone-no caste, creed or religion.

Installation Process:

- Write once.
- Chant 3 times
- Do this 108 times.

You can use Red or Blue ink

You have to follow the above process of installation they way it is explained.

1. There is no specific time to install these switch words.
2. Just be relaxed and find a silent place while you are installing these V SW.
3. You have to install these Vedic Switch words (V SW) in one go - means u should not get up till u finish installing one switch words i.e. Chant one. write 3 times, like this 108 times need to write.

4. There is no need to install all the switch words in one day. You can do it as per your convenience and whenever you wish to use them. Only thing to remember is before using any Vedic Switch word you need to install it first. This will make you connected with the switch word and will give you better results.

5. There are no side effects of these switch words(mantras). These are sacred mantras so should not be used for fun purposes.

6. You can use as many switch words you wish to use at one time.

7. You can even use multiple switch words or even combine the switch words and use. Be clear and specific in intention while using them.

8. You can even use multiple SW for a single purpose/issue. The thing to remember is those switch words should be installed before using.

9. You can even chant Switch words for others. For this you need their permission. This is called PROXY CHANTING. Only exception is that the parents can chant for their children without permission.

10. As these switch words are very sacred and Sanskrit words -women during periods, people after drinking alcohol or after eating non-veg should not use these switch words in any form.

11. You can chant this anytime -no time restrictions.

12. You may even write these V SW.

Some Do's and Don'ts

- These Vedic Switch words should not be written on body parts during monthly periods. U can chant.
- These SW can be installed only after 3 during monthly periods.
- These switch words should not be written on your private body parts.
- These switch words should not be written on the lower body parts-below the waist line.

- Your clients, friends, family members need not install these switch words before using. Once you have installed them they can use your energy.
- Only when you teach the whole course to anyone then that person has to install all these switch words before using them.

Rules of Writing Vedic Switch words and How to use them.

1. You can write these switch words on the left side of the body but not on the lower part of the body.
2. You can even write these SW on a paper or notebook.
3. You can even stick it on your water bottle, coffee /tea mug or on the wall.
4. You can even chant these V SW over water and drink the water.
5. You can even chant these V SW over water and sprinkle the water in the place where you feel negativity (this method can be used when the V SW is for negativity removal or black magic removal.)
6. You can use the above method (point 5) when the V SW is for the health purpose for your kids or when its not possible for the person to drink this charged water.
7. You can even use it as a coaster.
8. You can make them as your password.
9. For kids you can write this V SW on a paper and keep it under their pillow, mattress. You can even stick it on their study table, their book shelf.
10. If at times it is not possible to write with a pen you can even write it with your ring finger on the left side of the upper body part.
11. You can even make an Energy Circle (EC) and get it laminated and can use it to charge your liquids, food, medicines with these Vedic Switch words to work for you.

Switch words Connected to Gods

1.   Tan (टन)

Connection - Lord Brahma

Uses

- Female Problems (Reproductive organs, Uterus issues, monthly periods)
- Neurological Problems (Paralysis, Parkinson)
- Any physical Pain (write with black ink on that part)
- Endocrine system
- Epilepsy
- Boost immune system (cold, cough)
- Migraine (Write at the back of the neck -3 times)
- Stomach ache (write with ring finger -11 times)

2.   GAM (गम)

Connection - Ganapathi (Vighnaharta)

Uses

- Invisible Fear
- Sudden Obstacle
- Bad Dream
- Sudden dispute in relation
- Pending work

3.   Shreem (श्रीं)

Connection - Mahalakshmi

Uses

Any type of Money Issues

- Blocked Money
- Money problem
- Money Gain
- Lended Money
- Livelihood

4.   Kreem (क्रीं)

Connection - Goddess Kali

Uses

- Protection
- Black Magic

- Grief
- Evil Eye
- Spiritual Issue

(You can even write and put on your house's main door for protection.)

5.   Hroum (ह्रौं)
Connection - Lord Shiva
Uses
- Incurable Disease
- Chronic Disease
- Death like situation-when a person is not able to leave the body - to get Release.
- To cut the Karma
- Moksha

6.   DAM (दं)
Connection - Lord Vishnu
 Uses
- Health
- Wealth
- Success
- Prosperity
- Victory

7.   Ayeim (ऐं)
Connection - Goddess Saraswathi
Uses
- Education
- Knowledge
- Concentration
- Wisdom
- Music
- Slow Learners, Late Speech
- Stammering

8.   OM (ॐ)
Connection - Brahma/Vishnu/Mahesh
Uses

- All in One
- Peace
- Spiritual
- Soul Searching

9. Hreem (ह्रीं)

Connection - Mata Bhuvaneshwari

Uses

- Illusion
- Dispeller of Sorrow

10. Fraum (फ्रौम)

Connection - Lord Hanuman (Can write no-58)

Uses

- Protection
- Strength
- Bad Spirit
- Fear

11. Bhram (भ्राम)

Connection – Bhairav

Uses

- Strength
- Protection
- Victory
- Health

12. Dhoom (धूं)

Connection – Dhoomavati

Uses

- Enemies
- Strength
- Fortune
- Protection

13. Hleem (ह्लीं)

Connection – Bagulamukhi

Uses

- Elimination of all Enemies

- Power
- Victory
- Fame

14. Dhham (धम)

Connection - Kuber

Uses

- Wealth
- Monetary Gain
- Fortune
- Success

15. Treem (त्रीम)

Connection - Goddess TARA

Uses

- Financial Gain
- Fortune
- Fame
- Unlimited Wealth
- Happiness

Switch words Related to Chakras

1. **Lam (लाम्)**

Connection - Root Chakra

Uses

- Security
- Survival (Lack in Basic needs)
- Basic needs (Food, Sleep, Shelter)
- Self Identity
- Safety

2. **Vam(वाम्)**

Connection - Sacral Chakra

Uses

- Feeling
- Sensual Pleasure (both Men/Women}
- Expression of Sexuality
- Creativity
- Conception (Issues related to Reproduction)

3. **Ram (राम्)**

Connection - Solar Plexus

Uses

- Decision Power
- Will Power
- Responsibility
- Self Confidence

4. **Yam (यं)**

Connection - Heart Chakra

Uses

- Fear of Betrayal
- Jealousy
- Selfishness
- Hatred

5.   Ham (हं)

Connection - Throat Chakra

Uses

- Communication
- Expression (can't express, shyness, stammering)
- Fear
- Throat (Any type of Throat related issues)
- Thyroid
- Tonsillitis
- Cough, Cold

6.   Ksham (Earth Element) (क्षं)

Connection - Earth elements

Uses

- Eating Disorder
- Gynecological Disorder
- Irritable Bowel Syndrome
- Gastritis

Switch words Connected with Gods

1. Swaha (Wife of Agni) (स्वाहा)

Connection - Mahesh Mahadev

Uses

- To end the Problem
- To end Disease
- To end negativity/thoughts
- To cut the cord
- To end any unchanged Patterns

2. Varun (वरूण)

Connection - Varun

Uses

- Loo Lagna (To cool the body)
- Defame
- Dehydration

3. Saraswati (सरस्वती)

Connection - Saraswathi

Uses

- Knowledge
- Wisdom
- Music
- Aim

4. Ashwina (अश्विना) (Ashwini Kumar-Surya Putra) Called as Doctor

Connection - Ashwini Kumar

Uses

- All in one Doctor
- To get right Doctor and right Healing

When you are not getting any right doctor or proper treatment, to know the right diagnoses, right medicine.

5. Indra (इंद्र)

Connection - Indra

Uses

- Money

- Wealth.
- Prosperity
- Material Bliss

6. Vaayu (वायु)

Connection - Vayu Dev

Uses

- Breathing Problems (Asthma, Lung Issue)
- Communication
- Telepathy
- Grief-Want to come out of it.

7. Soma (सोम)

Connection - Som Ras

Uses

- Insomnia
- Tiredness-You are not getting sleep
- Distress
- Relax (Relaxed Sleep)

8. Agnay (आग्नेय)

Connection - Agni Dev

Uses

- Purification (when you need to do purification of something)
- Energy
- To consume negative habits, Black magic, disease.

Wherever there is negativity, for purification we need Agni.

Switch words Connected with Mahabharat

1. Divya Drishti (दिव्य दृष्टि)

Connection - Bhagwan Vasudev

Uses

- To develop intuition (When you feel you lack intuition)
- To develop Accuracy (Related to predictions)
- To develop your Psychic Power.

2. Akshay Patra (अक्षय पात्र)

Connection - Shri Krishna

Uses

- Annapurna
- Prosperity
- Abundance
- Richness
- Food Gain

Tip - When there is a party at your place suddenly increase in guests and u feel food is not enough-chant Akshay Patra.

3. Kavach Kundal (कवच कुंडल)

Connection - Surya Dev

Uses

- Divine Protection
- Protection from solar and lunar eclipse
- Protection from all psychic attack
- Rahu Ketu Kaal
- Mental protection

Even for kids when you want protection for them.

4. Shri Krishna (श्री कृष्ण)

Connection - Shri Krishna

Uses

- To attract
- Sudden Crisis
- Flickering Mind
- Lack of Focus
- Help in spiritual Growth

- Love and Romance (when you feel lack of love and Romance in married Life)

5. Brahmastra (ब्रह्मास्त्र)

Very powerful Switch word

Connection - Brahma ji

Uses

- Use only when it is most necessary
- It gives Positive or Negative results
- It never goes Empty

Please Note - This switch word is very powerful. Should not be given to anyone. Only the person who installs can use this switch word. This definitely gives you the result-result can be positive or negative. When you are ready to face and accept the results/effects only then use this.

6. Surya Dev (सूर्य देव)

Connection - Lord Suryah

Uses

- Medical problems. Medical emergencies
- To make possible any medical impossibilities
- For getting pregnant (when finding difficult in conceiving)

7. Gandiv (गांडीव)

Connection - Arjun/Agni Dev

Uses

- To get victory-to win any competition, sports/exams
- To defeat enemies
- To remove obstacles
- For court cases, office politics.

8. Indrajaal (इंद्रजाल)

Connection - Indra Dev

Uses

- To create temporary illusion
- To create any manipulation
- To hide things Temporarily

Switch words Connected to Shiv Puran

1. **Sapta Ganga (सप्तगंगा)**

Uses

- To purify land
- To enhance the effect of any work
- To ease the release of soul
- To evoke before doing switch words

When you do something auspicious use this switch word
You can take any tap water and chat this switch word over it
with full faith and belief, this can become as Gangajal. You can
use this if you don't have Gangajal with you.

2. **Panchamrit (पंचामृत)**

Connection - Five Elements
(Milk, Curd, Ghee, Honey, Sugar)
Uses

- To protect from Psychic attack
- To heal Food poisoning
- To increase the effect of Medicine.
- To balance Tridosh (Vatta, Pitta, kappa)

3. **Saptachiranjeevi (सप्तचिरंजीवी)**

Uses

- Long life
- Chronic Diseases
- To gain willpower during disease
- To remove all diseases.
- Health

4. **Sapta Rishi (सप्त ऋषि)**

Connection - Vashishta, Kashyap, Gautam, Vishwamitra,
Bhardwaj, Atri, Jamadigni.
Uses

- Education
- Knowledge
- Wisdom
- Moral Value

Kids too can chant this

5.   Panchkanya (पंच कन्या)

Connection - Ahilya, Draupadi, Sita, Tara, Mandodri - these ladies were of highest virtues.

Uses

- To avoid unwanted affairs.
- To create /enhance good character.
- To increase Moral values
- To increase dedication, love towards spouse and devotion. Male/Female can chant.

6.   Swayamwara (स्वयंवर)

Connection - Shiv/Parvati

Uses

- Love, Love Marriage
- To get desirable Husband
- To attract a soul mate.

7.   Kalpvriksh (कल्पवृक्ष)

Connection - Heaven

Uses

- Good achievement
- Fullfilment of Desire or Wish

A Tree That fulfils all our wishes can be said as Kalpvriksh

Our Brain can also be like a Kalpvriksh.

8.   Nachiketa (नचिकेता)

Called Judge for Gods.

Uses

- Social Justice
- Knowledge
- Spiritual upliftment
- Spiritual quest
- Discrimination

Right perspective towards what you are thinking, will get correct direction, Selection for right career (can be used by Kids)

9. Kumbh Karan (कुम्भकरण)

Connection - Kumbh Karan

Uses

- Insomnia
- Bad Dreams
- Sleep disorders

You need to use this switch word with intention for a specific issue. Once the result is achieved you should discontinue its use.

10. Nal Neel (नल नील)

Connection - Vishwakarma

Uses

- To make household repairs (mechanical, Plumbing, Engineering, Electrical)
- Technical issue.

Other Switch Words

1.   Baal Gopal (बाल गोपाल)
Connection - Shi Krishna
Uses
- To attract good soul
- Good for pregnant Ladies

2.   Radha Krishna (राधा कृष्ण)
Connection - Shri Krishna
Uses
- Love
- Love Life
- Not getting Married
- To attract soulmate
- To attract Chemistry

3.   Raas Leela (रास लीला)
Connection - Sri Krishna
Uses
- Love Life/Love
- Romance
- Good sex life
- Happy Love Life/Romantic life

This switch word only for married people not to be chanted by unmarried people or will lead to Adultery.

4.   Ram Raj (राम राज)
Connection - Shri Ram
Uses
- Peace
- Prosperity
- Social Security
- Crime free

Can be used for workers to work honestly, even in office, for smooth functioning.
You can even use charged (Chanted) water and sprinkle in these areas.

323

5. Riddhi Siddhi (ऋद्धि सिद्धि)

Auspicious switch word

Connection - Ganpati

Uses

- Success
- Family Happiness
- Peaceful life
- To resolve Issues

6. Subh Labh (शुभ लाभ)

Connection - Ganpati

Uses

- Growth
- Benefit
- Success
- Family happiness

7. Swastik (स्वास्तिक)

Connection - Sun (Surya)

Uses

- Success
- Growth
- Benefit

Can be used by students also

8. Samyak Marg (सम्यक मार्ग)

Connection - Buddha

Uses

- Solution
- Compromise
- Negotiation
- Meditation
- Balance

When you are not getting any clarity for any particular issue, not finding any solution. Don't understand what to do/How to do, For deep Meditation.

9. Kamdev (कामदेव)

Connection - Kamdev

Uses

- For Happy Married Life
- Good for sexual pleasures (Only to be used or chanted for married couple)
- Natural beauty
- Romance

Please Note-This should not be chanted for too long.
Husband/wife anyone can chant for their partner.

10. Vashikaran (वशीकरण)

should not to be given to everyone
Connection - Indra Dev
Uses

- If want others to listen to what you say/value your saying
- Power to control opponents or enemies in any field.

11. Ucchatan (उच्चाटन)

Connection - Indra Dev
Uses

- To develop disinterest-Person's mind, place, property or object.

Use this very Cautiously

- Can be used for addiction

12. Vidhweshan (विध्वेषण)

Connection - Indra Dev
Uses

- To create Disputes
- To worsen Relation
- To break Friendship

Don't use it for Self-Ego

13. Stambhan (स्तम्भन)

Connection - Indra Dev
Uses

- To stop (for anything to stop like a pole)
- To stop any work/machine/enemy/Noise Pollution
- For addiction (to stop)

14. Mohan (मोहन)

Connection - Indra Dev

Uses

- To attract
- To influence
- To impress

Switch Words Related to Mantras
(Bonus and miscellaneous)

1.   Chhu Mantar (छू मंतर)
Uses

This is a main switch word of Sanatan switch words.

This should be used only by the students who learn this course. This switch word has the auto intelligence to switch any required switch words automatically. If you are in any hurry or any emergency u can use this switch word. This is a master switch word.

2.   Vasmukhi Rajmukhi Swaha (वाशिमुखी राजमुखी स्वाहा)
Uses

- For attraction
- Chant whenever you wash your face-will give glow to your face

You can even chant this while applying your face wash, face cream.

Anyone of any age and gender can use this switch word

3.   Shantam Papam (शांतम पापम)
Uses

1.To reduce anger

Chant this switch word over water or any liquid and drink, can even give to others if you want to reduce the anger.

4.   Jeewam Raksham (जीवन रक्शम्)
Uses

- For protection -acta as a protection shield

After bath when small kids wearing their undergarments chant this mantra, it works as a shield. Can be used by adults too.

5.   Vam Pam Lam Ram (वं पं लं रं)
Uses

- For dry skin

Chant this over water and drink, can even use while applying any cream or oil.

6. **Pasupadhim Mahadevam** (पशुपाधिम महादेवा)

Uses

- To leave any addiction, carving, infatuations, Habits,

7. **Vallabham Gajananam Ekdantham** (वल्लभम गजाननं एकदंतम)

Uses

- For courage

When u feel lost. No way to go.

8. **Vajrajeshawari   Vamadevi   Vayo   Awastha ViVarjeetha.** (वज्रेश्वरी वामादेवी वयो अवस्था विवर्जित)

Uses

- To look young and beautiful
- Full body to look beautiful
- Reverse your age

9. **Ambika   Andinidhana   Aswarudha   Aparajitha** (अंबिका अधिनिधाना अश्वरूधा अपराजिता)

Uses

- To get success in any interview or any negotiation.
- Success in any exam

Can be used by kids for any type of exams.

10. **Laghima** (लघिमा)

Uses

- For weight loss
- To decrease fats
- To heal obesity

11. **Garima** (गरिमा)

Uses

- To increase weight
- To Gain Fats
- To increase muscle mass

12. **Apavighna** (अपविघना)

Uses

- Remove obstacles from any aspect of life.

Person of any age, Male/Female or child anyone can use this.

13. Vinineeshate (विनीशते)

Uses

- To get rid of any addiction/or person/or any situation or anything which you need to remove from your life,

14. Saanasi (सांशी)

Uses

- To bring wealth (Money) or Blessings

15. Pushpita (पुष्पिता)

Uses

- For manifesting our Desires
- To get success in any manifestation
- To boost our wishes

Can be used with any mantra -it increases the power of any mantra.

16. Pravaal Prarudhakesha (पुरवल प्ररुद्धकेश)

Uses

- For Long and Beautiful hair

17. Skandaaya (स्कंदये)

Uses

- To get success in any competition
- To win over your mightiest enemies/rival/competitors and get success

18. Siddhiyog Sugati (सिद्धि योग सुगति)

Uses

- To balance all planets and get their protection

You can combine any planet with this which you feel problematic.

19. Tattwadhigata (तत्वधिगत)

Uses

- For students of any age group
- People who are in research work -to get success

- Those who wish to learn more in their profession with excellence.

20. Durantadeva (Master Switch word) (दुरंत देवता)
Uses
- If any Vedic switch word is not giving you desired results, then before chanting that Vedic switch word chant 'Durantadeva'.

You can use this V SW in combination with any other switch word.

21. Virosh (विरोश)
Uses
- To be free from Anger.

22. Sanrunaddhi Ghargharaayate (संरुणद्धि घर्घरायते)
Stop Snoring Noise of Yourself/Anyone

23. Siddhapraaya Rudhirvarnikaa (सिद्धप्राय रुधिर वर्णिका)
Perfect Haemoglobin

24. Parinaishthik Rutukaal (परिनैष्ठिक ऋतु काल)
Perfect Periods/Menstrual Cycles/Delayed Periods.
Chant when needed. Write this switch word on the left hand wrist when needed.

25. Jayati Koshtha (जयति कोष्ठ)
Remove clots/lumps/cyst from anywhere in the body. Write on the left hand.

26. Sanskaroti Rudhir Nipid (संस्करोती रुधिर निपिड)
For High/Low BP or To Balance BP.   Chant daily. Write on the left wrist with a Blue pen.

27. Sansiddhi Naadi Nipunam (संसिद्धि नाडी निपुणम)
Varicose Veins

28. Yaapayati Dudaankura (यापयति दुदांकुरा)

Piles

29. Yaapayati Vivar (यापयति विवर)
Fissures (Chant 70times daily)

30. Yaapayati Anaamaka (यापयति अनामाका)
Haemorrhoids.

31. Safaltava (सफलतावा)
Success in any work/relation/Monetary issues/or anything. This V SW can give you success in whatever you wish to, for students, employees, employers, small/big business, love, relationship, getting married etc.

32. Lobhayati Grahakai Falabhogin (लोभायती ग्रहके फलभोगिन)
Attract customers /clients/service/Business and increase Profits.
Write this V SW on the main door of the office/Home in a way that whoever enters may look at or read it.

33. Adhikarupavat Sucharman Paamaghna NutanaYauvana (अधिकरूपवत सुचारमन पामगहना नूतनयौवना)
Remove skin Disease/spotless skin/look young and beautiful.

34. Samvinayati Koshthana Dukhanan (संविनयति कोष्ठाना दुःख हनन)
Remove Cyst and Pain.

35. Sthirkaroti Pravas Aadhikaarik Anugyaapatra (स्थिरकरोति प्रवास आधिकारिक अनुज्ञापत्र)
PR/Green Card ((Permanent Residency)

36. Sukshema (सूक्शमा)
Peace of Mind

37. Swaruchyaa Suparyaapta Vilaasgruh Saanasi (स्वारूच्या सुपर्याप्त विलासगृह सानसि)

Buy Dream Home in your Budget

38. To find lost objects - Name of the thing you lost + Durantadeva satyaraadhas sampraapayati upalabhate (दुरान्तदेवा सत्यराधास समप्रापयति उपलभते)+ name of the thing you lost.

39. Shubhradatt (शुभरदत्त)
White Teeth

40. Labdha Nidraa Sukha (लब्ध निद्रा सुखा)
Sleep peacefully/Insomnia

41. Shulaghaatana Ashthivat (शूलाघाटना अष्टीवत)
Knee pain

42. Man Prasad Shashvachchhanti Nirudvega Nishchinta (मन प्रसाद शश्वच्छान्ति निरुद्वेग निश्चिंता)
Free from Anxiety and Depression

43. Durantadeva Kaamada Vidyaalaya Praveshan Sumnya (दुरान्तदेवा कामदा विद्यालय प्रवेशन सुमन्य)
Get admission in Desired School/College/University in any Country.
Write this V SW on a yellow paper and encircle it. Keep child's photo on it, keep everything in the North or North East.

44. Durantadeva Adhivaasitaa Videshavaasa (दुरान्तदेवा अधिवासिता विदेशवासा)
To settle Abroad.

45. Rutukaa Stripushpa Rajodarshan (ऋतुका स्त्रिपुष्पा रजोदर्शन)
To get regular Periods and normal flow.
Write this V SW on the left hand with a Red pen.
Stop writing and chanting once the period flow is good.

46. Gyn (ज्ञन)
Whenever you need to strengthen your Belief.

Chant write in your hand whenever you are in doubt.

47. Santulit Paittav (संतुलित पैत्तव)
Cholesterol
Write this V SW with Blue pen on left hand wrist. This is for any age/Gender.

48. Abhaya Abhiru Prashamana (अभय अभिरु प्रशमन)
To remove Fear of any kind in Adult and Children.

49. Maargaitavya Janak Shinghram Aagchhat Yathakshipram Nirminioti Ishvariya Shabda (मार्गइतव्य जनक शिन्ग्राम आगच्छतु यथाक्षिप्रं निरमिनिओती ईश्वरीय शब्द)
To get back the missing Person. Write these words on a Brown Paper with Orange Pen, cut it in a circle and put the photo of the missing person on it.

50. Shariryashti Paichhilya (शरीरयष्टि पेछिलया)
Be slim
Write this on the left hand wrist.

51. Tvachishtha Paamaghna (त्वच्चिष्ठ पामगहना)
For Beautiful Skin and Face

52. Subhruta Pratidinam Suvitta (सुभृता प्रतिदिनं सुवित्ता)
To get more Clients in the Occult Field.

53. Anushilit Mahaavigya (अनुशिलित महाविज्ञा)
For getting high scores in any kind of exam by any age.

54. Saadhya Yaapya Kshatchina Apgatakaalaka (साध्य याप्या क्षतचिना अपघातकालका)
For removing any kind of scar and spot from skin and body.

55. Durantadeva Vachyati nipun (दुरान्तदेवा वाच्याती निपुण)
For any kind of speech disorder, Stammering, delay in speech, confidence in speech for all age – adults and children

56. Sidhyati Sukhasaadhya Arbudaroga (सिध्यति सुखसाध्य अर्बुदरोग़ा)

For any Cancer of any type/any age/any gender.

57. Aparaardhya Vipanan Laabhakara Prakarshit Panyafalatava (अपराध्र्य विपणन लाभकर प्रकाशित पण्यफलतवा)

High sales/ Online or offline / high profit in any type of Business.

Write on a round yellow paper with Green and stick one each on each wall of Home/ office/ Godown, etc.

58. Durantadeva 'name of the Student' Kramaka Samvinayati aasakti ch tandraa (दुरान्तदेवा _____________क्रमाका संविनयति आसक्ति च तंद्रा)

For students of any age group who have lost interest in Studies and is Lazy.

Write V SW on a paper with Red Pen encircling it and keep the photo of the student on it in the North East corner. Ensure the student sits East or North East facing while studying. Chant over water as many times as u wish and give the water to the child.

59. Saurajya Karmasadhak Karmacharin Vidmanaapas Krutaarthikaran (सौरज्या कर्मसाधक कर्मचारिन विद्मनापास कृतार्थीकरण)

When your paper /documents are stuck anywhere, Government or private and u want to move it fast.

60. Arjati Lobhaniyatam Sharir (अर्जति लोभनियतम शरीर)

For a healthy Fit and Attractive body (for Men, women.and Children of any gender.)

61. Durantadeva Apohaati Mahaavaatvyaadhi ch Prabhanjana (दुरान्तदेवा अपोहाती महावातव्याधि च प्रभंजना)

For autism

Write it on a round paper and encircle it. Keep a photo of the patient on it, Keep all these things in the North.

62. Nirdukhatva Shulagaatana Arvata duribhoota Koshtha (निर्दुखैवा शुलगातना ꕔरवता दुरीभूता कोष्ठ)

For cyst in any part of the body.
Note - This is not an alternative to surgery

Switch Words Connected with Ram Charit Manas

1.   To control the angry person

Nath Sambhu Dhanu Bhanjan Hara, Hoyiye kou ek daas tumhara.

बयरु न कर काहू सन कोई
राम प्रताप विषमता खोई ॥

2.   For success in exam

Jehi par kripa karahi janu jaani, Kavi ur ajir nachavahi baani.
Mori sudharihi so sab bhanti, Jaasu kripa nahi kripa aghati.

जेहि पर कृपा करहि जनु जानी।
कवि उर अजिर नचावहि बानी ॥
मोरि सुधारिहि सो सब भांति ।
जासु कृपा नहि कृपा अघाति ॥

3.   To attain Lakshmi (Money)

Jimi sarita sagar maahoo jahi, Jadyapi tahi kamna nahi.
Timi such sampati binahi bulaye, Dharmseel payi jahi subhaye.

जिमी सरिता सागर माहू जाही।
जद्यपि ताहि कामना नाहीं ॥
तिमि सुख संपति बिनही बुलाये ।
धर्मसील पाई जाहि सुभाये ॥

4.   For attainment of Riddhi Siddhi

Sadhak naam japhi laye laaye, Hohi siddhi animadik paaye.

साधक नाम जपहिं लय लाएं।
होहि सिद्धि अनिमादिक पाएं ॥

5.   To grow love

sab nar karahi paraspar preeti, Chalahi svadarma nirat shruti niti.

सब नर करहिं परस्पर प्रीति,
चलहिं स्वधर्म निरत श्रुति नीति ॥

6.   To acquire wealth

Je sakaam nar sunahi je gaavhi, Sukh sampatti nana vidhi pavhi.

जे सकाम नर सुनहि जे गावहि,

सुख संपति नाना विधि पावहि ॥

7. To gain knowledge

guru grah padhan gaye raghurai alpkaal vidya sab aayi.

गुरु गृह गए पढ़न रघुराई।
अल्पकाल विद्या सब आई ॥

8. To win in debate

Tehi avsar suni shiv dhanu bhanga, Aayau bhrigukul kamal patanga.

तेहि अवसर सुनि शिव धनु भंगा।
आयाउ भृगुकुल कमल पतंगा ॥

9. For success in adversity

Rajiv nayan dharen dhanu sayak, Bhagat bipati bhajan sukhdayak.

राजीव नयन धरें धनु सायक
भगत बिपति भंजन सुखदायक

10. To have a child

prem magan kausalya nisi din jat na jaan. sut saneh bas mata balacharit kar gan.

प्रेम मगन कौशल्या निसिदिन जात न जान।
सुत सनेह बस माता बाल चरित कर गान ।

11. To remove poverty

Atithi pujya priytam purari ke, Kamad dhan darid dwari ke.

अतिथि पूज्य प्रियतम पुरारि के।
कामद धन दारिद दवारि के ॥

12. To avoid premature death

naam paharu divas nisi dhyan tumhar kapat,Lochan nij pad jantrit pran kehi baat.

नाम पाहरू दिवस निसि ध्यान तुम्हार कपाट ।
लोचन निज पद जंत्रित प्रान केहि बाट ॥

13. To avoid diseases

Dehik devik bhautik tapa, Ram raaj nahin kahuhi byapa.

दैहिक दैविक भौतिक तापा ।

राम राज नहिं काहुहि व्यापा ॥

14. To eliminate poison
naam prabhau jaan shiv niko, Kaalkoot fal deenha ami ko
नाम प्रभाव जान शिव नीको।
कालकूट फल दीन्ह अमी को ॥

15. To find lost items
gayi bahor garib nawazu, Saral sabal sahib raghuraju.
गई बहोर गरीब नेवाजू।
सरल सबल साहिब रघुराजू ॥

16. To make an enemy a friend
bayaru na kar kahu san koi Ram Pratap vishmata khoyi.
बयरु न कर काहू सन कोई
राम प्रताप विषमता खोई ॥

17. To escape the fear of ghosts
Pranvyau pawan kumar Khal ban pavak gyan ghan Jasu hriday aagar bashin ram sar chaap dhar
प्राणवऊं पवन कुमार
खल बन पावक ग्यान घन।
जासु हृदय आगार बसहिं राम सर चाप धर ॥

18. To apologize to God
Anuchit bahut kahenu agyata, Chamhu chama mandir deyu bhrata.
अनुचित बहुत कहेउँ अग्याता।
छम छमा मंदिर दोउ भ्राता ॥

19. For a successful journey
Prabisi nagar kije sab kaja, Hriday rakhi kosalpur raja
प्रबिसि नगर कीजे सब काजा।
हृदयँ राखि कोसलपुर राजा ॥

20. To wish for rain
Soyi jal anal anil sangata Hoyi jalad jag Jeevan data
सोई जल अनल अनिल संगाता ॥
होई जलद जग जीवन दाता

21. To win a case

pavan tanay bal pavan samanaBuddhi vivek vigyan nidhana.

पवन तनय बल पवन समाना ।
बुद्धि विवेक विज्ञानं निधाना ॥

22. For marriage

Tab Janak Pay Vasishth Aaysu ByahSaj Sanvary Ke | Mandavi Shrutkirti Urmila Kunary layi hunkari ke ||

तब जनक पाई वसिष्ठ आयसु ब्याह
साज सँवारी के |
मांडवी श्रुतकीर्ति उर्मिला कुंअरी लई
हंकारी के ||

23. To destroy tribulation

haran kathin kali kalush kaleshuMahamoh nisi dalan dineshu

हरण कठिन कलि कलुष कलेशु,
महामोह निसि दलन दिनेशु

24. To end the crisis

din dayal biridu sambhari harahu nath mam sankat bhari

दीन दयाल बिरिदु संभारी।
हरहु नाथ मम संकट भारी

25. Peace for trouble

Sakal vighna vyapahi nahi tehi Ram sukripa bilaukhi jehi

सकल विघ्न व्यापहि नहिं तेही ।
राम सुकृपा बिलोकहिं जेही ॥

26. Khed naash

jab te ram byahi ghar aaye nit nav mangal mod bataen

जब ते राम ब्याही घर आये,
नित नव मंगल मोद बधाये ||

27. To put an end to worry

jay raghubns banaj ban bhanoo. gahan danuj kul dahan krisanoo

जय रघुबंस बनज बन भानू ।
गहन दनुज कुल दहन कृसानू ॥

28. To ward off evil forces

pranpau pawan kumar khal ban pavak gyan ghan, Jasu hriday aagar bashi Ram sar chaap dhar.

प्राणवाउ पवनकुमार खल
बन पावक ग्यान घन ।
जासु हृदय आगार बसहिं
राम सर चाप धर ॥

29. To have good intelligence

Take jug pad kamal manvayu, Jasu kripa nirmal mati pavau.

ताके जुग पद कमल मनावउँ ।
जासु कृपाँ निरमल मति पावउँ

30. To relieve mental pain

hanuman angad ran gaje Haak nukrit rajneechar bhaje.

हनुमान अंगद रन गाजे ।
हाक सुनकृत रजनीचर भाजे।

Extra Switch Words

1. For all tooth problems
Rogantak dantya (रोगान्तक दन्त्य)

2. Insomnia, sleep disorder
Nidrakar Sushupti nirbharnindra (निद्राकर सुषुप्ति निर्भरनिंद्रा)

3. Knee pain
Shaamayati Jayati Jaanusandhi (शामायती जयति जानुसन्धि)

4. Anxiety/Depression
Man Prasad Shashvachchhanti Nirudvega nishchinta (मन प्रसाद शश्वच्छान्ति निरुद्वेग निश्चिंता)

5. For all kind of fever
Aruj Yaapayati gatajwara (अरूज यापयति गतज्वरा)

6. For child's anger and aggression
Lalit avasruj ati "person's name" Virosh (ललित अवसरुज अति_______ विरोश)

7. Weight and inch loss
Vdyanukodar (वदयानुकोडर)

8. For height increase of child
Vruddhi uttungatta (वृद्धि उत्तुंगट्टा)

9. For squint eye and clear vision in children
Netrarogaharan (नेत्ररोगहरं)

10. For getting pregnant
(wife's name) + Garbham upalabhate suwam (गर्भ उपलभते सुवाम्)

11. For cold and cough
Kaasamarda kaasaghna (कासमारदा कासघ्ना)

12. For liver and kidney issue

Vigada yakrut vrukka agadyati (विगड़ा यकृत वृक्क अगद्यति)

13. Spondylitis
Durantadeva Jayati vayurujaa attidah vishalyalkrut shoolaghna
(दुरंतदेव जयति वायुरुजा अत्तिदह विषल्यालकृत शूलघ्न)
NOTE: Those who don't have spondylitis but just any pain can remove "vayurujaa"

14. For overall good health and long life
Man prasad Shashvachchhanti Nirudvega nishchinta
(मन प्रसाद शश्वच्छान्ति निरुद्वेग निश्चिंता)

15. To increase memory and concentration in child
Smrutivardhani ekaagrichittena (स्मृतिवर्धनी एकाग्रचित्तेना)

16. For good husband and wife relationship
Priyaarha pritivardhana (प्रियारहा प्रीतिवर्धना)

17. For alcohol addiction
Parityajati Vyasana Devabala (परित्यजति व्यसना देवबाला)

18. To buy property
Durantadeva vasuprada (दुरान्तदेवा वसुप्रदा)

19. To sell property at good price –
Vikrayanam Adhikamulya Aashishaa (विक्रयणं अधिकमूल्य आशीषा)

20. To win a court case
Kaartaviria (कार्तवीर्या)

21. To increase sales in any business
Mangalsuchak dhan Bhagya yog nirminoti (मंगलसूचक धन भाग्य योग निर्मिनोति)

22. To increase salary and promotion
Dhanavruddha roruhyat dhanam Urdhwagaman Atmarupine
(धनवृद्धा रोरुहयात धनं ऊर्ध्वगमन आत्मरूपिणे)

23. To increase confidence
Khagaaya Pushne Aatmarupine (खगाय पूष्णे आत्मरूपिणे)

24. For profit in shares
Samruddhi vandra aparilop Prakarshit panyafalatva
(समृद्धि वंद्र अपरिलोप प्रकाशित पण्यफलत्व)

25. To get job
Durantadeva manorathasiddhi shripada viniyoktavya
(दुरान्तदेवा मनोरथसिद्धि श्रीपदा विनियोक्तव्य)

26. For unexpected money
Samruddhin prachurta susampada (समृद्धिं प्रचुरता सुसम्पदा)

27. To attract customers
Swaddhyambhava (स्वड्ध्यम्भवा)

28. To reduce fatigue
Ashramam (आश्रमम)

29. For all heart problems
Niraj hriday (नीरज हृदय)

30. Weak eyesight
Durantadeva Stat drishti tyajyate upanetra aatmarupine
(दुरान्तदेवा सतत दृष्टि त्यज्यते उपनेत्र आत्मरूपिणे)

31. For thyroid
Mrutunjaya Aruja Agad (मृतुन्जय अरूजा अगद)

32. For diabetes
Kalya Aruja Madhumedh (कलया अरूजा मधुमेध)

33. To remove obstacles
Apavighna (अपविघ्ना)

34. For sciatica pain
Sidhyati Katishool (सिध्यति कटिशूल)

35. For Parkinson's A neurological disorder
Aruja Chetaa Sanhita (अरूजा चेता संहिता)

36. To attract good and true friends
Bandhookrut suvandhoo shuchi (बन्धूकृत सुवांधू शुचि)

37. For beautiful skin
Tyachishtha Paamaghna (त्याचिष्टः पामगहना)

38. For pain in almost entire body
Nirdukhatva Shulagaatana sarvata duribhoota Koshtha
(निर्दुखैवा शुलगातना सर्वता दुरीभूता कोष्ठ)

39. For backpain and other pain related to it
Pramunchate prushthavedana (प्रमुञ्चते पृष्ठावेदना)

40. For good staff/maids
Daasakarmakara padaatilava dirgharaatram vasati
(दासकर्मकारा पदातिलवा दीर्घारात्राम वसति)

41. For gastric and constipation
Geruvachoghna (गेरुवाचाहना)

42. For heavy period flow and pain also for cyst in uterus and fallopian tube
Vyaadhighna Abhugha krnini supachar (व्याधिघ्ना अबहुघा कर्णीनी सुपचार)

Some Examples for Combinations

- Aiyem + Gandiv = For hyperactive child (ASD)
- Vashikaran + Mohan + Nachiketan (optional)
- Ucchatan + Vidhveshan = When we want to break something
- Kamdev + Mohan= Attraction
- Tan + Surya = For headache
- Tan + Vam + 6 or Venus (Shukra) = Urinary issues, Kidney
- Hum + Dhurantadeva + Pushpita = Thyroid
- Laghima + Ashramam = Weight loss
- Pushpita + Saansai + Dhaam + Shreem = For money
- Shantanpapam + Virosh = To control anger

इति ॥

Touching Billion Lives

+91-8929127575 , +91-7838133555, +91-7838104104

https://astrometry.in
https://courses.astrometry.in
https://astrometrytalk.com

facebook.com/astrometry.in

Instagram.com/astrometrytalk

Youtube.com/astrometry

Twitter.com/astrometryin

Linkedin.com/company/astrometry

Quora.com/profile/Astrometry-1

astrometrytalk

astrometry